Black Lives and
Digi-Culturalism

Black Lives and Digi-Culturalism

An Afrocentric Perspective

Kehbuma Langmia

LEXINGTON BOOKS
Lanham • Boulder • New York • London

Published by Lexington Books
An imprint of the Rowman & Littlefield Publishing Group, Inc.
4501 Forbes Boulevard, Suite 200, Lanham, Maryland 20706
www.rowman.com

6 Tinworth Street, London SE11 5AL, United Kingdom

British Library Cataloguing in Publication Information Available

Library of Congress Cataloging-in-Publication Data

Names: Langmia, Kehbuma, author.
Title: Black lives and digi-culturalism : an Afrocentric perspective / Kehbuma Langmia.
Description: Lanham : Lexington Books, [2021] | Includes bibliographical references
    and index.
Identifiers: LCCN 2021011238 (print) | LCCN 2021011239 (ebook) |
    ISBN 9781793639738 (cloth) | ISBN 9781793639745 (ebook) |
    ISBN 9781793639752 (pbk)
Subjects: LCSH: Digital media—Social aspects—Africa. | Digital media—Social
    aspects—United States. | Technology and blacks—Africa. | Technology
    and blacks—United States. | Communication—Technological innovations—Africa. |
    Communication—Technological innovations—United States. |
    Internet and activism—Africa. | Internet and activism—United States. |
    Computers and civilization. | African diaspora.
Classification: LCC HM851 .L345 2021 (print) | LCC HM851 (ebook) |
    DDC 302.23/1—dc23
LC record available at https://lccn.loc.gov/2021011238
LC ebook record available at https://lccn.loc.gov/2021011239

Dedication
This book is dedicated to George Floyd, killed by a White
police officer in the United States, and others like him that
have placed the fate of the Black race on the world map.

Contents

List of Figures

Acknowledgments

The inspiration to write this book came from my doctoral scholar forum students, the critical mass in the CCMS program at Howard University. We have regularly come together to assess the path of Black scholarly journey yesterday, today, and tomorrow. To these students, I say thank you for always providing the touch light for which we must rely on if we as a people want to reach our goal of studying and teaching at the Mecca, Howard University. Each time I left the discussion with the students, I found myself thrust into another debate of why our voices are sometimes not heard, no matter how shrill they are in the academic wilderness. This book continues to be our baby steps to lift every voice, the Black voice hoping that the echo will reverberate, and the new vista of hope will comfort the incoming generation.

Each time I publish a new book, I never hesitate to thank my family. Without my family, no academic juice can be squeezed out from my brains. They have ceaselessly provided the psycho-social freedom at home for me to write. This is not something I take lightly. I will never trade them for anything on planet earth. Since the colonial language is poor in capturing my gratitude to you, my wife and two sons, Brandon and Gabriel for all what you have done to me, I will, in words of Mungaka, my mother tongue say NJIKA JAMU!!

Foreword

Africans in the Diaspora and Africans on the continent are making new digital narratives studded with budding Wakandas of light that are increasingly finding their way into the contemporary imagination. Kehbuma Langmia, one of the leading scholars in communication, has placed this movement in the middle of the scenarios of speculative and digital futures. Exploring the limits of "techno-determinism" and various social media platforms and their usages by African people in *Black Lives and Digi-Culturalism: An Afrocentric Perspective.*

There is no one else that I can think of who could have produced such a profoundly engaging interpretation of the way social media, the Internet, techno-futures play out in the lives of Africans who have been often victimized by digital exploitation and colonization whether in Nigeria, the United States, Ghana, Cameroons, South Africa, Mali, the Caribbean, or other loci of African people. Langmia demonstrates how the convergence of Black Lives, digi-culturalism, and Afrocentricity might be seen in the explosive nature of new media platforms and digital futures.

Reading Langmia's brilliantly crafted language, I am reminded of my conversation at dinner with Marshal McLuhan several decades ago in Monterrey, Mexico. We had both been invited to the Instituto Tecnológico y de Estudios Superiores de Monterrey, also known as Tecnológico de Monterrey, to give major lectures on the future of communication. Of course, McLuhan, the superstar of the media in the late seventies, enthralled me and other younger scholars with his intriguing arguments about the nature of hot and cold media, the use of color on television, and the growing superhighway of information being built at the time. But as the evening grew older with good Mexican wine and lots of laughter, McLuhan started a monologue about the military structure of the glasses, plates, spoons, and candles on the table at the restaurant. McLuhan spoke eloquently with tropes, similes, and metaphors of cutlery, silverware, and glassware as he intoned about the martial nature of the dinner table. When I read Langmia's description of the age we are in with social techno-deterministic and speculative realities, I was as intrigued by his gifts as I was by those of McLuhan a generation or two earlier. Here is a volume that brings together for the general and expert reader the dynamic nature of the communication scene where Black Lives not only matter but also participate in the digi-cultural world of the future.

Staking his claim on the grounds of agency Langmia disentangles the hegemonic complexities found in the ever-increasing technocultural reality that has dominated our lives. In some ways, the digital dilemma speaks to the inherent issues identified in the social dilemma because the essential core of African inventiveness is about values manifest in the marketplace of ideas and behaviors. Who you are says a lot about how you will employ your knowledge of the digital structures that engage societies? Indeed, Langmia understands the interactions between cultures as well as the need for people who are the creators of culture to have a firm value base to make our lives meaningful regardless of the new tools in our toolbox.

Clearly, we know that the social media markets that trade in human futures have rarely considered the agency of Africans except as parts of the algorithms for control. Over the years, and especially since the turn of the century, African people have expressed the necessity for the character to fill the emptiness of actions without values. The greatest concern with African philosophy has always been the character. If character can exist or rather if character exists then the digital realities will be infused with meaning for humanity and not be used to destroy humanity.

There is no reason for us to see anything else in Langmia's creation of the tropes of contemporary and future society than his regard for the profoundly African way of beneficence in the created spaces that confront the masses of people. To call his book *Black Lives and Digi-Culturalism: An Afrocentric Perspective* highlights his regard for the fundamentals of human relationships.

Africa is not merely the birthplace of humanity, but of civilization, and it is probable that the first digitalization may have been found on the African continent. If we connect the Lebombo and Ishango bones to the story of digits themselves, we will see that African people have always been at the heart of the creative spirit seeking to make meaning out of our lives. In fact, we know that the Lebombo bone constitutes one of the earliest, if not the earliest examples of mathematics in the world. Around 44,000 years ago, Africa women made incisions on the fibula of a baboon to indicate their menstrual cycle in the area located in the mountains between Swati and South Africa. The notches on the bone may have been a part of some ritual practice since in the history of the world ritual has always brought about invention and transformation participation in rituals. So now we have evidence that the lunar phase might have been counted by women in Africa long before any other example. Similarly, in the Congo region, the Ishango bone calculator was created nearly 20,000 years ago with notches in several sections to indicate digital reasoning.

In some ways, the meaning of communication through digits might indicate manipulation of human society. Here is where Langmia shows us that the use and usage of the digital moment must mean the protection, sustaining, and enlivening of human lives. It is the central core of the Afrocentric perspective that agency resonates with any interpretation of reality. Africans are not marginal to any human phenomena, and our experiences must be told as narratives of reality in this moment. The fact that Kehbuma Langmia, with his keen insight and wit, has taken on this role as a lead philosopher of communication helps to reorient much of our thinking toward the relationship between culture, technology, and digits, hence, digi-culturalism in its clearest sense.

Molefi Kete Asante
Author of *The Precarious Center, or When
Will the African Narrative Hold?*

Introduction

Black Lives and Digi-Culturalism is a book that has used several lenses to thoroughly examine the role of African Americans and Africans on the new communicative superhighway called cyberspace. The cybernetic revolution has taken the entire world by storm, and we are all using it for almost all human communicative needs. The Black person appears to still be a victim in what Thomas McPhail in 2006 eloquently described generally in his Electronic Colonization Theory (ECT), as a pariah in almost all facets. As a result, s/he has tended to face the sins of digital communication victimhood, what Fuchs and Hovak (2008), two years after the publication of McPhail oeuvre, have aptly termed "digital apartheid" (104). Nevertheless, whether the Black person is on cyberspace as a pariah or a contributor to the advancement of humanity in general is open to debate and that is the subject of this book. On this new digital highway, all human race on planet earth have bought tickets to be onboard and each passenger's destination is different from the other. On this journey, there are cyberhawks (omnipresent content creators), cyberneophites (beginners who need help), cyberimmigrants (new entrants), cybercitizens (intermediate users), and cybernetizens (expert users) all eager to belong, to fit in, and be respected. All human beings, regardless of race, value their dignity. That is why being on board is one thing and being comfortable is another, and all that depends on one's cybernetic acumen. Cybernetic skills in accommodating the constant changing demands with respect to one's cultural aptitudes and vicissitudes on either the World Wide Web or the Internet as the case maybe are often based on age, educational level, gender, class, ethnicity, sexuality, and to some extent political affiliations. Most of the intricacies and affordances with respect to all these human ideological and cultural categorizations that are often present in the in-person world are also visible, in one form or the other, online; creating what is now

popularly known as digital or mobile divide. Anthony Giddens's structuration theory that argues in favor of these two platforms maintaining some form
of linear/curve linear relationship is to be commended. Therefore, Marshall
McLuhan's dictum of the medium is the message is still relevant in today's
new digital communication world. When it comes to users in the subaltern
as argued in this book, it is no longer access and information divide but an
epistemic divide that warrants attention if indeed, as it is often the case, all
humans are created equal. Apart from the cybernetizens who have mastered
and have acquainted themselves with the virtual communicative intricacies
on issues like cookies, spams, trolls, cat phishing, and all other forms of
scamming schemes that take place on the Internet, the other "newcomers"
are carried away by the allure of digital technology and so do face insurmountable challenges to fit in. On the other hand, the roles of each user on
the digital communicative plain field are different. Each user has an agenda,
and this agenda can be realized or not because this new human-to-human
communication is further compounded by the fact that capitalistic modes of
human exploitation have creeped into the online public sphere, and the political economy of the digital media is still alive and well.

The sudden shock wave of an unprecedented paradigm shift in human
communication brought about by the ramifications of COVID-19 pandemic
has empowered virtualization of communication. It is now an inevitable
form of human communications. Zoom, an international video conferencing
tool that recorded barely about 12 million users before March 2020 has suddenly spiked to 173 million after the pandemic because everyone, including
schools, have gone online. But what about schools in some remote areas of
Africa, Latin America, South East Asia, the Caribbean, and other parts of the
world that also shut down in-person instructions in favor of other modes of
digital communication when no structures were already in place for such a
sudden transformation? Zoom, Facebook Messenger rooms, Webex, Google
Meet, and so on are tools that are now being used as the new digital communicative public sphere and counterpublic sphere, especially to those who
can afford them. Other Black virtual interactive sites and movements on the
Internet like #BlackTwitter, #TWiB (This Week In Black Nation), #BLM
(Black Lives Matter), and so on have also seen spikes in user activities. In
the era of renewed street protests triggered by the brutal murder of George
Floyd by a White American Police Officer Derek Chauvin, these sites are
being inundated with diatribes aimed at the government, congress, elective
officials, and other law makers to undertake police reforms in the United
States. This and couple of years of Black disenfranchisement, marginalization, subjugation, discriminations that started with issues related to the voting
rights act, the Jim Crow laws, segregations, lynching, and many other forms
of inequality have all become the focus of these digital communications on

cyberspace. Blacks in Africa have not been left out in all this online communication saga to redress the situation that confronts the Black race in general. From the Arab Spring online galvanization that saw the physical toppling of dictatorial regimes of Ben Ali of Tunisia, Hosni Mubarak of Egypt, and Colonel Mourmar Kadaffi of Lybia to the cyberspace mobilization of citizens in Tropical Africa like in Cote D'Ivoire, Burkina Faso, Kenya, Nigeria, Cameroon, and especially South Africa with #RhodesMust Fall and #FeesMustFall that brought down Cecil Rhodes Monument, the digital realm of communication is now a potent force for the future.

The perspective that this book has undertaken juxtaposes Eurocentric and Afrocentric ideological stances with preference for the latter because the former has eclipsed the universe of thought for some Blacks in the Diaspora and those on the continent. The Eurocentric ideology that was planted in the minds of the Black race from the fourteenth to the fifteenth century with the Atlantic slave trades and the arrival of Portuguese explorers, then the Dutch, the British, and the French on the continent itself became a reality at the 1884/1885 Berlin conference to partition Africa for themselves. Since then, Eurocentric culture has occupied a central position in the cognition of the Africans, African Americans, and other Blacks in the Diaspora and that has affected their language and communication in the offline as well as the online platforms as will be seen throughout this book. In order for the Afrocentric view of themselves to gain potency after years of political, cultural, social, and economic incarceration, there needs to be a paradigm shift in their ontological, epistemological, and axiological view of themselves and the world. Therefore, what is uploaded on some of the Black Internet sites, the debate that are carried out are examined to ascertain whether they reflect the reality of the Black personhood whether living on the continent or outside the continent. The ultimate aim of any individual on this earth is to maximize his or her livelihood by not losing his/her dignity.

Chapter 1

No Retreat, No Surrender

Africans and Blacks at the Crossroads of Digi-Culturalism

BEFORE THIS TIME, YESTERDAY

Techno-determinism has now become the socio-cultural telescope for human-ity to predict the future. Gone are the days when religio-cultural barometers were used by European missionaries and colonialists to determine the des-tiny of those within their territorial boundaries and those outside, especially in Africa, Caribbean, or the Americas often referred to as the subaltern. By using dogmas and existential philosophies, Greco-Roman prelates and sub-sequently French and British explorers and Christian missionaries sought to convince Africans that the world was made up of heaven and hell (James, 2017; Asante, 2015; Soyinka, Amin, Selassie, Mugo and Mkandawire, 2015; Oyewumi, 1997; Hochshield, 1998). If one failed to conform, s/he was doomed to perish in hell. Generations upon generations of people of African descent have visualized their lives through those lenses either through lan-guage imposition, what Thiongo (2009) calls linguicide or educationally what Whitehead (2016) calls epistemicide. This situation arose because Europe was good at imposing all those principles in the various curricular for schools all over her colonies in Africa, Caribbean, and Latin America. Today, educational quests are gradually shifting. The world now revolves around a system of electronic and digital technologies. Machines now act as the mediating—invisible actor—force to human communication, where the journey to the moon and Jupiter can be done by a click of the mouse. This is possible because according to Nichols (2000, 90) "the computer has come to symbolize the entire spectrum of networks, systems, and devices that exem-plify cybernetic or 'automated but intelligent' behavior." But the Black per-son, though still soaked into these Europeanized experiments of brainwashing has continued, to an extent, to practice interactive communication rooted in his base on the continent or in the Diaspora. The Black person appears to still be a victim in what Thomas McPhail describes eloquently in his electronic colonization theory as dependent (McPhail, 2006). Nonetheless, whether the Black person is on cyberspace as a pariah or a contributor to the advancement of humanity in general is open to debate and more of this will be explored in the chapters ahead.

The Black person has intergenerationally garnered traceable unique forms of communications from the continent of Africa and in the Diaspora. The uniqueness lies in the awareness of cosmic realities bequeathed to him/her by the forebears who were deeply religious. Anyone of African descent is a spiritual being (Mbiti, 1969, 2011; Halloway, 1991; Skinner, 1999). Technocultural communication, the new norm to interpersonally, interculturally, and cross-culturally transmit messages between humans through the mediating force of the digital machine has drastically altered prior human-to-human in-person interaction. The tendency to conform to norms on cyberspace interacting virtually with netizens have transformed and transcended human-to-human communication as we knew it in the last decade. Wole Soyinka, the Nobel Laureate in literature says this about spirituality and this new form of communication:

> today, for instance, with the penetration of computer technology in everyday life, the only problem might be to decide whether the computer belongs to Ogun, the god of electricity, or to Sango, the god of metals. I suspect it will be Ogun of the Cyber-Superhighways. (Soyinka, Washington Post, 1995)

This is the mindset both internally and externally that informs the African, mostly those in and from the Tropical regions, on their involvement with the cybernetic forces of communication. To be cybernetic is to assume a different persona and, to some extent, transplant one's true self on a new communicative platform because the Internet has a White male omnipresence (Daniels, 2013, Gray, 2012 and Kress, 2009). The question that naturally circles one's mind after learning that the Internet has a White male omnipresence is where then is the White female presence? And naturally, where is the Black male/female presence? If all of them are present, as one would expect, does it mean they are under the surveillance of the White male dominance because he is omnipresent? These questions have reawakened the debate of race and gender with respect to communication on the superhighway. It has also raised the sleeping lion in mankind's cognitive universe who is battling with selfhood: virtual (online self) and in-person (offline self). The debate that is continually raging is whether the two selves can dovetail (virtual and in-person) to transmit true reality both to in-person/virtual audiences and viewers. The answer is complicated because those who "tweet" about Black Lives Matter

(BLM) will at the same time, if given the opportunity, jump on the street for in-person demonstrations transmitting new messages that would eventually wound itself online in another form. Consequently, these two new worlds of communications are complementary to each other. But at what levels? This is one of the main preoccupations of this chapter because before, this time yesterday, humankind (Africans and Blacks inclusive) were used to in-person verbal and non-verbal communications and later electronic communication before the birth of digital communications. The Black communicator faces a communicative dilemma in this day and age especially as s/he interrogates, engages, and confronts Afrocentric concept of communication on any given terrain. By Afrocentric concept we base our assumptions on the basic tenets that characterize the un-westernized African citizen communication. Those assumptions are based on the premise that an African communicator/communicologist has been imbued—from birth—with ways of communicating with the community, elders, peers, parents, and hierarchy.

THREE SELVES IN ONE

Communication through machinic tools and where algorithmic manipulations are somewhat alien to an average user in Africa has opened another can of worms for inter-human meaning exchange. In the era of the COVID-19 pandemic, compounded by the race of various advanced industrialized nations to top the chart of who is the best on the list of creating the best smart city or has invented the most usable artificial intelligence (AI) technology for mankind, Africa is still struggling to wade off the dusts of neo-colonial influence still hovering on the skies of their various independent nations. An average African on the continent of Africa wears three lenses: virtual, physical, and psychological. The physical lens, that is culturally inclusive, seems to have been dominated by the Western realities on cyberspace. That dominance has contributed in changing the African's realities of his/her environment. Now it is no longer oneself but three selves communicating on cyberspace as well as the physical space. Riding an Uber in Africa one is immediately taken to the realm of artificialities, what Guzman (2018) calls "sassy Siri" (83). Siri takes control of the road and the driver follows the automated robotic gesticulations hoping for the best. Both the driver and the passenger are transformed into the world of "pseudomodernity" (Kirby, 2009). Imagine the sound of the "Siri" or "GPS" telling the Uber driver to make a right turn on street number 6 when there is no sign in the physical human world indicating any street by that name. In fact, it is a dirt road leading to a dead end. But the driver sighs and shrugs off the machine or in some cases shuts down the system entirely and uses the mobile phone (electronically) to call for direction at the destination. This is the fate of Internet artificial-driven world of communication pitted against the physical universe where Africans have been used to physical touch and smell for centuries. As the Uber driver is figuring out the "right" direction to the passenger's destination, the passenger's finger is busy navigating WhatsApp communication, texting where appropriate, and watching uploaded videos to while away time instead of engaging in a conversation with the driver. Anyway, the driver is driving, texting, and talking to someone at the same time keeping watch over street passerbys. This is the life of three selves operating in two worlds at the time, space, and speed. Psychologically, the Uber driver is dealing with stress of an accident and the resultant effect it can have on his life and large family that depend on the proceeds from his job. The Uber driver is also battling with the psychological torture of pleasing the customer, especially if the passenger is a foreign visitor from Europe and America. His reputation to making sure that he is in tune with modern technology is at risk in addition to reviews and evaluations. This is the fate of engaging one's selves within the multiple worlds of cyberspace. It is a pressure that no one had anticipated in Africa but for which one has to swim along. No one wants to miss the train departing at the train station and that is where Africa belongs now. She is confronted with catching up with the rapid technological changes in the world championed by China, the United States, Canada, and Europe in this race for producing smart cities and forming algorithms in almost all aspects of human endeavor. At the same time, inhabitants and rulers are battling the forces of abject poverty, malnutrition, hunger, unemployment, and colonial education that have continuously rendered them subservient to foreign cultures. As the world turns the page from postmodernity once more to electronic and digital globalization, dependency on developed world order continues to rock the fabric of African ontologies and that is complicated to unravel. The world of digi-cultural communications, where those who master that type of digital culture are netizens, is a challenge for Africa's educational landscape because she has to change the curricula to reflect the three selves in one epistemology in schools. How knowledge is passed through and how they are dispensed has shifted but the structure of the classrooms has not. There are still students in Africa who are taught under the trees (read Ali Mazrui's The Africans: A triple heritage). There are still students who do not have basic educational materials like books and pens to write with, let alone having computers in the classroom for each student. And so, as the world moves quickly as reflected in the structure and forms of urban cities in Africa, the rural and some urban parts of Africa are still left wallowing in the dark and that is far beyond the constant debate on closing the digital divide gap. The notion of the three selves applies even to the old, the weak, and the sick in the villages in Africa who have to wrestle with the language of the Internet, the cell phones, and their local languages in order to be able to cash money from their mobile money transfer sent to them from relatives in the cities of Africa or abroad in the United States of America, Canada, Europe, Asia, and Middle East. Their ways of life have been drastically changed without prewarning and training. These issues seem to be exacerbated with the onslaught of new westernized digital forms of communications. The problem becomes acute when language, the vehicle of communication is factored in.

When this three selves notion within the context of digi-culturalism crosses the Atlantic ocean to the Americas, we are confronted head on with not only W. E. B. Du Bois double consciousness saga plaguing the mindset of the African American in his/her daily interactions with the White domi-nant society, we are in the realm of what Homi Bhabha has aptly referred as staring at the world through the back mirror. Through the back mirror or through the broken mirror because of unforgiven trauma emanating from years of Jim Crow laws, years of insidious and pernicious segregation, years of mass incarceration of African Americans and yes the mirror continues to be broken because they have been stripped of their identities and so are forced to observe the world through another person's lens. Imagine the vary-ing degrees of the interpretation of the death of George Floyd by a White police officer, Derek Chauvin by an African and an African American. An African sees cruelty and inhumanity, and an African American sees public lynching. The cloud of history (psychology) and continuous brutal murder of Black men in America (racism) and the criminal justice system that do not dispense justice (physical reality) because only few African American judges exist with only one represented in the U.S. Supreme Court. An African's perception is rooted in the history of colonialism, neocolonialism, and dicta-torship. An African American's perceptual instincts takes him or her back to Trayvon Martin, Micheal Brown, Freddie Gray et al., whose murder resulted in no conviction for the White police officers in spite of their loud cry on digital media and on the streets. This is what Homi Bhabha, as earlier indi-cated meant by staring at the world through the back mirror. An African on the continent of Africa and an African American do not operate on the same wavelength, culturally and psychologically speaking on cyberspace because of the complex meanings associated with the signifiers they use (Langmia and Mpande, 2014; Langmia and Durham, 2007) to communicate in any given platforms. Anthony Giddens structuration theory affirms that one's identity formation in the in-person world can be transferred to the online public sphere successfully and unsuccessfully depending on circumstances (Haslett, 2012). The African identity creation and formation on Twitter, Instagram, Facebook, Snapchat, YouTube, Blogosphere, #BlackTwitter, #BlackLivesMatter, and so on is informed by the aforementioned triple selves quadrants from the African context. That of the African American triple selves presence is informed by changing culturalscape of the American politics at a given time. The Black race in Latin America and the Caribbean are carrying varying baggages too to the digital public sphere debate on all these platforms already mentioned. When all these messages are posted on cyberspace interpreting, reacting to the same happenings in the United States, each ethnic group brings along an epistemic and ontological baggage, including some sympathetic White Americans as would be seen in the subsequent chapters.

CYBERCULTURE AND THE LANGUAGE FACTOR

The tendency for the continent of Africa to consume without question what is imported from Western democracies has been a longstanding tradition, but this could be detrimental to the forces of development on the continent. From a language point of view, Cheikh Anta Diop is reputed to have said "no nation ever developed using the language of another people. Indeed, the nation that used the language of another people ran the risk of losing its own language and culture" (Babou, 2004, cited in Asante, 2007, 13) and Thomas Sankara has chimed in by insinuating that for Africa to continuously feed on the breast of the West (at least from a language point of view), despair will welcome us at the doorstep of success because "he who feeds you controls you" (Akomolafe, 2014, 66–67). Africa has lost both her languages and culture and if language is the steering-wheel of culture in any given setting, there is no denying the fact, whatsoever, that the continent of Africa is limping to her cultural grave as the death-knell of language and cultural disappearance is sounding loud and unambiguously clear. China, the new "colonial" master of the continent is imposing its languages and culture on the continent in the same way European invaders did in the late nineteenth century. For a continent like Africa, the origin of humanity to continuously suffer this fate is not only regrettable but tragic. We are still glorifying the colonial languages and culture even though other countries like North Korea, China, Republic of Korea, India and Arab States have stood their ground to grow their languages and culture in the face of marauding Western influences. Only few African Universities (mostly in East Africa and South Africa) have centers, departments, and schools that cater to their indigenous languages. The argument for the growing need to imbibe Western languages and culture is not to allow Africa to fall behind other advanced countries in the age of globalization. But if that be the case, has China fallen behind? Has the Republic of Korea and other Arab States fallen behind? What does it mean to fall behind, anyway? Development as Cheikh Anta Diop as well as Ngugi wa Thiongo emphasize is that of the mind and not physical infrastructures that impose themselves in our capital cities with no running water or twenty-four hours electricity and functioning elevators.

Africa has suffered this fate for more than a century now since the proclamation of forced partition of Africa by Otto Von Bismark in 1884 at the
Berlin conference that unconditionally brought European nations of Britain,
France, Belgium, Germany, and Portugal to the open shores and borders of
African countries in the name of "mission civilizatrice" (Nyamnjoh, 2012,
135). Granted, importing foreign goods and services creates healthy atmosphere for competition but when local industries are affected adversely, there
is bound to be monopoly. It is that monopoly which has propelled a good
number of Euro-American, Chinese, Indian, and Japanese products to flood
the markets in Tropical Africa before and after the 1960 independence of
most African states. What is worrisome and, to a much larger extent, painful
is that these products do not adequately reflect the socio-cultural life patterns
of those forced to consume them. Yong (2015) states inter alia that

> Non-Western countries have not, and *likely cannot* (emphasis, mine), construct
> a balanced global order because Google (including its Andriod operating sys-
> tem), Facebook, Twitter, and Apple's iPhones (iOS), as well as YouTube, are
> indices of the dominance of the U.S. in the digital economy and political culture.
> Again, several developing countries, such as China and Korea, have invented
> and advanced their platforms, but their use is mainly limited to their own ter-
> ritory or their own diaspora with a few exceptions. Therefore, it is not contro-
> versial to say that American dominance has been continued with platforms.
> Platforms have functioned as a new form of distributor and producer that the
> U.S. dominates. Arguably, we are still living in the imperialist era. (6)

The digital communicative platforms that have been developed by China and
Korea may be limited to their respective countries and those resident in the
Diaspora but the raison d'etre for their existence and survival underscores the
basic tenets of globalization of the media. Western domination of the media
does not satisfy the norms of globalization. Media globalization can be a
horizontal developmental concept whereby any nation state has a meaningful
contribution to the growth and development of the channels of communications. Western dominance creates verticalization of development, that is,
top-bottom approach where the producers and manufacturers are resident in
factories in Europe and America are dishing out forms of communication to
the rest of the world to consume without question. That form of development
fits perfectly with the dependency model of development and that can never
be healthy in the long term. When U.S. citizens intend to carry out communication on digital platforms with folks from China, about Chinese products
and culture, they can conveniently do that by using any Chinese social media
platforms. They do the same with English when they are coming to study in
the United States. The tendency to embrace Western taste at the expense of

local and national ones can have negative consequences because by doing that the inferiorization of non-European products becomes a reality because we have chosen dependency over collaboration. As a result, African consumers are compelled to become "petit bourgeoisies" or European "mullatoes" hoping to catch up with the West and be regarded by their peers as elites. Uribe-Jongbloed (2013) endorses this disparity between the West and the rest of us by stating that such a phenomenon arises "because imported cultural goods, or those elaborated by a majority culture, have the quality standards and supposed superiority granted to them by the hegemonic economic and structural advantage of the cultural industries where they were originally produced" (34–35). This is the reflective mirror as you casually take a walk on most African cities today in the age of Western social media communicative revolution. If young people, in the most part, are not peddling their fingers on their smartphones text messaging to loved ones, their ears are plugged with omnipresent earphones that transmit music into their ears. This is what I have witnessed in Marakesh, Casablanca in Morocco (North Africa), Lagos, Nigeria; Accra, Ghana; Yaounde, Cameroon; Nairobi, Kenya; Kampala, Uganda, and Harare, Zimbabwe, in Tropical Africa. No one listens to the daily breeze of the wind or the sound of the incoming car anymore. No one pays attention to the moos of the cows in the meadows or the clad of thunder in the distant sky signaling the arrival of raindrops anymore (figure 1.1).

Figure 1.1   Natural African greenery. Photo by Gwaivu Azed.

Heads are only facing downwards with focused attention on a two-inch rectangular-shaped device that contains all the secrets of one's lives. This is what social media communication have come to signify to most urbanized African residents. They have unconsciously or subconsciously relegated their erstwhile cultural communication systems to the background. The youths have no more respect for institutions as their minds operate simultaneously on their physical geographical settings in Africa and the invisible virtual far-off lands in the West where most of the data on their smartphones originate. There is no other way to electronically colonize a people according to McPhail (2006) than to seduce them with shimmering products, and in this case something that glitters like smartphones and other digital and electronic products emanating from the West. The most attractive gifts for anyone traveling to Africa now is to transport huge loads of smartphones, laptops, fitbits, and other complex computer systems that cannot only "transform" the lives of the natives but put them at par with Westerners thereby making them feel "modern" and absolve them from the pejorative primitive tag often levied to "uncivilized" Africans. To be modern in Africa means to appropriate and assimilate Western styles, tastes and values, and shun African ones as much as possible. In fact, acquiring Western taste is synonymous to being an elite in Africa and that elitism comes with wealth and status and you cannot acquire status just by the mere fact of being a traditional noble, prince, or princess. That status can only be sustained by punctuating it with Western tastes and style and those values cannot be garnered until you accumulate monetary wealth. That wealth can only come from the West.

With the omnipresence of social media communicative tools on the continent, efforts are on the way (though fruitlessly at times) to adapt these technologies to African life-world experiences. Language has become the main concern, as English and French seem to be the main channels of communication on the mediated platforms. English, Portuguese, Spanish, and French are not indigenous to Africa. They came with colonial masters who imposed them as official languages for instructions. So, extricating oneself out of it appears to be an uphill battle as they have sowed a lasting impact on the cognition of the people. That is why it is easy for Western manufacturers to export them easily to the continent without any consideration of adaptation as they would if they were sent to China, Korea, India, and most Arab countries. But there are more than 1,000 languages existing on the mother continent and the most prominent ones are Arabic, Hausa, Kiswahili, Wolof, Zulu, Yoruba, and Amharic. About the positioning of African languages in affairs related to Africa, Nyamnjoh (2012) makes this observation:

English and other European languages on the continent are given status by associating them with civilization and enlightenment while every attempt is made to

reduce African languages to gibberish and chase them out of the mouths, ears
and minds of African students born into these languages. (Nyamnjoh, 2012,
140)

This mentality of valorization of Western languages at the expense of African
languages is not limited to Africa but has affected those people of African
descent resident in the Caribbean, Latin America, and North America. All
attempts are being made by those in the Diaspora to throw their entire weight
on Euro-American languages because according to them that is where the key
of success is hidden. The obstacle to allow Africans all over to learn, speak,
and write African languages, according to Francis Nyamnjoh starts from
home: "There is resistance from parents who believe mother tongue education will dilute educational standards, as students are called to operate in a
globalized world and may eventually proceed to universities where instruc-
tion is almost invariably in colonial languages" (Nyamnjoh, 2012, 141).

Therefore, the hope for sustaining African languages in the digital communicative platforms to the level that can attain international stature is slim.
This may sound like predicting the doomsday, but what can one make of
the future of a language when the users themselves have already killed and
buried it alive and the rest of the colonial masters are watching with gleeful
faces and self-gratification. Regrettably, other Lingua Franca languages like
creole and pidgin do not occupy central places on social media that are being
exported to the continent of Africa and the Caribbean or Latin America. Users
must develop strategies to get around the already encrypted language codes
on the system to create usable communicative strands and tags to their cor-
respondences. This is a vexing phenomenon that rekindles the era of colonial
legacy in the minds of consumers from the African continent. Dependency
chokes because decisions are made on your behalf without conscientious
concern for your input. This is the fate that African consumers of new media
currently have got to wrestle with while anxiously waiting to develop their
African-centered culture-driven new media technology as echoes of it are
being signaled in South Africa with the soon-to be-created Smartphones for
Africans (Coatzee, 2016).

In an interview with some student smartphone users at Iganga, Uganda,
in East Africa in January 2020, one of the interviewees, Linda, provides her
views regarding mobile phones and African languages.

New technologies have not taken care of African languages. Personally, I don't
see the future for African languages. Reason being I look at my young nephew
who is about seven years and he can only speak in English because that is what
is used in school. When he goes to the phone, he downloads all those apps,
the children songs. They are all in English. At home we prefer to talk to him

in English because we say he needs to learn English. He needs to be where other people are. Reading in English. So, I do not see the future for indigenous languages . . . . So African languages and culture are gradually being eroded. (Linda, Iganga, January 2020)

This statement from Linda is a testament to the overall sentiment regarding African culture and languages in the age of new media technologies in Africa. The future for African languages according to her is bleak because her seven-year-old nephew only interacts in English at home and in school and since brain development begins at young age, that is what he will identify with in the next decades. So, the colonialist goal is still alive and well on the continent of Africa, even with the introduction of a communication tool like mobile phones. Another interviewee on this question of languages on social media chimed in:

The few Africans who use African languages on social media have to translate for the other people to understand. Most of the people prefer not to use African languages. Though personally, few times, if I post something or if I write something in Kiswahili then I will translate for other people who don't understand Kiswahili. But then, mostly it is not used because people feel like people will not understand what I am saying. They will think I am so traditional. (Grace, Iganga, 2020)

From Grace's interjection above, in addition to what Linda said about no future for African languages on social media, Africa is limping on the left foot toward the sunset of digital technologies. If language can define any given novel technology as is the case with Europe, United States, and China, then Africa has its work cut out for her to compete with the rest of the tech-savvy world. It will be outrageous for Chinese technicians sitting in a laboratory in Beijing and writing out new codes for AI or creating a new algorithm in another countries language. The same is true of the Koreas, Europe, or the United States. But the contrary is happening in Africa. Not only is Africa consuming finished mobile technologies from the rest of the "advanced" technological world in their own languages and at best struggling to translate them into African languages as Grace has eloquently stated above, Africa is "producing" and consuming new technologies in foreign languages. It is now over sixty years since the colonial masters packed their bags and left the continent and independence was proclaimed. That independence means that Africa was to be in charge of her own affairs and language continues to be a serious consideration if the continent intends to leapfrog into the twenty-first century with her head raised high in the sky and not bowed to the sting of the master. Language encapsulates one's visions for the future. It captures a people's value system and their *perception of reality.* Africa's reality in the new media communicative world cannot effectively be carried out if she is still rooted in colonial languages. As these interviewees (Grace and Linda) have interjected, no one feels comfortable speaking African languages and then strain to translate them on any of the platforms like *WhatsApp* for majority of the people for which the interaction is intended for them to understand. It is such a laborious activity given that the user has to adapt to the keyboard that is, more often than not unfriendly to African languages as well as the annoyance of auto-correct interruptions that hinder one from moving from one word to the other if "grammarly" cannot identify that it is accurate on *their* system. This is what Africa gets by not manufacturing their own technological gadgets using their own language coding systems but prefer to rely on Europe, America, Asia, and the Middle Eastern countries to dump their products to them and they then start the process of figuring out how they will adapt to it.

Black Prosumers/Consumers

The Black race in North America, Latin America, and the Caribbean equally share this burden of new media dependability. They have suddenly, or forcefully, made to become what Yong (2015) calls "prosumers" (15). By prosumers, the author insinuates that in this day and age American-led digital platform dominance has created a new form of imperialism. Gone are the days of military and political invasion and dominance when the European powers maintained their grip on the economy, culture, and politics of non-Western countries. Today, it is the invisible digital mediated platforms like YouTube, Facebook, Twitter, Instagram under the powerful media giant companies like Google and Apple making consumers to become content providers through Apps on their iPhones and Androids.

From W. E. Du Bois, double consciousness theory of African Americans being constantly haunted by this sense of "dual perceptions" in their relationship with America, the world and themselves, the roots of dependency have been sown so deep. The Black race, where ever present in Argentina, Columbia, Costa Rica, Jamaica, Dominican Republic, Brazil, Cuba, or Venezuela, is treated with disdain and disrespect (Dixon & Johnson III, 2019) and so making headways to achieve any semblance of freedom and receive dignity, they have to play the game of feigning inclusiveness. Hollington (2017) demonstrates this, especially in Jamaica using the in-person and digital consumer behavior of a t-shirt product sold offline and online. The word *cho* that is printed on this t-shirt is a short form for charity project. But when it is marketed on the digital platform the author states that "the digital discourse that emerged around these t-shirts shows how the meaning of *cho* is being renegotiated in the new context" (96). The re-negotiation is another example of double consciousness without which meaning can be misconstrued. The presence of the new media communication context has created another realm for users in this part of the world to be conscious of their African heritage, their *Caribbeaness* as well as the Western. To be included or counted as a human being, you swallow the bitter pill of dependency and consume without question what the hegemonic race is feeding you with. This tragedy has been echoed too by Frantz Fanon who in his book *Black Skin White Mask* seeks to dramatize the inferiorized Black race status. The same is true of the new digital media consumption for the entire world. The images of African/Black brothers and sisters published on digital platforms to represent the entire race has to be constantly debunked, but they are impossible to stop because by and large, they are not party to ownership in conceptualization, production, and dissemination of dominant digital platforms (Facebook, Twitter, Instagram, WhatsApp, etc.). Like all other subalterns in the world being caught unawares by the viral nature of social media platforms and other digital media outlets targeting consumers like the Black race, we are struggling to tell our own story but is someone out there listening or even paying attention? If ears were tuned to the cry of the subaltern and most especially the Black downtrodden folks in the world, we would not still be suffering the pangs of the recent FCC net neutrality rule that has turned the table of digital equity completely in favor of the rich dominant multinational media companies. The loud cry for inclusion in decision making on matters that affect the Black race has gone unheeded for decades simply because we do not call the shots. We are, according to P. L. O. Lumumba, not invited onto the dinner table as guests but as spectators. It is this stance of constantly taking the role of spectatorship that has rendered the Black digital media consumer a passive byproduct of the West, and the situation is only getting worse. As powerful as most Black find themselves in the political scenes in the United States; and as economically influential as some of them including billionaires like Oprah Winfrey are, they do not own and control any powerful digital media company in the likes of Facebook, Twitter, LinkedIn, Snap Chat, or Instagram that have dominated the mainstream global communicative media. But 2019 makes 400 years since the first contingent of Black slaves set foot in James Town in Virginia, USA. For 400 years and some of these years spent in servitude, time is not on our side to be players in the game of economic influence in the world. The Black person has remained a pawn in world affairs. This is how Fanon (1967) sums up the Black person's plight:

> His reality as a man has been challenged. In other words, I begin to suffer from not being a white man to the degree that the white man imposes dis-crimination on me, makes me a colonized native, robs me of all worth, all individuality,

tells me that I am a parasite on the world, that I must bring myself as quickly as possible into step with the white world, "that I am a brute beast, that my people and I are like a walking dung-heap that disgust-ingly fertilizes sweet sugar cane and silky cotton, that I have no use in the world." (p. 98)

This state of psychological uneasiness and neurological impact that the Black person has had to undergo since the dawn of slavery in the Western hemi-sphere has resulted in a fighting spirit within them that continues till this day. But that spirit continuously encounters boulders of emotional and cognitive effects all the way to the level that dependency seems to be the mantra that has eclipsed the minds of our people. The echo and the re-echo of the ubiq-uitous sound that you are of no use to the world should prompt unity among our people to set the records straight, but that doesn't seem to be the case. No one dares to confront dependency else, he/she becomes an economic pariah and political scapegoat. Indeed, no retreat, no surrender has been the fighting emotional spirit exemplified through the many years of civil rights movements in the United States and the long battle against Apartheid fought by the valiant Black civil and political activists in South Africa. Freedom has come at a cost. The cost of the Black person's delay and slow pace to catch up with the rest of the world. Some will argue and rightly so that if, indeed, freedom has come to the threshold of the Black person's door, is the Black person truly free today? Be that as it may, the entire continent of Africa does not presently have a colonial ruler. Independence, like Apartheid and civil rights struggles in the United States has brought "political autonomy." And if political autonomy is the mother of progress, then there is no reason why Africa cannot achieve economic stability, and with stability comes socio-cultural impact that exposes, articulates, and sustains one's identity. Africa and the Black race, in general, are still faced with mountain loads of emo-tional and psychological debt to their erstwhile colonial and slave masters that seem to mar their progress and blur their visions to be creative. Creativity from a media perspective takes will and determination. The government in place, especially in Africa, has, as a matter of duty, to invest in their media experts, so they can have the requisite resources that they need to invent and compete with the rest of the world. But that has not been the case; otherwise, social media platforms like the ones already mentioned: Twitter, Facebook, Instagram, Snap Chat, and LinkedIn should have been facing stiff competi-tion on the continent with local ones like *Chomi* in South Africa, *Naijapals*, and *Lenali App* in West Africa. But they are not. They enjoy the monopoly of being the only ones that have conquered the cognitive spheres of average African. There are burgeoning semblances of these digital platforms that are striving to make waves (more on this in the subsequent chapters), but the African governments do not support them and so this private sector economy is unable to overcome the ubiquitous influence of WhatsApp, Facebook, Twitter, Instagram, and other Western-driven platforms. This is where it becomes a painful arduous task to wean ourselves from the dominance of Western goods and services on the continent and there seems to be no end in sight. The lone hope for such an initiative to take root is only if consumers are ready to pour in unalloyed support. But as of now that support is still timid.

The wave of digital communicative revolution that has rendered us to be in what many called the "global village," Africa and the Black population at home and in the diaspora can only wish for one thing: that they, too, will contribute culturally relevant and identity-driven software applications for mediated communication that can be bought by others across the globe. This is the dawn of another revolution similar to the industrial revolution that transformed commerce in the world. Even though it started in England, other countries like the United States, China, Japan, and many other countries in Europe came out with unique products made in their countries. Africa was absent because they were at that time under the yoke of colonial control. With the digital communication revolution that started twenty years ago, Africa cannot afford to be a passerby consumer.

Chapter 2

The Place of Africa/Blacks
in Digi-Culturalism

Before we zoom into the discussion of the role Blacks play in general in this thing called "cyber space," this is a lengthy Internet homily on where Black people are doing in this space which Tyrone D. Taborn calls tricknology as cited in Everett (2009).

This scam involves the "digital divide." For years, we have been saying that African Americans are being left out of the technology revolution, that the tremendous wealth created by the New Economy is bypassing minority communities. Now, after billions of dollars spent in so-called national effort, we are seeing reports claiming that the digital divide is beginning to narrow, that Blacks are gaining in computer ownership, and more of us are getting online than ever before. We have done our job, these reports seem to say: soon every kid will soon have a computer right next to his or her Playstation. The folks promoting this nonsense—I call them "tricknologists"—are the high-tech equivalent of the three-card Monty dealers you see on street corners. The trick is simple: the first step is narrowing the definition of digital divide, by saying that computer ownership and Internet usage are how we measure minority participation in the new high-tech economy. In fact, all what these statistics prove is that minorities are closing the gap in being consumers of technology, not being producers or equal partners. [I]f we are not careful, by the time we figure the whole thing out, the only thing left for us will be jobs flipping computer-inventoried hamburgers at fast-food restaurants or cleaning out test tubes at high-tech labs (Everett, 2009, 151).

This should not be the everlasting fate of the Black race. If we are *humans* like the rest of the race on planet earth, we should meaningfully demonstrate our roles vis-à-vis inventions, ownership, imagination, and creativity in all aspects of human endeavors and that include cyber technological innovations.

Cybernetic autonomy has a direct correlation with ownership and skill. With respect to Africa and the Black race in general, it is a top-down process, whereby the material is introduced first by the West and then consumed by Africans and Blacks. Like slavery, colonization and purported independence of African states, democracy had to be imported and expatriates dispatched to the newly independent African countries to help craft their constitutions. A similar trajectory has been followed with media globalization and the introduction of electronic and digital means of communications. The server, hardware, and software have all been imported to the continent of Africa. Black people from the continent of Africa continue to play secondary or supportive roles in the creation, formation, and dissemination of electronic and digital media. Way back in the 1950s with the birth of television in the United States, the minority Black population were often seen on shows that depicted them as appendages to the rest of humanity. Since they did not, and still do not own more of these networks (Craig, 2014), they could not alter the stereotypical caricature of the Blackman perpetuated in them. The Minstrel show comes quickly to mind.

Writing about performers, Cashmore (2012) said this about Black performers on shows "many other performers either side of civil rights felt obliged to blanch their facial skin in order either to enhance their appeal to white audiences, or just to find work" (Cashmore, 2012, 136). Six years after the publication of Cashmore's research, Dates and Ramirez (2018) research on the Minstrel show depicts another side of the debate "Some white entertainers began to offer to white audiences clown-like images of African Americans, most often portraying them as comic buffoons" (26). So, to Cashmore, the Black person still plays the master/servant relationship, what Skinner (2001) calls "bastard of the West" (29) in order to fend for himself/herself and his family. To do that, his physical attributes have to be sacrificed because retaining his/her Black skin would not guarantee a job that he/she badly needs for survival. This also means that the Black race is incapable of absorbing him/her. On the other hand, Dates et al. (2018) reveal a situation whereby Whites were instead using the Minstrel show to commodify Blacks. This vexing situation still rears its ugly head in the political economy of the new media world. The capitalist chiefly controlled by rich Westerners would not entertain a Black face the same way they would with a White face. The Black race has been at the consuming end of the media revolution. In as much as a few Black financially well-to-do folks like Cathy Hughes and Oprah Winfrey have founded their own media houses (TV One, Radio One, and OWN), they are still being outnumbered by the majority White media ownership. So long as majority of new media organization are owned and operated by non-Blacks especially in the United States, Black presence in these spaces would continue to be marginalized. There is some glimmer of hope witnessed after the brutal murder of George Floyd by White policemen in Minneapolis, USA. The spontaneous outpouring of love and sympathy for the Black race on digital media and street protests have gradually changed the perceptions of the Black race. One of the notable examples has been some Blacks being appointed to posts of responsibilities that they have not been privy to before. For example, Alexis Ohana of Reddit immediately requested he be replaced by a Black person. So, on June 10, 2020, just days after the George Floyd murder and riots that sprung in all American cities and abroad, Reddit named the first-ever African American CEO Michael Seibel to replace Ohana. The same thing happened in the University of California. For over 152 years of its existence, the University named its first Black president, Micheal V. Drake, to replace Janet Napolitano on July 7, 2020, a month after the death of George Floyd.

THE POLITICAL ECONOMY OF CYBERCULTURALISM

Cyberculturalism tends to enmesh oneself with mind and spirit in the seamless virtual universe of digital communicative discourse. Consciously or unconsciously, the cybercitizen or the digital citizen (Luke, 2011), as the case maybe, is oblivious of the invisible power play of the institutional influence on how the new media operates. The fact that the new media user is never invited to the table of decision making regarding how he/she uses the cyberspace is a politico-economic calculation by the powers that be. The role of the political economist, in this instance, becomes inevitable. This is how Robert McChesney sums it up: "Political economists of the media believe that assessing policies, structures, and institutions cannot answer all the important questions surrounding media, but they believe their contributions are indispensable." (McChesney, 2008, 12). Therefore, assessing and putting into perspective how new media communicative sphere seeks to undermine collective democratic principles of involving all stakeholders in matters related to economic survival and political freedom is crucial for the future of interactivities between all relevant parties in the virtual realm of inter-human communications. The fact that someone is called upon to release confidential information like social security and credit card information for C2C or B2B transaction in cyberspace is enough currency or license for him/her to know where all the information is secured and protected. The cybercultural tendency of giving big corporations benefit of the doubt that all is well with respect to security of data transmission on the Internet is the reason why breaches occur on a rampant basis on the Internet. This is fundamentally why identity theft abounds in cyberspace as well. The perspective of the consumer is hardly taken into consideration when crucial decisions are to be taken. In 2018, the FCC turned a blind eye to equality of Internet usage by overturning the net neutrality rules (https://www.nytimes.com/2018/06/11/technology/net-neutrality-repeal.html). This is a testimony to show how the voiceless Internet consumer, abiding by the ethics of human virtual communication dynamics, is thrown under the bus, yet monthly bills continue to pile up, including the value-added taxes. When it comes to international network operations, the situation is fluid and dicey, especially with respect to Africa. Exorbitant cost of accessing the Internet on a PC or Mac in Africa still constitutes a major setback to the development of new media in the continent. Mobile technologies have flourished (Asongu, 2018), and social media platforms with access through Wi-Fi have slowly gained ground on the continent (Rodney and Wakeham, 2016). But the problem of low bandwidth (Osuagwu, Okide, Edebatu, and Udoka, 2013), especially in some parts of Africa with limited access and speed, still affects the continent today. Until and unless the citizens are able to have reliable power supply and steady Internet supply in their various homes and offices, digital divide gap will hardly close in entirety in Africa.

CYBER-CULTURE IN AFRICA AND COVID-19

COVID-19 has accelerated online activities in Africa even though the rate of access still remains relatively low compared to industrialized nations. Cyber-culturalism is practiced more by students in universities and businesses in Africa (Langmia and Hammond, 2018). The rest of the population use their mobile phones for smart technology interactions. These phones like Android and iPhones contain most of the applications that can be downloaded and uploaded. They are powered by the Internet. Others are still using their cell phones that do not have these features that are inbuilt in smartphones. Before the pandemic struck the continent, educational activities have been largely carried out through in-person interactions within the confines of a classroom setting between students and teachers. Since the entire world went on shut down spree, so did Africa. The problem that arose was what to do with online education that most developing countries in Europe and America were switching to. Students were languishing at home with little-or-no information on what was to be done for school age kids, say in the elementary schools. This action to shut down schools came as a surprise to everyone in the world but some countries had planned way ahead with installations of online Learning Management systems in place like Blackboard and Canvas. Africa had to figure things out. There have been success stories like the case of the 4IR technologies in South Africa, as opined in the study carried out by Mhlanga and Moloi (2020). This advanced technology though at first shunned by some in South Africa rose to an eminent position as primary and higher institutions turned to them for online education for students stuck in their homes for fear of transmitting the virus to other people. The success story in South Africa has not been replicated in other countries in Africa. Other countries in Tropical Africa used the popular WhatsApp interactive communication for lectures and others used their national television to program lectures and demonstrations, especially to the kindergarteners. COVID-19 has, therefore, taught a bitter lesson for the continent of Africa. The continent should have learned from the Ebola virus pandemic that something similar can strike the continent. Cybercultural activities are not limited to money transfer, business transactions, social interactions where various interdependent cultures between nations and individuals are transmitted and exchanged. It also involves attuning to virtual changing cultures online that warrants curricular changes in the schools in Africa. Before students hop on the bandwagon on cyber national and international journeys, they should be able to respond to the exigencies of the demands of cyberspace technologies and demands that may qualify them as netizens and not mere online citizens bent on glossing over chatrooms and posting intermittent messages. It should be an attempt at immersing oneself through managing and controlling one's customs, traditions, values, and languages within the given structure. It is an activity where passivity is disallowed and where commitment to promoting ones' culture to the global universe is wholeheartedly welcomed. This pandemic that plunged the entire world on its knees has taught every nation on planet earth the tough lesson of making plans for the unknown and not allow the outside agenda-setting countries to control another nations destiny through their creative technologies. This pandemic is the time for Africans on cyberspace multifarious chatrooms to ponder on the fate of their nations, the fate and significance of the continuous colonial education passed down to younger generations still in the kindergarten and those that are still to be born. The future remains uncertain and Africa needs to test her technological know-how on online platforms that transmit Afrocentric educations to her children, so that by the time they embrace Western education, they are fully entrenched in their individual national cultures. This notwithstanding, a recent study by Hope Micheal et al. (2020) has provided some light at the end of the tunnel, even though there are still challenges:

> Although it is too early to assess the strength of the COVID-19 response in Africa, African countries, despite limited resources, have also adopted measures worth imitating, such as simplified triage strategies and proactive screening (Uganda), handwashing stations at transport hubs (Rwanda), WhatsApp chatbots providing reliable information and rapid testing diagnostics (Senegal), and

volunteer-staffed call centres and celebrity campaigns to promote responsible actions during the pandemic (Nigeria). Yet relatively little has been heard on the global stage about these efforts or from African veterans of the Ebola epidemics in west Africa and central Africa, even though COVID-19 appears to spread in similar ways—through family clusters. (Hope Michael, Raptis Constantine, Amar, Hammer Mark and Henry Travis, 2020)

As evidenced from this study, WhatsApp applications that is being used by millions of Africans have been used as a vehicle of dishing out information to the population on how to cope with the pandemic. The problem is that not all online users of mobile technologies in Africa have smartphones that can enable them to download the App. A majority of Africans are still using cell phones that transmit SMS and audio messages (Langmia, 2020). During this pandemic, digi-culturalism should be transformed into a marketplace for ideas to flow, debated, and challenged so the destiny of a people who have suddenly been thrown into another digitalized universe manufactured by the West do not become victims of neo-colonial scape-goats. Since COVID-19 has been a health pandemic, the use of online platforms by the government and private sector organizations has been key to spreading information to people who have been locked down and told to practice social distancing and to stuck up food. There has not been any inkling of socio-cognitive awareness on the part of members of the World Head Organization that there are people in Africa who cannot stuck up because they lack basic necessities of life like constant electricity supply let alone owning a refrigerator. When information is posted on Twitter, Facebook, Instagram, WhatsApp in Western languages, there has to be an infrastructure in place within WHO to translate all that into the millions of languages of the world otherwise interpretations and translations by some untrained individuals can lead to misinformation. Most people still to this day in Africa receive information not by radio but by word of mouths. People who live in the Sahara desert need to be part of this information dissemination because they do receive constant visitors from abroad. They have become the cyberspace underdogs.

CYBERCULTURAL UNDERDOGS

Africans and Blacks in the Diaspora like other users from developing countries facing digital divide or not are not operating in the same equal plain field as their rich White counterparts in Europe and United States of America. A lot of cybernetic activities require regular updated software servicing that impact the way users navigate the Internet. A user in a remote village in Africa is faced with power supply challenges that could impact quick and convenient usage. That is not the case in the West. The user in Africa is wrestling with download-able and upload-able speed issues on his/her smart phones, and as result would not quickly respond to platform changes let alone updating applications on smart phones. Access and language challenges affect users in Africa than in Europe and America. These and couple with the fact that they are digital citizens eager to become netizens (Luke, 2011) with all the rights and privileges that come with it affect some users. A lot of them are disenfranchised. The Internet operates freely as in a democratic terrain where all and sundry are presently being treated with fairness. There are no restrictions for obtaining a netizen certificate for usage, rather users are called upon to sign disclosure statement that forewarns them of potential repercussions that they can face in case of transgressions. These laws transcend national boundaries in Africa and many other developing countries whose regular citizens are connected to web activities. In a truly democratic virtual society, participant countries have to agree with manufacturers and other interested parties on rules and ethical conducts on the net before access is guaranteed. These iniquities have prompted van Reijiswoud and de Jager (2011) to make these revelations about ICTs:

Computer hardware, software, and the methods and techniques for the design and the implementation of information technology are almost all invented or developed in the West (Europe and North America). Environmental requirements and conditions become integral part of the design of these technologies, and this factor limits the transferability of the technology to other different environments. (60)

If the Internet revolution spreads its wings to peripheries outside the Western world, contextual implications have to occupy central stage otherwise the rest of the world will have to resort purely to adaptability to new techies from Europe/Northern America. That is, the recipe for unequal access and use that can continue endlessly until the rest of the world create user-friendly and user-conscious hardware and software materials that the people for whom they are designed can find comfort in them. This is what occupied members who crafted the New World Information Order and according to McPhail (2006) it had three objectives:

1) An evolutionary process seeking a more just and equitable balance in the flow and content of information, 2) a right to national self-determination of domestic communication policies, and 3) at the International level, a two-way information flow reflecting more accurately the aspiration and activities of less-developed countries (LDCs). (McPhail, 2006, 12–13)

Aspiration and activities of the LDCs exemplified in the quotation are nothing short of contextualization that van Reijiswoud et al. (2011) earlier insinuated above. There could be various school of thoughts as to why this is not taking place but be that as it may, client-producer relationship in any given economy needs to be established for effective transaction to occur. But when it comes to LDC, the formula does not apply. This is what continuously fertilizes the soil of dependency in Africa and with most Black media consumers abroad. Africa is being taken for granted mainly because they still harbor/share socio-economic and cultural traits with their former colonial masters. This is what has triggered Marcus Breen to cite Charles Tilly in his description of the Internet age as the act of proletarianization. To Charles Tilly "proletarianization is the set of processes that increases the number of people who lack the means of production, (*in this case Blacks/Africans*, addition mine) and who survive by selling their labor power" (Breen, 2011, 13). When the Black user from the continent of Africa, living in Africa has to sell his/her labor on the Internet by subscription to various services and paying for it through mobile banking systems, he/she has no clue as to whether the pay is equal to the services rendered. There are no metrics or criteria for leverage for the Internet user. Their labor and consumption are not in parity with complementary contextual cultural consideration. In other words, their socio-cultural and political context of operation do not dominate let alone be at par with the West even when they are using the Internet in their various countries and cultural spheres. This is quite unfortunate. The hegemonic Western powers determine consumption pattern for the subaltern and the latter has not turned its back to those products and that is similar to the processes of colonization but this time it is what McPhail (2006) aptly describes as electronic colonization. There seems to be no end in sight until the time when power will shift and the Black race takes charge of her own affairs and wield recognizable power in global affairs. That can happen through concerted effort in a similar style like the 1919 Pan-African congress in Paris that was attended by political activists and Afrocentric hardcore Black individuals from Africa and the Americas. At that conference, W. E. B. Du Bois stressed the need for Africans and African Americans to strive for unity of purpose that would inevitably lead to a modernized Africa and according to him "the chief effort to modernize Africa should be through schools" (Contee, 1972, 15). The year 2019 marked 100 years since Du Bois discussed this issue in the form of a memorandum at the 1919 Paris PAC and there has been subsequent Pan-African Congresses (PAC) like the 1945 PAC in Manchester; 1974 in Dar es Salaam, Tanzania; 1994 in Kampala, Uganda; and 2014 in Accra, Ghana. At all these conferences, one thing always stood out, that is, the empowerment of Africa as well as all those that call Africa home. That empowerment came in the 1960s when a major cataclysmic shift resulted in the independence or most African countries. They relieved themselves from the direct politico-economic and cultural influence of the West on the continent of Africa. This is when the school system according to Du Bois could have experienced a major shift in the process of modernizing Africa but 100 years has gone since 1919 and Africa and Africans and others in the Diaspora that are directly or indirectly affiliated to the continent are still suffering under the yoke of imperialism and neo-colonization and that empowerment that started with the memorandum from Du Bois at the Paris PAC has vanished into thin air. The educational system on the continent has not empowered the African person to catch up or marched in equal footing with the modern technology of Europe. Consequently, the resultant effect is that those conversant with Western modes of education in Africa and in the Diaspora are able to easily navigate the cybercultural systems on their communication gadgets that are imported to the continent or the Caribbean or Latin America. Those that are non-Western educated or literate in the cybernetic parlance of the west are left in the periphery to self-educate or find alternative means of communication and that is how the concept of digital divide has continuously gained momentum. One would have assumed that with the subsequent congresses that have brought Africans and Blacks from all parts of the world for deliberations that will eventually help the Black race, the shadow and pronouncements of the Du Bois, Kwame Nkrumah, and Julius Nyerere would have been haunting the delegates meeting at these various locations especially on the continent of Africa to take major steps to wean Africa from colonial vestiges. When Ngugi shocked the African literary world by coming up with the now famous book "decolonizing the mind," he was responding to the dictates of the various PAC that have been holding since 1900. Since the 1884/1885 Berlin conference to partition Africa for Western appetites, something had to happen to drastically shift the minds of Africans who for all these while have become Western surrogates in their own land. This is still true with the arrival of these new forms of communications. Dependency even after more than 100 years of colonialism for Africans in Africa and the plantation experience of 1619 for African Americans in the Americas, is the ghost that continues to lurk on the continent and its Diaspora. The economic, cultural, and political dependence that constituted the life-world of Blacks at home and abroad has affected them adversely and that is why with this new wave of cyber communications, Africans still find themselves at the mercy of their Western hegemonic forces as they play the piper and dictate the tune for them as manufacturing of the products and dissemination originate from the west. That is why with the growth of new communicative Apps that are seeing the light of day in Africa (more on this in subsequent chapters), it is time for consumers in Africa to do justice with what they themselves are producing. This way the Black race becomes a producer, participant, and contributor.

BLACK USERS AND DEPENDENCY

Dependency for Africa has accelerated even after the continent gained independence from colonial masters in the 1960s. Francis Nyamnjoh, one of Africa's topmost scholars says this about African scholars with respect to dependency: "African scholars are doomed to consume not books and research output of their own production or choice but what their affluent and better-placed counterparts in Europe and North America produced and enforced" (Nyamnjoh, 2012, 144–45). Unfortunately, a similar trend is being observed with the emergence of the cyber revolution on the continent. It has swept the entire continent of Africa like the eastern whirlwind of multiparty-ism of the 1990s that brought change to the political establishments on the continent. Again, with an interview conducted with some students at Iganga in the outskirt of Kampala, Uganda on January 4, 2020, important revelations were made regarding the use of smart phones in Africa. One of the interview-ees who was quoted in chapter 1 by the name Linda had this to say when asked about the role of smartphone technology on the lives of the people on the continent:

> *It is efficient. It has also improved communication in terms of speed, in terms of the distances. You know in the past in Africa, people used to communicate using letters which could relay false information or even give a different inter-pretation of which it will bring some issues here and there. I think modern communication has made everything so easy and fast.* (Linda, January 4, 2020)

So according to this mobile technology user, life has been made relatively easy because people on the continent now have speedy communication that has reduced distances between them. It has also resolved the issue of what she calls "false" information that was often relayed in Africa prior to the emergence of digital communicative technologies. When questioned about the effect of new communication technology on African culture, she goes on to state that:

> *It has improved past communication system. If you look at it from a cultural per-spective it has changed a lot. In terms of interpersonal perspective, you realize that now people prefer to speak over the phone rather than having a face-to-face conversation. I could be sitting with you here and we are talking but I am still on my smartphone, on my WhatsApp and I am talking to someone else. So, it has eroded the real meaning of interpersonal relations. And it has brought so many other things: We no longer eat local, we see people posting and they are eating Pizza. You wanna be there and so you want to abandon what you have been eating, the local foods and you start eating other things else. Our local foods no*

longer have meaning because simply we have borrowed some Western cultures
including the foods we eat. (Linda, Iganga, January 4, 2020)

Pizza is an international Italian dish that never flooded the restaurant markets in Africa during and after colonization. But the emergence of visual online media has made it possible for African consumers to develop interest in that dish and according to this interviewee, they hunger for local foodstuff has diminished. Dependency according to Linda in this interview has triggered a switch from cultural norms of interpersonal communicative relationship whereby listeners and talkers play respective dependent and interdependent roles accordingly; meaning that when someone is talking the other person listens attentively. But the introduction of smartphone has created a notion of distraction between listener and talker. This distraction has been manifested in the way the listener pays attention to her online texting on WhatsApp while simultaneously engaging in dialogue with an interlocutor. This is a new dispensation with respect to interpersonal communication that is quite new to the people of Africa. Their total embrace of it has further engineered the Western dependency dialogue currently going on in Africa. It has also reminded Africans of the arrival of multiparty politics in the continent in the early 1990s that shook the foundation of politics in the region.

Dictators that have ruled the continent since independence with one party system mentality saw their powers eroded as opposition parties sang hymns of praise as the wind carrying the olive branch of change blew across the mother continent. For the first time, national conferences were being organized from north to south and east to west in Africa about party politics plurality. Since the constitutions of most newly independent states in Africa were modeled from that of their colonial masters in Europe, it was equally easy to amend them in their national assemblies as the need for change came knocking at their doors. This is what dependency does to nascent democratic nations. You cannot afford to stand on one leg when the other leg is being dragged by a force more powerful than your one leg can withstand. With Internet revolution, when Europe sneezes, Africa catches not only cold but instant pneumonia. Smartphones have inundated entire households in Africa and landlines telephone subscriptions rate have dwindled (Bornman, Bryen, Moolman and Morris, 2016). But at what cost—culturally and socially—for the average user as well as the government? More on this in chapter 6 (Black Cybernetizens and inequalities). Dependency theorists (Mazrui, 1987) all agree that media globalization using the top-bottom approach increases the tendency for dependency. For instance, James Carey admonishes while citing Harold Innis that

The increasing facility with which electronic media penetrated national boundaries worried Innis because it increased the capacities of imperialism and

cultural invasion. Innis considered "monopolies," whether of electrical technology or, for that matter, rigid orthodoxy, threats to human freedom and cultural
survival. (Carey, 1992, 135)

The monopolies of transnational and multinational communication companies especially in the developing world has asphyxiated the growth of local
companies and this has been one of the painful media tragedies plaguing the
entire Black continents. Blacks in Africa and in the Diaspora have suffered
major setbacks to their self-worth and development starting with Arab slave
trade to European slave trade/colonization (Nkrumah,1964; Rodney, 1982;
Asante, 2007; Rabaka, 2009) that they do not seem to be conscious of the
effect of foreign dependency any longer. The same dependency mindset
has gripped the souls of the continent as Silicon Valley digital communicative technology has ushered in new forms of interpersonal communications.
Africans owned iPods, iPads, laptops, smartphones, tablets, and many other
technology-driven gadgets to help them hook up with inter-human virtual
communication like the rest of the world. But interestingly enough, neither
the hardware nor the software meant to power these machines have been or
are presently being exclusively manufactured in Africa. Consequently, users
have to depend on Western techies to bridge them through for global outreach.
All the URLs and domain names have been given to them from overseas.
They are obliged to communicate using the colonial languages—English,
French, Spanish, Portuguese—the same language that was used to colonized
them for effective transnational transactions. This is the pain of dependency,
when you have no control over your communicative airwaves. The worst
pain that a human can suffer is that of being relieved of his/her natural tongue
for official national transactions. Indigenous African languages only enjoy
meaningful status in the confines of homes and tribal meeting groups. The
data they transmit on airwaves both electronically and digitally are in foreign
languages. In fact, tons of data archived all over the cloud include millions of
messages originating from Africa, from Africans posting photographs, videos, and texts to loved ones across the globe. They do not have access to these
data. Even if they were to have access to them, they may need translation into
tribal languages that are spoken by the vast majority of the population on the
continent for it to have significant national effect.

KNOWLEDGE AND INFORMATION DEPENDENCY

During the seventh annual social media conference at Howard University
in 2016, Michelle Ferrier, the keynote speaker, described the social media
consumption pattern for people of color as inundating themselves with more

information while acquiring little knowledge in the process. She said we are filled with the sea of information, but knowledge desert is still around us. The ceaseless use of information technology through mobile phone use, especially by some African Americans, has made them addictive and this addiction has affected their cognitive health. In this study by Jin, Jones, and Lee (2019), Internet addiction for African Americans has a high correlation with depression. African Americans, Blacks on the continent and in the Diaspora constitute a significant majority on the superhighway technology, and the effect on their interpersonal in-person communication as well as their societal cultural relationships is supported by Linda in the interview already mentioned.

In the same interview referenced above, Linda continues on this theme by stating with respect to the future of digital communication in Africa that

> With the new communicative devices face-to-face communication will radically reduce. The more smartphones the young people have the less they will be able to have face-to-face conversation. (Linda, Iganga, January 4, 2020)

And if the youth are the future of fragile continent just experiencing sixty years of independence from colonial rule, there is every reason to feel the pain of the erosion of in-person communication what the respondent has referred to as face-to-face (FtF) conversation above.

On the question of whether we understand ourselves more in Africa by having in-person communication or by using smartphones, this is what she said:

> *I feel both help us to understand ourselves. With the new communicative device you are able to google something in terms of allowing you to know who you are. Take for example when you want to do a self-awareness test and the device through google give you the opportunity to fill a questionnaire. You are able to understand who you really are. At the same time when you look at the negative side, we want to keep up with new technology, we want to keep up with everyone in New York or keep up with everyone in Nairobi. So it makes you change who you are to fit in societies. (Linda, Iganga, January 4, 2020)*

Like any new invention or creation, users learn to adapt. They enjoy the benefits but decry the setbacks. In this case, Linda referenced the issue of google which helps curious minds to gain self-gratification when they google and take the "self-awareness test" that she has referenced above. The result *could* be self-gratifying if only the user knows the source of the instrument and whether cultural differences have been factored on that instrument before being distributed widely on the Internet. That instrument may have a Cronbach's alpha of 0.71 and above for people resident in the West and may not have been pilot tested with people on the continent of Africa or any other developing country. But the user would not know this but will be satisfied with the self-awareness test results and adjust his/her life accordingly. This is the implication of consuming materials from cyberspace without questioning the source and rationale. This is another classic example of top-bottom dependency approach to digital communication in Africa.

No doubt, Vaidhyanathan (2011) forewarned us ten years ago about googlization in his book titled *"The googlization of everything: (and why we should worry)"*:

> Google gives us Web search, email, Blogger platforms, and YouTube videos. In return, Google gets information about our habits and predilections so that it can more efficiently Target advertisements at us. Google's core business is consumer profiling. It generates dossiers on many of us. It stores "cookies" in our web browsers to track our clicks and curiosities. Yet we have no idea how substantial or accurate these digital portraits are. (Vaidhyanathan, 2011, 9)

Therefore, the effect of dependency is a never-ending saga of downward spiral of Western-driven media consumption on the continent and the worse of part of it is that the tool that has taken over one's communicative life is ostentatiously being used as a weapon of racism as opined by Safiya Umoja Noble in her much recent book titled "Algorithms of oppression." She has revealed a rather stunning observation when she stated that "you should see what happens when you google 'black girls'" (17). She did this way back in 2011 when she wanted to show images of Black girls on the Internet to her stepdaughter. She was shocked to find mostly lewd images for the so-called Black girls being displayed on the screen. This is just one of the many indirect effects of reliance on a tool where the Black race has little input in the designing, ownership, and dissemination of contents. Linda, our interviewee herself, admitted this in the later part of the interview when discussing the negative aspect of the digital media that implicitly and unconsciously pushes them to behave like people in New York when they consume a lot of material online on New York and Nairobi an urban city and capital of Kenya. When asked about the role of the seniors or elders residing in the rural parts of Africa on their consumption pattern on digital media she has a different response. With respect to older people when answering my question on the older generation of African users being left out on the new communicative devices, She says:

> *With the old people they are not left out. When I look at my mom, the only use she has with the cell phones is to make calls. So, I feel like she is not being left out. Most of her life she has already lived it. She only needs to speak to the people who are close to her. Her daughters, her brother, her grandchildren. She*

doesn't need Facebook, she doesn't need Instagram etc and I think she enjoys
it because I realized that the face-to-face communication is more efficient with
the older people.(Linda, Iganga, January 2020)

Linda sees her mom as one who should be contented with a life well lived in
the past and not worry about new digital media communication expecting her
to download various Apps for Facebook, Twitter, Instagram, and so on. She
should practice traditional in-person communication rather than worry about
sending emojis on Facebook or Instagram. That was not meant for her. So,
she confirms the digital divide as not being a sin for manufacturers of smartphones. But this goes contrary to inclusivity and diversity that any invention
meant for human consumption should yearn to achieve and that is exactly
what democracy calls for.

But do social media interactions and posts on a daily basis with friends,
colleagues, loved ones, and relations the shortcut to importing real democracy to Africa such that freedom can ring from the north to south and east to
west? The answer is still blowing in the wind. How can Africans interacting
say on WhatsApp bring the much-needed freedom of communication for one
another? A sense of oneness that can be translated to knowledge autonomy to
displaced groups on the continent? We have seen how political mobilization
was carried out by urban youths in North Africa to galvanize the people to
permanently install tents at the Tahrir Square, for instance in Cairo, without
the dictators' sting? More of this is discussed later in the book.

BROADBAND/MOBILE ACTIVITIES

Access to cyberspace counted as one of the main indices of digital inequalities
that was often referred to as the digital divide (more on this in chapter 6). A
study by Mossberger, Tolbert and Anderson (2017) carried out in the suburb
of Chicago with low-income African Americans and Latino online users indicate that African Americans are more frequent mobile online users on matters
related to job search, buying tickets, searching for homes, and so on. Other
activities like taking online classes or downloading requisite materials, say
from a doctor–patient interaction requiring broadband access using laptops or
desktop computers were low for African Americans. Reasons given for such
a disproportionate result were attributed to their low-income status. Laptop
computers with broadband access and desktop computers were less affordable to this group of people. It is not surprising too from their findings that
African Americans prefer to use their mobile phones for multivariate activities than subscribe for home broadband. The affluent African American family residing in the urban centers could afford those luxury items. Cyberspace

was conceived to virtually help human-to-human communication that could be facilitated online and make life convenient to all and sundry. It should be noted that in as much as the rate of mobile phone ownership has increased significantly for African Americans and most especially with Africans on the continent of Africa, the kind of activities that they do on mobile phones must also be taken in consideration in matters related to racial online discussions. As will be discussed further, Black cyberspace users, especially the digital citizens and netizens, use platforms like Twitter to construct dialogue with those they are familiar with as well as those that they are not like politicians. Twitter appears to be a very powerful tool, especially for African Americans to constitute a counterpublic discourse, especially with the role of Black Twitter (Rosenbaum, 2018).

CONCLUSION

Cybernetic communicative structure and pattern have unique purposes and aims. They depend on users' priorities and intent to manipulate or be manipulated by the invisible forces that are ubiquitous on the "netosphere." This virtual netospheric communication world, wherein humans and machines are both caught up in a tidal wave of who controls message flow, has reshaped mass/group/interpersonal/intercultural communication for the foreseeable future. Netizens have all been transformed by the exigences of this new form of communication. Users of all category and caliber now operate in a binary cognitive universe of thought when it comes to crafting, drafting, and posting messages by text, image, audio, or video since they need to factor where and when the message is being received (individual or group or mass). This process of communication has increasingly compounded the notion of public sphere as originally envisaged by Jurgen Habermas. He saw the public sphere from an in-person, interpersonal perspective, whereby certain group of citizens would answer present say in salons to discuss affairs of the state and chart trajectories for a much more palatable political future of a given state. That public sphere was limited to mostly the European world. With the emergence of Internet revolution, there is now a new form of communicative dialogue emerging where gender, race, class, citizenry, and nationality are all visible in given sites on cyberspace. These groups belong to either the developing or the developed world of political and economic influence. This chapter discussed affairs that pertain mostly to those in the subaltern, the underprivileged, the Blacks and African cyber users caught between their innate socio-cultural, political, and economic world of influence and that of the Western-dominating influence across the board. They may choose to align themselves with what others in the Western world are using, including language use and culture or choose to exert their influence. The conclusion is that they can hardly exert their influence because they seem to have entered the electronic and digital realm of communication with one foot only and that foot being their Western educational mindset and they are only few of them in number. In a continent boasting over 1 billion population, only a handful have the privilege of acquiring Western education due to colonial influences and indoctrination. Those in the periphery who are resident mostly in the rural parts of the continent and also in some Latin American countries and the Caribbean need extra critical Western educational training to fully participate meaningfully in all the various forms of digi-culturalism.

Another aspect worth mentioning about this chapter is the issue of decolonizing the mind so users can be able to decipher Western demagoguery and African or pro-Black activities on cyberspace. Since the colonial enterprise instilled an unavoidable slave-mentality on the psyche of all members of the Black race on the continent and in the Diaspora, there needs to be a mechanism to re-claim, and re-center their dignity that has severely affected their self-worth. This was seemingly endemic outside the continent as recounted below by Reiter (2019): "Nowhere do we have accounts of slavery stripping a person of his or her very personhood, taking away their names, language and culture as consistently and violently as in the Americas" (47). When their minds are decolonized, their approach to the consumption of Western forms of communication will be different. They will assert themselves and be aware of the consequences of Western dependence and the effect on their well-being for the long haul. When new forms of communications are introduced, there is ultimately a source and in the case of cyber communication, it is the Western hegemonic forces operating under the push and pull factors of Western politics, social, cultural, and most importantly, economic aims that can better be termed virtual forms of capitalism. This form of capitalism that has manifested itself on the lives of Africans, especially on the continent, Caribbean, and Latin America, continuously reduces the Black person to the level of a digital communicative pauper.

Chapter 3

Black Confluence of Digital and In-Person Spaces

Cyberpolitics can be a potential deal maker or spoiler. In-person communication spaces, according to Jurgen Habermas, the last surviving Frankfurt School critical scholar, accorded and amplified political dialogue among communities in the 1960s. Today, that space has become more digital. African Americans and Black activists have taken to Twitter, Snapchat, Facebook, Instagram, and so on to vent their anger after the senseless police murder of George Floyd, Travon Martin, Freddie Gray Michael Brown, Breonna Taylor, Philando Castille, Eric Garner, Tamir Rice, the recent Wisconsin shooting of Jacob Blake, and so on. In fact, according to Chen (2017), this action "demonstrates the interplay between social media and race and how technology offers new avenues of communication for people who may have lacked the means to express themselves in more traditional media channels" (117). Given the omnipresence and the apparent fluidity of identification associated with virtual communication, oppressed groups have taken to online platforms to express feelings of discomfort. These digital spaces, including platforms on Twitter like #TWiB (This Week in Black Nation), have now become avenues for "self-definition and self-representation" (Florini, 2017, 330). It also operates podcast and radio outlets. The two interfaces provide readily available media for Black people to express feelings about their race. TWiB is founded by Elon James White and its primary objective is uplifting Blackness. This, of course, throws the wet towel on the often-contentious discourse of race and colorblindness. Anything tagged with Black presence presupposes that there is equally and, fundamentally too, another digital space for "Whiteness." But years of unjust and poor treatment of Blacks by Whites throughout American history has given room for such confined spaces to exist among Black people and the attempt at fashioning parallel structures in the name of racist or pejorative readings of such venture continues to deny the very significance of open democratic spaces for marginalized folks to air out grievances and uplift their spiritual mindsets. Years of suppressed anger and disgust at the dominant hegemonic White leadership that have, on a consistent basis, relegated Blackness and Black people to the lowest rung of human achievement has triggered an onslaught of reactions in the in-person as well as the digital spaces. They have resorted to search for their voice to retell the history of the Black person and his struggles to move from one rung of the ladder unto the next in the face of grueling racist chants from the dominant White race. Statistics about traditional media ownership by minorities and more especially Black media ownership in the United States in radio, television, and newspaper is at a dismal single-digit number and so the welcome relief of digital platforms for interaction among them that could provide space for their voice is a welcome relief. But that too maybe problematic since there is no Black ownership of the major national and international digital platforms own and managed by a Black person. Ownership gives one license to control the narrative; it gives management an editorial agenda on what should be posted, what should be censored, and what should be allowed and disallowed.

BLACK INTERSECTIONALITY SPACES

Blackness exists in various interrelated forms online and offline. The migratory journey that started with massive transatlantic slave trade dispersed millions of Blacks from the continent of Africa to far-off lands of the Americas and Europe. As a result, the term "Black" has undertaken different semantic undertones depending on context and issue at hand. The United States has become the confluence of Blackness by bringing Black people from Latin America, South America, Europe, the Caribbean, and the mother African continent. Thus, online and offline spaces have been created to cater to pertinent needs affecting different sections of these various Black groups. Sometimes these issues intersect like the constant police brutality in the United States targeting mostly people with Black pigmentation and sometimes they don't intersect. When issues affecting the collective race are brought into the public sphere virtually or offline on Blacks, the world overreacts in unison as was the case with Trayvon Martin and George Floyd, but this does not mean that they are a monolithic group. Far from it. It must be borne in mind that being Black does not equal to pigmentation; rather, it is a social construct based partly on White dominant ideology on what constitutes Blackness and also a psychological burden for an individual who chooses to belong to the Black race regardless of parentage or matrimony. Other matters that affect this specific group are, by and large, drug-related crimes, immigration, incarceration, and deportation. The same is true especially with Black women in Africa. Organizations have been created as well as several blogs on the Internet to educate men as well as women on the negative consequences of Female Genital Mutilations (GFM) in Africa (see psmag.org).

BLACK SOCIAL MEDIA SPACES

Social-mediated platforms are used for uploading videos, images, and texts by everyone in the world. Ever since the launching of social media platforms such as Facebook and YouTube in the mid-2000s, mobile Internet users have stormed these sites. Others have also mushroomed within this decade like WhatsApp, WeChat, Instagram, Snapchat, and Twitter. Black users in Africa have also continuously demonstrated a voracious appetite using mostly their mobile-to-mobile communication handsets. Becker (2017) has revealed that just within a space of two years (2012–2014) South Africans increased their subscription rate on another popular social media platform called Instagram from 100.000 in 2012 to 1.1 million in 2014 (104). What is even more intriguing, to say the least, is that some Africans using Instagram on social media have created an alternative visual culture of artistic display known as "Every Day Africa." "Everyday Africa [that] shows images by both amateurs and professionals in an attempt to counter mainstream perspectives with images of the ordinary" (Gorin, 2015, 5). So, digital spaces for Black Internet users serve dual purposes: Social movement public sphere congregation and platforms to promote virtual unique cultural artifacts. These spaces are a direct reflection of the in-person spaces in the offline world of human activities. But sometimes representations of reality in the hyperreality universe of chatrooms and simulated audio, image, and video can be complicated. That is why interpretation of items uploaded on the transient and seamless space called the Internet could be a little bit deceitful. With deceit comes artificiality, and both can jettison the ship of communication on the tumultuous high seas. That is why a special virtual space knowledge site is expected to completely decipher the difference between truth and falsehood when materials are uploaded for consumers on the Internet. The same problem that beset Western users of cyberspace also confronts Black users at home and abroad. But this is not to dispute the fact that these spaces have provided the much-anticipated voice to the underrepresented Black users. As already argued with respect to the case with George Floyd, Tamir Rice, Trayvon Martin, Michael Brown, and so on, these spaces have opened the vista for age-old Black problems to finally crash on the threshold of the overwhelming White dominant society. The Internet provides the window for all to consume materials that would have otherwise been confined to the privileged few. A case in point is Black Twitter, as would be discussed below.

BLACK TWITTER AND CYBERSPACE

Black Twitter is a virtual "public sphere" for mainly African Americans and Blacks to exchange ideological stances on issues affecting the Black community. It came about after the brutal murder of unarmed African American teen, Trayvon Martin, in 2012. It is a place for racial identity (Harlow and Benbrook, 2019) construction. In the 1990s, African Americans were demographically outnumbered by White Americans on Internet access. But twenty years later, their acquisition of smartphones with Internet access made them narrow the gap between them and Whites when it comes to Internet access (Clark, 2014). According to Smith (2014), African Americans have now surpassed the Whites in the use of Twitter. The narrowing of the gap has equally resulted in creating a space using Twitter hashtags to microblog content relevant to mostly the Black community. In an interview on State News Service of Waco, TX, Moody Ramirez, the co-author of a groundbreaking book titled *"From Blackface to Black Twitter: Reflections on Black Humor, Race, Politics, and Gender,"* acknowledges that Black Twitter is an online grassroots movement particularly for African Americans. Hotbutton socio-political issues that are ignored by the mainstream media in the United States are discussed and debated online using the various hashtags like #BlackGirlJoy, #blackboyjoy, or #blacklivesmatter (White, State News Service, 2019). Black Twitter seems to mirror the offline 1960 civil rights movements in the United States, where Blacks who have consistently been marginalized, discriminated upon by the majority White American community took to the streets to demand equal rights and freedom. That movement that saw the rise of prominent African American activists like Martin Luther King Jr, Malcolm X, and John Lewis forced the government to come to the negotiation table with the Black communities. This is what subsequently gave birth to multiple abolition laws enacted in the United States, most especially that of Jim Crow, voting rights, and desegregation of schools in the country. With the emergence of the Internet revolution, virtual movements like the Arab Spring in North Africa brought dictators like Hosni Mubarak in Egypt, Ben Ali of Tunisia, and Colonel Muammar Gaddafi in Libya to their knees. They fell from power because social media galvanized young folks to tweet and facebooked each other mainly in the urban cities to organize street protest (figure 3.1).

Nevertheless, Black Twitter configuration and tapestry of in-group dialogue is dramatically different from the Arab Spring hashtag that was

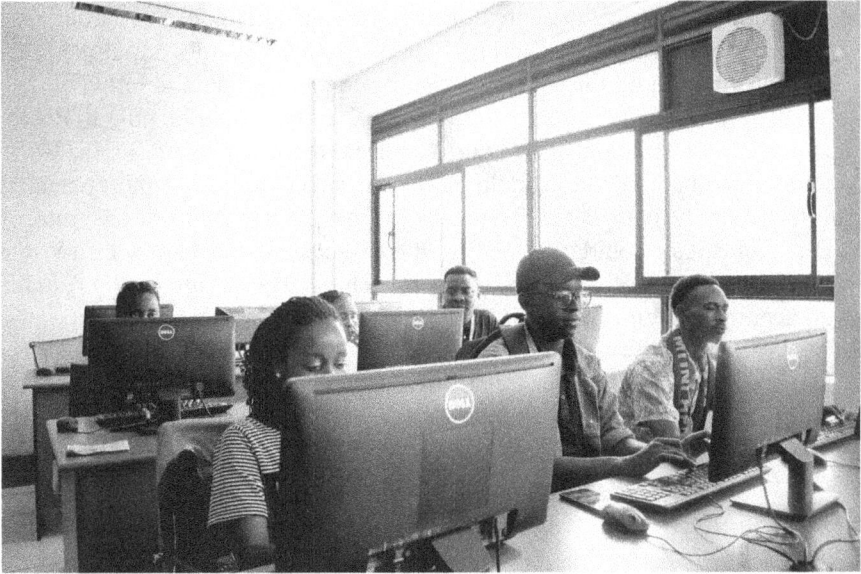

Figure 3.1   Photo by Agnes Lucy Lando.

centralized with religio-cultural affiliations as content markers. Almost all the followers identified with the Muslim religion and their nation's citizenship including Arabic as their official language. The discourse that goes on in the various hashtags on Black Lives Matter may be tainted because some users/ contributors may be "speaking, acting, and tweeting black" (Maragh, 2018, 592). Others could be tweeting Black and acting White and that could seriously jeopardize concrete physical action to redress political and social issues plaguing the Black community. The virtual forms of grassroots movements as espoused by Moody Ramirez aforementioned can hardly mirror in totality the 1960s civil rights movements that were non-virtually carried out. An inauthentic Black community member can easily be spotted during a Black church gathering after service or during a rally through the words that he/ she utters regardless of pigmentation, but that could be a daunting task for us to decipher with virtuality where people are sending messages using their smartphones, laptops, tablets, desktop on Macintosh, and PCs. It is so easy to disguise and imitate or role-play any given topic(s) that is being discussed but in real life, this user could be an anonymous spy. Imagine the nature of the discourse if the ownership of Twitter was Black and authentic certificate issued to members before they can gain entry to Black Twitter site. Imagine if this #BlackTwitter was entirely under the supervision, directorate, and organization by Black Internet users. By Black we do not mean to essentialize, rather to authenticate such that any posts on Black Twitter could easily be identified by source and content. But anonymity abounds, and participants contribute from all over the world. Ownership, organization, and dissemination of information on this site could have been manageable in terms of data sourcing such that a researcher studying the hashtag could be able to distinguish users' contribution from Latin America, the Caribbean, Africa, North America, Europe, and the Middle East. The supposition that the content is king to the analysis of Black Twitter could not be further from the truth. A content contributor could be tweeting Black issues but he/she may be a White European, not even White American and such data sets could hardly provide us an accurate picture of the significant effects of Black communication on Black Twitter. Consequently, online discourse that can purely be categorized as directly from a cultural or racial reference to the Black community with no irony intended by the contributor could be difficult to decipher. This is because contributors "acting White" could purposefully redirect discourse to a particular focus in order to ascertain reaction from Twitter fans and that user could retweet such discussions and forward to the global community. When it reaches the global community that is when the mainstream media would get into the spin mode of analysis, thereby minimizing the impact of Black Twitter that is a space meant to consciously discuss issues facing the Black community.

As opposed to the street protest in North Africa and the Middle East that was largely triggered by social media push and pull factors, it is difficult to state with conviction whether the Occupy Wall street and Black Lives Matter street protests in the United States were spurred by #occupywall street or #BlackLivesMatter online discussions. Being consciously aware of posts online on such platforms could be another dilemma affecting analysis of constructs and dialogue on Black Twitter as opined by Brock (2018). He says "I have consistently found that articulations of digital/online Blackness draw from offline understandings of racial identity (Black and non-Black), technocultural representations of Whiteness in code, and beliefs about 'appropriate' technological use." (5) This is problematic in that offline socio-cultural awareness informs the user's choice of expression online so as to conform or not to conform. It, therefore, means that before contents are uploaded on any of the sites for Black consumption, the context of the message sender, the identity of the messenger, and his/her cultural affiliation are factored into the message, but this may be difficult to assess because an African American who lives in Durban, South Africa and who reads, and is constantly updated with African American affairs here in the United States is not different from one who has lived in the United States all his/her life. But their offline socio-cultural identification may not be the same. The user from South Africa may have been assimilated by the Black protest movements of the African National Congress and the subtext of his/her dialogue may be influenced by that. That contributor could stir the discussion to another angle that could trigger angry reactions from some African American residents in the United States. Also, there are multi-racial members of the Black Twitter whose contributions could be sympathetic to both Black and White race with respect say to the killing of George Floyd by Derek Chauvin in Minneapolis, Minnesota, Rayshard Brooks by Garrett Rolfe, in Georgia or Marcus Brown of Ferguson, Missouri by Police Officer Darren Wilson. This contributor could be taken for White and a barrage of tweets sent to counter his/her viewpoints. This is the conundrum with online protest site like Black Twitter that stands to further the cause of Black Lives Matter.

Another area of contention when looking at the confluence of in-person action versus online activism for the Black race is that place, time, and setting are determined when dealing with in-person movements. In the 1960s, African Americans and some White sympathizers participated in the march to Washington. The Black Church and other gatherings of African Americans were used to rally sympathizers. With virtual space like Black Twitter, millions of users can tweet and retweet about an action that could culminate in the march to the White House. But those not resident in the United States may not be party to the ground movement that can actually provide legitimacy and credence to the struggle. In order for the numbers to increase, additional effort has to be implemented to recruit foot soldiers to go from door to door to bring sympathizers, but that could be difficult because those who tweet may not be willing to disclose the home addresses even though Twitter can detect the cities from where they are sending messages. This is one of the struggles of online activism for Black Lives Matter movement. Conversely, not all users online can actually be called cybernetizens (fully committed). Most of them are cybercitizens gaining access and reading contents online—more on this below.

BLACK CYBERCITIZENS AND CYBERNETIZENS

Cybercitizenry is the process of gaining access into the cyberworld through login id acquisitions, but cybernetizenry is "active" presence in that world. In other words, you are in the process of becoming a cybercitizen when you undertake computer literate courses, say in a rural cybercafé in a remote village in Malawi or Cameroon. When you sign up with login ids into any given Internet domain for cyber activities, you become a cybercitizen. But you may not yet become what Luke (2011) calls a "digital citizen" (90). You are still a neophyte in cyberspace. This idea is partially in consonance to that of Luke's (2011) general conceptualization of cybercitizen and digital citizens. We now seem to have dual citizenships: one in the electronic communicative twenty-four hours' republic and another in the in-person non-electronic communicative republic. To become a cybercultural guru takes a longer process of epistemic know-how of cybernetism. This applies to Black users on the continent of Africa and abroad. The concept of digital divide, whereby lots of potential cybernetizens on the continent of Africa have been neglected due to access/educational difficulties, plays a significant role in reducing the flow and subsequent preponderant role of Black cyberactivism. Similarly, the lack thereof of monetary wherewithal in the Diaspora for African Americans and other Black individuals from Africa, Latin America, and the Caribbean hampers their significant contributions on cyberspace. Given that most immigrants Blacks in the United States, Europe, and Canada must be gainfully employed in more than one job, so as to put food on the dining table, care for the elderly, send kids to school, and also send remuneration back home to needy extended families have equally greatly affected their day-to-day activism on some given sites like Black Twitter or TWiB. But their activities in cybersubcultural sphere on matters related to their kith and kin at home and abroad have seen increasing participation on mobile telephonic Apps like WhatsApp, Viber, Imo, and Facebook. When they do become active citizenry on any given cybernetic discourse, they transplant their offline cultural traits with them. The transplantation may not necessarily yield dividend in the sense of complementarity, but certain features of "black speak" (Brown, 2002) are evident in lexicon and other iconic representations in text, images, audios, and videos. True, the keyboard can become a hindrance to transplantation as well as language, but sometimes they do find a way to go around it. This is what gives unique qualities to Black netizen cultural communicative transactions on cyberspace and that should not be confused with stereotypes or racism (see chapter 7, Digi-Culture and Racism). To be a Black netizen means one engages actively in the process of netizenification, which involves encoding and decoding messages on virtual space that comply with the concept of communication competence. There are several users of the net who barely communicate competently across, within and between platforms. To be competent is to follow canons of communication within a certain given context, sphere, and applying ethical standards where necessary. Most users are effective communicators on cyberspace and those could be termed citizens because they master the language of communication, but when they are oblivious of given rules of play, say from a moderator of a given site, blog, listserv, and platforms, they fail to achieve communication competence and that cannot make them netizens. Classic examples are scammers and spammers who are constantly blocked on some sites, and they have to keep figuring out how to target users and get wanted information that can be used for malicious effects.

When someone is resident in Latin America as an Afro-Latino/Latina or in the Caribbean, North America, Europe, and Africa and engages in either "black speak" on any given site that brings Black people together like #BlackLivesMatter or the past #RhodesMustFall and many other sites on social media, that is already an indication that that person is a Black netizen or follower because he/she has mastered the vernacular of the populace registered on that site. Very rarely do you have people from other races that have mastered "black speak" like Ebonics, Creole, Pidgin, or any African language. Apart from the linguistic taxonomy that could be an indicator of netizen Black user on the cyberspace, there is also the familiarity with customs and culture, especially with those in Africa who have the tendency to still maintain and respect cultural hierarchy online. A certain user could identify himself or herself as representing a clan or tribesmen and women and those familiar with such a warrior could use ritualistic tags to honor his/her presence and that is what communication competence from a netizen is supposed to be like. There are social media platforms in Africa like NaijaPal for users from Nigeria, Jamii Forum from East Africa, Chomi for South Africans, and Lenali App for those from Mali. In these platforms, those who constantly interact there are netizens who master the culture and languages that are employed on the site and those who are identified with specific titles and positions they hold in the society are upheld and respected. Other Black social media users say from other parts of the world may not find it easy to join those sites because they will not be able to follow the discourse from the contents that are uploaded and the style of discussants. In these sites, you can hardly find "outsiders" as you might, say, on Black Twitter.

ORALITY (LENALI APP) AND SOCIAL MEDIA

Lenali App is an oral-interactive site created by Mamadou Guro in Mali to cater to the needs of those that are Western-written language deficient to go on Facebook. The Western literacy rate in French, the official language from France, the colonial master of Mali is relatively low. Only between 5 and 10 percent of Malians are fluent in the French language that is supposedly the official language of the country because Mali was colonized by France and like all other French colonies in Africa like Togo, Benin, Cameroon, Gabon, Congo, and Senegal, the French language was imposed as the main language of education, politics, and commerce. This was a direct rebuke to the people who, from pre-colonial era, have been used to their mother tongues in the oral and written forms. In Mali like all other French colonies in Africa, majority of their population speak mainly native languages. The Bambara tribe of people, that are the majority of the population, speak the Bambara language. This language is spoken by almost 80 percent of the population. The Tuareg of the northern regions speak Tamajaq and Tamasheq. The Dogon in the south speak the Dogon languages. Since they too have to communicate on social media or any other digital platforms, social media—a Western creation—has not taken their language deficiency into consideration. This is what prompted Guro to create this software in the capital city of Mali, Bamako, to bring in more social media users since it was becoming a daunting task to have more people participate as netizens on Facebook and Twitter. Only a tiny fraction of the Malian public mainly in the capital city and proficient in the French language could actually be active on social media site. With this platform users are able to speak out information in their various traditional or native languages and they get instant translation that are then transmitted to the receiver and the latter's preferred language. This App became a welcome relief as more and more subscribers jumped on board orally transmitting messages to loved ones at home and abroad. The full site can be accessed using this URL: https://play.google.com/store/apps/details?id=ml.lenali.lenafrica &hl=en_US.

With such a site, members can hardly not be affiliated with the customs, traditions, and rituals that go on in Mali. It may be difficult to sustain dialogue on such an App without prior knowledge of the cultural systems in place. The oral component of the site gives ample room for credibility because users are encoding messages using the local languages and the platform staff are translating or interpreting to the receivers and vice versa. This kind of message transfer actually vindicates the relationship between online communication and offline communication coming together for the mutual benefit of all parties involved. The question of ownership of content and site that was discussed earlier among Black users of the social media sites on cyberspace can actually be resolved through this medium. This is the Black race seizing what has been created in the West and adapting it to their cultural and traditional realities in Africa. If such sites could mushroom all across Africa, the Caribbean, and Latin America, then it could be quite easy to close the digital divide gap in digital communication. This way, Africa will stop paying lip services to imported materials from the West. They will interrogate them and find pathways to adapt and integrate to the needs of the people. Such an adaptation can take into consideration palpable scientific considerations on the ground through a study of communication needs, style, boundaries, and context before new communicative devices are introduced to the people. Like most other development initiatives that go on in Africa, Latin America, and the Caribbean, fact-finding mission workers are deployed to the countries and regions before new products, systems, and technologies are introduced. This could have been the case with digital technology before cell/smartphones and other accompanying devices were exported to the various regions. This could have resolved part of the saga about the digital divide from the viewpoint of access, gender, class, age, literacy, and culture. There are other social media platforms created by Africans for Africans and other Blacks in the Diaspora. They are mainly culture-specific. There is the *Naijapals* social media site where users narrate stories about their plights in Nigeria and outside Nigeria using contents that are easily recognizable mainly by those born and raised in Nigeria. *Chomi* is another App that is based in South Africa and being used by South Africans at home and abroad. There are other languages beside English that can be used on this App. The same is true of *Jamii Forum* that is based mostly in East Africa. Although Facebook, WhatsApp, YouTube, Twitter, LinkedIn, and Instagram are dominating the social media platform communications in the continent of Africa, followed by Naijapals, Chomi, and Jamii Forum, there are other startup platforms that are equally making headways. They are *OurHood* and *Medishare* in South Africa, *Slickr* in Egypt, and *Guumzo* in Tanzania, among others.

AFRICANS/BLACKS AND DIGITAL DIVIDE

There are numerous approaches and definitions of digital divide but what is common among them is that the issue of access, technological know-how, and availability constitute elements of digital divide (Langmia and Lando, 2020; Ragnedda and Mutsvairo, 2018; Graham and Dutton, 2014; Grosswiller, 2013). As far back as 2003, Lister et al. (2003) describe digital divide as the continuous presence of the "technology rich and technology poor" (180). I may go further by saying digital divide occurs when some communities are denied access through multivariate forces. These forces, in some cases, are governmental because they clamp down on users by shutting down the Internet. Blacks especially in some parts of Africa have suffered these consequences, especially in Egypt during the Arab Spring rising and Cameroon during the Anglophone Cameroon crisis. The government stifles free speech on the Internet when their interests are threatened by the angry populace who take on social media to disseminate images of torture by government forces. Digital divide coinage is equally problematic to unravel in a given context as Rimini (2011) posits. According to her, there is an apparent supposition that users are already in the digital domain after the analog debacle. But in truth, they are not and so to claim it resolves the digital divide debacle could be a misnomer to some sectors of the social and economic realm. When it comes to the Black economic standing in the global affairs, we may be overstretching it to talk about the digital divide when the lines of inequality, even in the analog communication era usage, were glaringly unequal. Be that as it may, the millennial Black population on the continent and abroad are on the bandwagon of digitalization, but they may not always be operating at the same wave-length, given that income distribution equally affects access, especially at home, abroad, and in some cases in Africa. Home and the school environment do not always provide economic leverage to users eager to join the global call for change or movements. Most users of digital gadgets are mobile phone owners, but they too have certain limits to the kinds of materials that they can download and upload on the World Wide Web for the world to see. Take for instance, a user following a political riot or military operation in a remote area in Africa has to deal with various challenges ranging from bandwidth, access, power, and censorship. And not only that, I also believe Doueihi's (2011) firm stance on digital literacy as a major contribution to digital divide as well as acquiescing Livingstone et al. (2010) definition as "a multidimensional construct that encompasses the abilities to access, analyze, evaluate and cre-ate online content" (Livingstone and Helsper, 2010, 311). This is so relevant to the Black user context because knowledge of emoticon, meme, trolling, phishing, texting, image, audio, and video uploads demand certain skills with respect to given platforms. Instagram posting in any given form is radically different from posting on Twitter or Snapchat. How to use Facebook wall and live posts are not the same as posting on WhatsApp, LinkedIn, or YouTube. They all demand certain restricted rules, and that by themselves constitute a divide and that is why it is possible to agree with Lister et al. (2003) that most of this depends on geopolitical context with respect to the technology rich and technology poor. There is no gainsaying the fact that even without statistics to back up claims, the so-called Western democracies, from where the Internet originated, are technologically richer than non-Western democracies like Africa who are technologically poor. Consequently, the percentage of folks deprived of digital know-how is no doubt higher than those in the West. So, any discussion of a digital divide is disproportionately in favor of improving conditions for those in the fringes outside Western capitals. The same goes to rural folks and income poor Blacks in the inner cities in the United States and Europe. Any inequality resulting from income directly impacts social activi-ties like cyberculture. Digital divide implies that what has been garnered in the in-person world that could become visible and attract global citizenry reaction may be stifled because users are unable to transmit information. When citizens uploaded disgusting photographs of police brutality of youth uprising in the Anglophone part of Cameroon, the government responded by shutting down the Internet to the North West and South West regions of the country where protest was rife (Pommerolle and De Marie Heungoup, 2017). The government believed those sites were sending gory photographs to the international community to ask for sympathy for their cause to secede from La Republic du Cameroon. As a result, ninety-three days passed with little-or-no footage of police brutality in the form of arbitrary arrests, abductions, murder, and rapes. For ninety-three days that users experienced digital divide brought about by no access imposed by the Internet Providers (MTN, NEXTEL, ORANGE, etc.), folks had to record some images, travel to nearby cities that have accessibility to upload, and send to the entire world including the BBC, Aljazeera, and the CNN. But they had to send these images surreptitiously because crossing from the North West and South West regions of the country, police and other men of uniforms inspected cell phones for possible questionable images, audio, and texts. The reason for Anglophone Cameroonians to upload these pictures and send through social media to other Cameroonians, especially in Diaspora, is because for decades the national television and radio stations are owned and operated by the government of La Republic du Cameroon and any message deemed offensive to the regime is quickly censored and the sender arrested and jailed and in some cases killed without anyone's knowledge. The emergence of social media communication is, therefore, a welcome relief to youths in Tropical Africa. But when dictatorial regimes impose a digital divide when the Eastern part and the Northern part of the country like Cameroon is allowed to have Internet access while the Anglophone sector that is in the west is cut off, the entire concept of the digital divide that began with the issue of access only acquires another new meaning.

BLACKS AND DIGITAL DIVIDE IN THE UNITED STATES

The COVID-19 pandemic has created another debate surrounding Internet access, costs, and computer accessibility for low-income families in the United States. Both Whites and Blacks have all agreed through a Pew research study by Vogels, Perrin, Rainie, and Anderson (2020) that Internet has been essential with the outbreak of the pandemic. But how many poor-income Blacks do have access and can afford the huge costs of Internet at home? With most schools going online, kids of low-income parents cannot afford to have their kids learn from a home computer with Internet access. In this same study, 36 percent of Blacks are worried about paying broadband Internet at home as opposed to 21 percent of Whites. When it gets to the low income it rises to 52 percent. From these statistics, it is quite evident that Black families fare far worse than Whites and with the rate of unemployment more for Blacks than Whites, especially as over 30 million Americans are out of work, the digital divide gap may be widening even further. The COVID-19 pandemic has also affected the African American and Hispanic families more than White Americans. It is crucial to understand that the notion of the digital divide that affects the minority population in the United States as earlier discussed should be limited to access and not be expanded to include motivation and creativity. Ellison and Solomon (2019) in their study have displayed the perceptual differences with examining this concept from different races. In their study they concluded that "the narratives about African Americans and the digital divide have displayed evidence of racist and stereotypical stories over time by disproportionately focusing on the access—or lack thereof—of populations of color" (238). It is often believed that since the African Americans in the United States are often faced with poverty and unemployment, they are the ones that are also being affected most with issues related to digital skills and awareness. But this study that has focused primarily with African American children and families has demonstrated the shortsightedness of stereotyping one ethnic group of people over the other or lumping them under a certain umbrella viewpoint that helps to feed generalities. The children in this study by Ellison and Solomon (2019) were skillful, adept, and creative with computer and Internet usage when given the possibility to perform given tasks. So, it is always counterproductive to lump a certain group of people under a certain mental rubric of assessment when empirical studies have not been carried out to validate assertions.

That notwithstanding, it should be pointed out there are several categories of Blacks in the United States. The notion of Black immigrants is often associated with members of the African, Afro Latina, and Afro-Caribbean families that reside as residents or as citizens in the United States. But most studies classify Blacks to include African Americans as well, and that is why getting a representative picture of who is impacted most with the issue of digital divide is more or less a daunting task. However, a much more recent study by Ndumu (2020) highlights the level of technology availability, access, and affordability between African immigrants and Afro-Caribbean and Afro Latinos. Her findings have more or less dismissed established norms of the Black community suffering more than the other race with respect to Internet affordability:

> Despite the prevailing view that immigrants lack ICT resources, access and skills, ACS data supports that Black immigrants primarily turn to mobile technology, though they maintain multiple forms of ICT and Internet access. Cellular data plan (70.4%) is the most prevalent form of Internet access for this group, and nearly the same amount had hi-speed Internet access (68.2%). The majority of households had access to smartphones (80.6%) and desktop/laptops (78.6%). Thus, Black immigrants' ICT and Internet behavior appears to be multidimensional. (Ndumu, 2020, 81–82)

Therefore, it can be deduced that the Black community in the United States is not a monolithic group and that there are other groups like the Black immigrant groups studied above that are on the train ride of digitalization. On the flip side, what could be troubling with this type of data is that it can be misconstrued as indicating that the digital divide gap—related to access—for the Black community is closing, but that is not the case. There are several angles to discuss the digital divide. Access is just one of those angles, but the other areas that have arisen in the age of the superhighway and coupled with the emergence of the COVID-19 pandemic, the other directions of examining the notion of digital divide with respect to access, availability, and costs are gender, age, and social status. The other divide has to do with knowledge. Affordability and availability can be a no-brainer for the Black immigrant community evidenced from this 2020 study aforementioned. But media literacy and education are the other aspects not to turn a blind eye when dealing with the issue of digital divide. While others can afford and do own these gadgets, what they do on them is another debate. There is increasing mobile divide (Langmia and Glass, 2014). There is a plethora of installed Apps on users' smartphones from Android to iPhone to iPods and iPads that users hardly use and have no use for them, yet they keep updating their IOS features that include all those Apps and they pay huge monthly data fees for them. There is also the situation of uploading and downloading applications for the smartphones that some users perform on their phones and others don't. Even when some users have successfully installed an App like Facebook, they have no clue on how they can get rid of spam and misinformation loading on their systems simply because they have not updated their settings or profiles. The use of emojification on smartphones do not represent all cultures on planet earth, yet these products are exported with similar content to users all over the world (Bangura, 2020; Langmia, 2020; Lando, 2020). The same statement applies to language. These are some relevant issues that do affect the concept of the digital divide because there cannot be any inequality (Ragnedda and Mutsvairo, 2018) on the seats of the bandwagon of the train of technology that is providing valuable services to humankind, especially in the era of too many traffic on the virtual pathways. Inequality breeds marginalization, whether intended or unintended. It is this marginalization that, more often than not, creates representational race imbalance. The Black race has for centuries now decried the wanton marginalization and subjugation that they have been subjected to for decades and the COVID-19 pandemic coupled with the outpouring of love that have been exhibited on the Internet and on the streets all over the world. This tendency of conscious marginalization has pricked the consciences, and some companies are struggling to create race diversity at the workplace (more on this in chapter 11). It is impossible to discuss the concept of digital divide affecting the Black community in the United States without discussing the issue of power.

Historically, traditional media, including television, newspapers, and movies, have offered two avenues for people of color—invisibility or marginalization. Critical Race Theory argues that the reason for this is that racism is not an aberration but is embedded in our culture as a means of reinforcing the power structure of the dominant white group. (Chen, 2017, 117)

The backdrop of traditional media marginalization of African Americans has spilled over to the digital media's sphere. Wilson II, Gutierrez, and Chao (2003) maintain among other allegations that power dynamics in the inter-play of African American marginalization within the context of the media has a long history with traditional mediated new coverage, wherein they did not place Blacks, and most importantly African Americans, as a significant race at the center of economic and political progress in the United States. To them "lack of coverage of peoples of color in mainstream news media had the effect of asserting their lack of status, a powerful social psychological message delivered to Whites and non-Whites alike" (117). The potent force of the media can have a deleterious effect on the viewer if tilted to favor one group over the other. Imagine watching the news media—mainstream for that matter, and to make matters worse, watching prime time when a majority of Americans are out of work and consuming news and not having a single African American as a news anchor. The recent appointment of Joy Reid to anchor a prime time MSNBC program titled "The Reid Out" has been a tiny drop of water that has splashed into the large ocean because this is a cable ser-vice broadcast station and only the working class have access to it, and, more importantly, mostly liberals are tuned to it. Mainstream media outlets like CBS, ABC, NBC, and Fox do not have a Black prime time broadcaster. The psychological effect can be palpable. It goes without saying that the Black community is there to play on the margins and push the dominant White com-munity to their preferred destination. This is what Gandy (1998) has observed about media on African American males in general:

The tendency of the media to focus on African American males in reports on violent crime has produced a widely held belief that Black males are danger-ous. Indeed, the judicial standard of reasonableness has on numerous occasions incorporated this distorted impression as a justification for a White person shooting a Black male in "self defense." (23)

So, power dynamics in favor of White Americans on the media to arrogate to themselves the potent force of the media is equally encapsulated in the multiple directions of discussing the digital divide because it is all couched in the notion of marginalization and its psycho-economic effects. The psycho-social negative effect, especially on the younger generations of Whites and non-Whites, can be immeasurable and that is what is being seen played on digital media. Joy Reid was recently appointed to anchor the 7:00 p.m. new feature (Prime time) on MSNBC, and it has happened after the scandalous resignation of Chris Mathews over a sexual harassment complaint from one of his staff members. At the dawn of the COVID-19 pandemic and the spillover to street protests over the killing of George Floyd, the American community is coming to terms with the unwanted, unjustified, and illegal marginalization of African Americans in almost all areas of human endowments in the United States. That is what has accounted for the appointments and gift donations to Black organizations, charities, and HBCUs by mostly wealthy White Americans. It appears they have decided to examine their consciences and view the world not from a broken mirror but from a lens that magnifies the image of the American society. Everyone can see the ulcer on the wound of the country. No more dressing of the wound with bandages that are nothing but palliatives; rather, we should carry out intensive care surgery to cure the wound forever. Whether this task can be achieved at this moment in time is another topic of debate. Whether this act of examining the conscience of the nation after the death of George Floyd can be possible is another issue entirely especially as we fold our hands hoping that this act can be sustainable for the new digital media that have multiple functions. New media have become the mainstay and digital media is now the tube that has been transformed to become the workplace and school for mankind on planet earth as a result of the pandemic. If we don't engage this media efficiently and do it collectively, then our identity, ie human identity will continue to be in crisis.

Chapter 4

Cyberculture and Black Identity

Figure 4.1   Mpesa Kiosk in Kenya. Photo by Agnes Lucy Lando.

CONCEPT OF IDENTITY/IDENTIFICATION

Identity is a complex subject from a human-to-human communicative perspective. While others may perceive one species of humanity from an essentialist/fixed viewpoint, others may see the predominant impact of reflexivity and processed change (Bell, 2001). In the in-person world of communication, certain attributes characterize individuals from a given cultural background, race, gender, sex, and class. These attributes are fixed ideological constructs in the mind of the preceptor that have been there for ages. There are extenuating and external variables like family upbringing, educational orientation, and media consumption that are responsible for these stabilizing forces on human minds. The only way to decenter these forces and allow social experience to act as informant to individual in the process of deconstructing these "fixed" perceptions is re-education. Hans Georg Gadamer would refer to as "bracketing one's prejudices" (Regan, 2012). This is why the question of identity and identification are complex to unravel. This is not to say that human beings do not possess what is often considered the real self. This real self is the core of who we really are and to some, this issue is heavily tied to religio-social upbringing. The impact of religion on the development of the self is extremely powerful and that constitutes identity. In the secular world, the identity of an atheist and the entire concept of identification in a given situation might puzzle believers of a certain religion. But to them they are exercising their experiential rights of being seen in that light. That is the same with gays and transgendered folks who have developed themselves and assumed different persona from what they had originally been known say at early childhood. This is a classic example of shifts in the notion of identity and identification. It is even more complicated when examining Black identities and identification on cyberspace.

Identification is much more complicated. Identification is heavily fed by stereotypical frames of mind. These frames could easily emanate from wrongful physical interpretation of one's outlook by the society as well as in-group factions in a given culture. Identification originally starts with someone presenting an identification document but that document has elements of physical attributes, including hair/ eye colors, sex, weight, and height. But increasingly, identification has gone beyond physical outlook to include accent, religion, body color, and groups that one has been admitted into. During a crisis like the hunt for Bin Laden after the 911 terrorist attack on the city of New York, regardless of the identification card that one holds, all those wearing hijabs and turbans were immediately classified as sympathizers of the religious fundamentalism. They were stereotypically classified as dangerous and people not to be trusted. Some were harassed at work (Gohil and Sidhu, 2007; Tindongan, 2011: Fadda-Conrey, 2011). This shows that identification is not only socially constructed but is politically constructed depending on circumstances and perceptual inclinations of a people. Some of these inclinations are spurred primarily by media exposure and socio-cultural affinities that one identifies with. Self-identity has bi-polar lenses. One's lens is innate to the individual and the other to the society. Blacks and many people of African descent go through the process of double consciousness (Du Bois, 2014). So, identity and identification for the Black race either in the United States, or the Latin Americas, the Caribbean, and Africa are complex concepts to unravel by a single definition. Ferenbok (2011) remarks on the concept of biometrics that can be very complicated to determine accurate identification:

The trouble is that biometric systems are measures of probability, the probability that the new input is the same person as the enrolled image, and therefore these systems can never be absolutely accurate. The face, when compared with fingerprints and iris patterns, is relatively dynamic physiological trait. Faces change considerably with lighting, viewing angles, and position, and with time, emotional states, surgery and trauma. Therefore, face recognition technologies confront a number of technological challenges when comparing faces. (Ferenbok, 2011, 127)

So, technologies can never solve the riddles of identity certainty. They depend on both context and content, space and time, nationality and pseudo-nationality, nature and nurture, education and the lack of education. Imagine the identity configuration of a Black immigrant child adopted by a White family in the United States who has White-acting proclivities or a biracial family being a victim of the one drop of Black blood mentality? How is that person supposed to address identity and identification in communication, let alone virtual communication?

IDENTITY AND CYBERSPACE

Being in cyberspace is synonymous to flying to an unknown destination and before you can acclimatize you must familiarize yourself with the rules of survival in that new setting. That is what virtual world of human communicative existence requires of all newcomers into cyberspace. The netiquettes of interpersonal, group, and mass communication must be learned before effective and competent communication and transaction either from B2B or C2C can be carried out. The ethics of these transactions can be defined by the site operators, moderators, and founders by any given group or persons. Black users of cyberspace are not immune to these requirements.

"Black Speak," as already discussed or rather the ways Black people interact offline has cross-pollinated to the virtual online realm from a socio-psychological perspective. The tendencies to code-switch or better still to imitate their daily offline interactive routine are clearly evident in the numerous listservs, news bulletin sites, discussion groups, and social media online communities that have been created from South Africa with Chomi to the United States on sites like Black Twitter and TWiB. According to Grosswiler (2009) "people everywhere prefer their own media in their own language" (118). So, it goes without saying that African media consumers deserve their own mediated spaces in their own languages. It is using language effectively and competently that one seeks to exert a certain amount of identity credibility online. Since users are not physically present to use both verbal and non-verbal gestures to demonstrate one's character that is central to validating identity, language is the only metrics for identity construction online, especially in a given space. If those spaces are only confined to small audiences of that language community, so be it. When matters of great importance transpire through that medium of communication, then people will learn that language to get into that given community. Although "social media have revolutionized our use of language" (Jones, 2013, xi), users would quickly identify patterns of change in their electronic language use than with another language. Western cyberculture has homogenized users—at least from a language point of view—such that it becomes almost impossible to decipher fake news from real news, fake personalities from real personalities, intruders and lurkers on the various platforms on the Internet and social media because a clear majority of users are sending and receiving messages in Western languages. As Grosswiler (2009) insinuated above, users are coerced to use these languages for communication because that is the only choice they have to reach the masses and also because the physical keyboards on most gadgets are one of the limiting factors. And When Cheikh Anta Diop says no nation can develop by using the language of another nation, it speaks to the dilemma with most Black cyberculturalists on the mother continent of Africa and abroad. #BlackTwitter supposedly houses the Black public sphere interactants and so would manifest a given cybercultural trait reminiscent of Black-on-Black in-person communicative dialogue. Suler and Barak (2008) observed this trend about the geo-socio-psychological effects of cyberspace-human communication:

> People experience and behave in the new cyberspace environment in a way that requires fresh innovative psychological conceptualizations, which entails exploiting old psychological knowledge, as well as formulating new ideas, to understand and explain human behavior and experience in cyberspace. (p. 2)

This presupposes a certain psychological shift in mindset when users transcend their imagination from the in-person human world of communication to the virtual realm in cyberspace. The same goes for Black Twitter users intending to maintain status quo of their erstwhile communicative traits on the site or rather for those non-Black users of the site to code-switch by assuming a different personality so as to sound and be perceived as Blacks on Black Twitter. The situation becomes more problematic because according to Nakamura (2002) the Internet has made it possible for cultures to be "transcoded" (3). So, to decipher an intruder on the site from a non-intruder could be an arduous task and when that becomes difficult the question of transparency on the net looms large. Digi-culturalism creates another dilemma with respect to identity when suspicious entries on the site can raise red flags. But users tend to believe that when they encode the decoder on the other side of the virtual world would understand their perspectives and can act accordingly.

CYBERSPACE AND PSYCHO-METRIC VALUES

When Sigmund Freud came up with the triangular concept of id, ego, and super ego, we thought it was limited to in-person characteristics of individual attitudes and behaviors. That is no longer true within the Internet public sphere where most people now spend most of their days at work than at home. The concept of the id, ego, and super ego are internal concepts that are exhibited by human actions. Now with online communication, how are those three concepts to be measured virtually. Psychologically speaking, it is a herculean task to decipher someone's instinctive attitude or behavior online from a 120-character text on Twitter without accompanying photos, videos, and audios. Even with those features from a one-time post, it could be foolhardy say for an employer to deny a good candidate for a job interview because his/her Twitter page is pregnant with photographs, texts, videos, and audios of himself paying say allegiance to someone like Osama Bin Laden. That could have been hacked, somebody could have gotten hold of his/her password, and decided to sabotage and assassinate his/her character, and employers do not have time, money, and energy to invest in a third-party organization to dig out the truth. The tendency to misinterpret, misjudge one's identity is far greater within the confines of digi-culturalism because images are sometimes cropped and photoshopped. The naked eyes can quickly find out if someone who pretends to be Black is putting up a mask or talking using a false accent offline than online. Human communication online, especially with the intermediary being the machine, the justification for authenticating identity formation, is problematic. Breen (2011, 71) states inter alia that as a result of this new mediated form of communication, "the Internet becomes a kind of knowledge broker for one's identity, where technology operates across the material, the social and the psychological domains of subjectivity." The psychological subjectivities stem from the source of data posted on a given site on the web and the content of the data. The encoder of messages can hardly conjecture the reaction of the decoders, particularly given the fluidity of messages and their senders. The fluidity comes about because multiple characters may have dictated the messages to the one sender who implicitly or explicitly believes that people will interpret the uploaded data from the same lens of understanding. This happens mostly with sites like Black Twitter or specified groups on Facebook dedicated to a given cause. From a psychological standpoint the reader will have to wrestle with his/her brains to take those messages with a grain of salt that they were not scripted by an attorney so as not to be implicated in one way or the other. When messages are anonymously sent on some sites, receivers will be able to determine through psychological gymnastics whether the sender's message and not the sender is authentic. So, anonymity has its place, especially when people are afraid of being immediately tracked down by readers, even technology experts who can trace message sources and senders are still capable of doing that. But that could be a long shot.

Another area of concern for identity as a psychological concern on the Internet is with material possession and autonomy of message. One's message carries weight on a group site only when the identity of the sender is psychologically associated with capital wealth. Cultural wealth may have its place in some areas, especially within the subaltern discourse, but in large groupings, people will quickly click on messages whose sender is already known to possess material wealth. The Internet is the new capital-intensive sphere since business can be carried out from persons to persons without any physical contact in the offline world. So, from a psychological point of view, users quickly react to messages from domains or sites whose sender can command some degree of economic standing in a given society. A case in point is the WhatsApp social media interactive site that people subscribe to as members of a clan or society. Since members associate themselves in the offline world but are resident in various parts of the world that prevents them from meeting in person, those who have established a priori connection with members of the group as economically wealthy individuals react to their messages in a quicker manner and those in search of jobs link up with them by sending private messages to their inboxes. Here identity has a direct correlation with a priori socio-cultural affinities. In other words, when sending messages on such a site unlike on Black Twitter or TWiB, the sender already knows the receiver (s). An ex-student Facebook chat group or WhatsApp or GroupMe chat rooms commands respect, a priori acquaintance, and affiliation from members of the group, making it possible for feedback to be measured. The burden of psychological stress of guessing how messages are to be received or reacted to is less in known-participatory sites as opposed to one that welcomes people as a result of race, gender, or class affiliations.

THE SELF AND DIGI-CULTURALISM

According to the Canadian Scholar Marshal McLuhan, the Internet is the "Extension of man" (McCluhan, McCluhan and Lapham, 1994). By extension, it means the transplantation of iconic symbols of one's non-virtual mind into the seamless cyberspace of interaction. How effective the process of transplantation can be is subject to contestation but suffice it to say some elements of the mind, body, and soul are present in the communicative interchange between two or more living beings on the Internet. The question now becomes whether pigmentation or the social construct of race that differentiates a Black user from a White user in the physical in-person universe of communication plays similar or dissimilar roles in the virtual space of communication. The answer to this question should inform identity creation, formation, and perception on any given platform of human communication on social media or the Internet in general. But what about Gray (2017) blunt assessment that "the Internet offered a space in which race and other identifying markers could remain hidden or ambiguous" (110). This is true only to a limited extent because advance in technology has provided ample tools to deconstruct and reconstruct the so-called hidden lurkers on the cloud. If WikiLeaks can deconstruct what seems unredeemable by all experts, there is little room for anonymity now in the cybernetic universe of communication.

Synchronous and asynchronous cybernetic transactions can offer platforms for a defined group of people like the Black race to self-disclose as well as pour out information that would otherwise not be disclosed in the "real" world of interpersonal, inter-group, or intercultural communication. The reason for such an attitude could be attributed to the fact that in general people tend to open up to things when they are in the position of being unidentified. Cyberspace seems to be that comfort zone especially on forums like Black Twitter or other exclusive sites for Black issues only. African American cyberspace users according to Dixon (1997) at the dawn of technological innovation should interact meaningfully with technology. They should "be 'intelligent consumers of information' rather than passive consumers of technological coolness" (Dixon, 1997, 147). By being "intelligent" users, Dixon probably implies engagement that constructs, reconstructs, and deconstructs their Blackness in any given MUDs, listserv, or platform that they congregate to advance a cause. There is the tendency for self-defined groups on cyberspace to use technology to learn about each other's ethnicity, region, religion, and social affinities that could instead spur racial or more ethnic discomforts. Though there is apparently nothing wrong in intersubjective assessment of personhood on electronic media, but that space could be more helpful if it is utilized for collective self-empowerment of the Black race. Instead of isolationism, whereby each group independently strives to advance a cause or seek to understand themselves in the Diaspora or at home, they could liaise with similar online groups to form a common Facebook platform. This is the case with the Southern Cameroon Ambazonia United Front site that brought in other affiliate online groups like SCAPO, SCNC, SCYL, and so on under one online roof so they can act together. All of them are Black Africans of Southern Cameroon region fighting for independence from La Republique of Cameroon in West/Central Africa.

There are various lenses to determine the magnitude of selves on the display dashboard of social media platforms in cyberspace. The Black selves display sentiments and advance information that could benefit a certain defined group of Blacks, say in the United States. Black Twitter is a good example. Other Black selves within the U.S. social media landscape could be the silent minority advancing the cause of gender equity within the Black community. All Black feminist groups on Facebook, Instagram, and Twitter are cases in point. The LGBTQ of the Black voice (https://www.facebook.com/blacklgbtandsgl/) and within this LGBTQ is another group for women LGBTQ. All these sites transmit messages unique to the causes that they are fighting for and since some of them are restricted, the impact of what they seek to address may only be felt through another means, mostly outside the virtual realm. The projection of different versions of selves can also be felt, especially when someone identifies as transgender but not gay. In that case, it could be far more difficult to discern from posted messages if the sender is transgender but following a different cause other than gay rights. It can only be discerned if the sender openly discloses to the group and in some cases the person can be expelled from the group. Another case in point is trans-subjectivities of selves where senders belong to multiple sites in cyberspace and post messages that respond to the needs of a given group. This case of multiple selves is similar to code-switching in the in-person world but even with code-switching you can only be one self in a given circumstance and unless you carry out transplantation or major face-lift you still would be identified primarily by folks who have known you for quite a long time as someone who is female or male and who belongs to such a race. But with the Internet, you sign up and portray multiple selves according to how you feel, thereby making yourself a multiplex individual in the cyberspace public sphere. So, when someone portrays Black feelings on Facebook and exhibits White sentiments on Instagram, we validate and vindicate Marshall McLuhan assertion that the Internet is indeed an extension of man. That extension has created two universes of existence for humans—the universe of offline earthly lives and the virtual online universe where livelihood and sustenance depend on the experiences of each netizen. Those who can hack and, in the process, get bank account numbers of other cyber immigrants, netizens, or citizens, and not get caught can extend their lifespan on the offline earthly lives. The pace of technological advances to create law and order in cyberspace is accelerated on a daily basis because each time new forms of encryption or data breaches occur, warranting measures to be taken to track down culprits. Imagine the task that awaits an Internet "police" compared to an offline police officer trying to gain access to all the multiple selves of one individual who has multiple passwords and login ids on various sites. Another complication has been echoed by Turkle (1997) when discussing the video game phenomenon on "Star Trek" when people spent many hours from across the world. "They create characters who have casual and romantic sex, who fall in love and get married, who attend rituals and celebrations. This is more real than real life" (143). When a character on a video game enjoys more of his livelihood on the virtual space than in the earthly offline space, that is seen as more real? This is what throws the entire concept of reality, hyperreality, and sur-reality with the introduction of online communication world for humanity. What to believe and what not to believe has become convoluted. Depending on what you are communicating about with whom, on what platform, in what setting determines your unique reality. What is real to a Black user on Instagram may be fake on Yelp for a White user. This is what identity has become in what Breen (2011) calls living in a "pixilated world" (282). As pixels vanish into thin air, so does our identity in the given cyberspace when there are none existent or deleted.

CYBERSUBCULTURE AND ETHNIC IDENTITIES

Spatiotemporal contexts on cyberspace provide avenues for cybersubcultural entities to mushroom and sprout. Blacks from different ethnic backgrounds exist virtually in self-defined spaces on cyberspace for multiple reasons. One of them, as already insinuated in the last paragraph, was for them to form a unified front to fight for self-independence from the majority population of Francophone Cameroonians in West/Central Africa. This group called the Southern Cameroon or Ambazonia, that is, #Ambazonia, is a subcultural entity within the larger entities on the Internet like Black Lives Matter (BLM) sites, Black Twitter, #TWiB, and so on. They have been fighting for the restoration of their independence from La Republique du Cameroon in West Africa for fifty-six years and counting. The raison d'etre for the creation of subcultural sites is to cater to the needs of specific groups within the Black community the world over. Homogeneity does not exist within any given race and that of the Black race is not different. The Black race today lives in socio-cultural and political mini incarcerated universes, and that by itself is making unity a far-fetched dream. That is not to say it is unattainable, it simply means the road has become much lengthier and rougher for a smooth ride to What Kwame Nkrumah, the former president of Ghana, dreamt of in 1963 as the *United States of Africa*. This explains, partially, the reason for the mushrooming of subcultural electronic spaces where they meet to fashion out common goals of their subgroups. This incarceration of the Black race began when millions of Blacks were uprooted from their natural setting in Africa and forcefully transported to the Americas and Europe without their consent. Those that remained on the mother continent became victims of colonization

200 years later, and that by itself constitutes what some have called rape almost as painful as the transatlantic slave trade. These two incidences in the life of the Black Diasporans have not only divided them into groups of disunited folks but in the larger scheme of things have made them to become denaturalized and disconnected from the continent of Africa.

Discussing the effect of that disconnection with respect to this new media technology, I conducted an interview with some students at Iganga in the outskirt of Uganda January 2020. In the interview referenced in chapters 1 and 2 that took place in Iganga, Uganda with young college students, another interviewee who goes by the name Grace noted the effect of smartphone technology and the effects on their African society:

> *It is affecting us a lot because most of the time when we are in a family meeting when I have my phone, I will not talk to anybody. It got to a point where I had to cut off using social media like for six months until I learn how to control myself . . . like realizing how it affected me I have reduced. Whenever I feel like going to the social media, I will read a book. It really affected me. It reached a time even if I want to think of something, I will not think, I just googled. That how much it affected me. After realizing that I told myself, this is not the way of life. I cannot put everything on the phone. So, I learned not to use the smartphone until I learned how to control myself. So, right now as much as I take it every-where with me. I can tell myself no. And when I am eating, I rather not carry it with me. So at least I can converse with the people that I am with.* (Grace, Iganga, January 2020)

The disconnection is felt at the level of interpersonal communication with Grace and her family and friends for which mobile technologies have colo-nized their personal spaces. In-person communication is indigenous to Africa and Africans. Non-verbal in-person communication is part of their DNA. But the smartphone has introduced a newcomer on the family meeting table and friendly chat and that newcomer is "silence" as they roam the virtual universe of social media. Grace's action above to resolve addiction and the disconnect she is experiencing with family and friends is to switch off mobile phone use for six months and read a book. And when she is with friends, she tries to initiate conversations in a bit to turn their minds off smartphones. Like most African youths, they are now in search of natural reconnection and rebirth. Whether this reconnection is going to yield meaningful fruits or dividends is anyone's guess. How long this re-connectivity is going to take is another dif-ficult question to answer, but as it stands now pockets of interrelated Black communities form spaces on the cyber universe to discuss matters related to identity, culture, philosophy, ethics, norms, traditions, social cohesion, politi-cal footprints, and economic survival. The real question lurking in the minds of onlookers and those impacted by these conundrums is whether something like cybercultural activism that North Africa experienced in 2010 can have a real-world impact. Right now, some examples of such actions are worthy of discussions like the Arab Spring cyber activism that saw the toppling of three African Dictators (Hosni Mubarak of Egypt, Muammar Gaddafi of Libya, and Ben Ali of Tunisia). Through the use of Facebook, Twitter, and blogs, citizens and netizens coalesced and constituted the critical masses that initiated the street demonstrations in these three countries. The overwhelming challenge came when they could not become a political force within the political system of the country and so conservatism still won as was the case with Egypt at the election booths when it came time to elect the successor of Mubarak. The Muslim brotherhood won overwhelmingly and that dealt a severe blow to the movement. The Tahrir Square in Egypt was the meeting plaza for the activists. All the mini cyber communicative platforms that generated discussions regarding the political atmosphere in the country directed people to physically demonstrate to show their disenchantment with the system by gathering at the Square. That is why at that Tahrir Square we saw women and men of different factions coming out from everywhere to congregate and listen to their on-the-spot purported leaders. Were it not for the social media push factor to galvanize the populace to stand firm against ruthless dictatorship, change would not have taken place that quickly. It could have been easy for the powers to censor messages coming either through traditional media outlets like radio, television or newspapers in these three countries because of state ownership, thereby killing the movement. But as fate will have it, or rather due to the unstoppable power of the virtual media platforms of communication that have given strength to youths, especially to debate issue after issue regarding their identity and personhood amid human rights abuses by state agents, change was bound to happen and it did. The aftermath could have been chaotic as was the case in Egypt, but the message had been made clear that no longer will dictatorial regime in Africa and beyond have their cake and decide which angle to cut a piece and give to its citizenry. The social-mediated sphere of communication has come like a volcanic avalanche to uproot the longstanding baobab tree that had stood firm for ages in the face of repression and oppression of ordinary folks. They can now enjoy a spacio-temporal sigh of relief while the government elites spend sleepless nights fashioning schemes to thwart the actions of the proletariat seeking justice, peace, unity, love, and equality. Marcus Breen is right when he opines that "the Internet has actively deterritorialized many people even while it has territorialized others" (Breen, 2011, 78).

Lindridge, Henderson, and Ekpo (2015) in their article on the Internet and ethnicity believe that racial discrimination that has been so prevalent offline has pushed most ethnic groups to carry out B2C online with much ease. They have used the analogy of a Black consumer having difficulties negotiating a good deal on car purchase in comparison to a White male. But online sales have been able to eliminate that. Nevertheless, the presence of coupons and other perks given to some exclusive club members for online sales of specific items, including airline tickets, is still discrimination from the offline world that has been transported to the online sale environment. This is probably why Leung (2017, 292) opines that the Internet is equally a theater where there is "ethnic objectification and White gaze dominates." As a result, most people of color find comfort by creating their own space as exemplified above. They also find comfort by creating their own space such that they can escape parental monitoring and regulations or ethno-cultural and political limitations imposed by the society in which they live (Milioni, Doudaki, and Demertzis, 2014). This is where they cultivate more identities.

ANONYMITY AND DIGI-CULTURALISM

COVID-19 pandemic has increased online interaction and the concept of truth and falsehood has been compounded by the very notion that the majority of human activities are now on the digital space. Internet trolls and phishing have infiltrated popular sites like Zoom that is almost used by the entire planet to zoom bomb individuals on conference meetings or classes. Even though Zoom has since improved on its security measures, there are still instances where anonymity has traumatized online experiences. With most schools, including the kindergarteners, to now have classes online, the fear for mankind is the issue of authentification. Who is on the other side of the screen? Who is eavesdropping using fake alias and so on? With Zoom, Google meet, Facebook messenger, or Microsoft Teams that have now become the favorite online video interactive platforms, users are provided with passwords that are supposedly secure before they can gain access into a group online session. But there've been cases where users are on their phones with muted video feeds and audio feeds and the host has to check and cross check whether those on the call have been authenticated. We have individuals sitting on the beach, riding bikes, tending to their dogs in the park or babysitting while taking part at the same time in a video conference. It becomes an arduous task to ascertain whether there is no other third-party listening in the background. This is a serious issue because the problem of security and privacy in the digital sphere has reached another level of scrutiny. In the era of facial recognition technology (more on this in chapter 9: *Blacks and AI (Artificial Intelligence)*) where Blacks have been disproportionately face different forms of bias. The concept of anonymity has become complex to unravel. The compelling case enunciated below is worthy of note:

Twitter and other social media are not necessarily anonymous but can seem to be anonymous. This characteristic means that people often feel free to post messages that would not be acceptable in other arenas. People may refer to President Obama or others with the N-word on Twitter but they are not likely to say that in face-to-face communication. The digital environment gives license to create an environment that marginalizes and devalues others in racial terms. Part of what empowers whiteness in the digital environment over and above other forms of racialization, e.g. blackness, is the imbalance in language. (Nakayama, 2017, 70)

Before people took to online platforms to use unpalatable words on President Obama, there was an offline exchange worthy of note during the run-up to the election between Obama and Senator John McCain. At a town hall meeting hosted by the Senator, one of the Republican attendees took the microphone and said the following about President Obama: "I can't trust Obama. I have read about him and he's not, he's not uh—he's an Arab" (Asante, 2016, 21). This is how the Senator responded after ceasing the microphone from the lady "No, ma'am. He's a decent family man [and] citizen that I just happen to have disagreements with on fundamental issues and that's what this campaign is all about. He's not [an Arab]" (Asante, 2016, 21). Needless to say, even though this was on live TV, when Barack Obama was elected into office, viral messages were posted on hate group blogs depicting him as "being born in Kenya" or that his long- and short-form birth certificate was fake (Jorden, 2018). Under the guise of anonymity, memes were circulated on the Internet depicting him as a monkey, especially after the Tea Party march on the White House on September 12, 2009, one year after he was elected into office. This is how the digital media on various platforms and the placards displayed at the rally described Barack Obama as captured by Enck-Wanzer (2011):

Obama is articulated as a racial threat in the posters and signs that circulate at Tea Party gatherings, are posted on walls in our cities, and are distributed through electronic means (e-mail, Facebook, etc.). Visuals such as (a) the "ObamaCare" poster featuring a dark "witch doctor" with Obama's face digitally sutured to the image, (b) the "Barack the Barbarian" cartoon featuring Obama as a hard-bodied barbarian wielding a Bronze Age axe directed at a scantily clad white woman with long blonde hair, and (c) the iconic "Socialism" poster featuring Obama in Joker makeup, all serve to mark Obama as a threatening, uncivilized, racialized Other without invoking the term "race" and while hiding behind the justification of "policy disagreements." Signs from rallies further mark Obama not merely as a racial threat, but as a racist threat, reading "Obama's Plan: White Slavery" and "The American Taxpayers are the Jews for Obama's Ovens," thus placing Tea Partiers within narratives of "reverse racism." One remake of the iconic Obama campaign "HOPE" poster retains the image but replaces "hope" with "R@CIST." Other signs visually figure Obama as a terrorist (e.g., one sign that shows Obama waving at armed Arab men standing on a backdrop of New York City with two airplanes in flight and the caption "Don't worry guys, I'll take it from here"), invoke the claims of the Birthers (who argue Obama is not a "natural born citizen"), reference so-called "death panels," or simply and unsubtly read "Save White America." (Enck-Wanzer, 2011, 26)

Similarly, other Black celebrities like Serena Williams have been depicted on the virtual platforms with masculine features or with racist derogatory cartoons like the 2018 one on September 12, 2018, originating from Australia depicting Serena Williams with monkey-like features. No one stepped forward to own responsibility for the cartoon even though it was traced to Australia. This and many such nauseating depictions of Black icons on the digital media have ignited the debate around anonymity and the digital public sphere. This form of virulent attacks on Black celebrities hiding under the guise of the anonymous synchronous and asynchronous streams of the digital communication flow, the future of human communication, especially as it relates to verisimilitude or credibility of online messages, are open to doubt. With new technology capable of altering one's facial expression through photoshopping, authenticity has become the victim. Little wonder most communicators still crave rich media communication, that is, in-person medium of communication. The debate on anonymity has just begun. Maybe McLuhan (1994) was right when he had advertently asserted that the media was indeed "an extension of ourselves" (7). If that be the case twenty-six years after this assertion when the world had not been knee-deep into digital communication, one can say without any fear of contradicting oneself whatsoever that people post messages on the cyberspace that reflect their inner core selves in the offline world. The digital plain field is only an extension of us as McLuhan has just stated. So, the vitriolic directed at the Black race especially to those who act like their role model: Barack Obama and Serena Williams are being denigrated by the negative anonymous hash tag postings on Twitter, on Instagram, Facebook, Snapchat, and so on. They are deliberate with the intention of stroking doubt to their accomplishments in a dominant White supremacy politically charged society like the United States. Anonymity in cyberspace has been exacerbated by the machinic creation of robotics who assume the function of humans when the physicalization of the human person is absent.

Therefore, according to Guzman (2016), machines are humans and humans are machines because the latter is the extension of human creation that acts alike. Human beings are natural machinic objects with parts in their bodies similar to those in man-made machines. Humans' continuous heartbeat is nothing short of machinic and the brain that acts like the central nervous system for the body acts just like the computer server. Andrea Guzman further alleges that "through automation, engineers and business owners created a system of machines with humans that replaced a system of humans with machines" (13). This confirms the conceptual, and to some extent, the interdependence of humans and machines. Worst of all, since we are more presently interacting online than we do with in-person communication especially in the age of the COVID-19 pandemic, the plethora of online attacks on people of color will be exacerbated especially as the Trump administration is anti-immigrants and minorities. With all these under discussion, no one has thought about how Africans and Africa are coping in these robotic communication changing times or whether they are still victims of digital divides. In the same interview conducted in Uganda, another interviewee by the name Ana interjected on how they sheepishly follow like blind users or have been left behind by the superhighway technology:

> . . . *also we definitely need classes because these are new things and when online communication came to us [sic], we just embraced it without knowing how negatively it can affect our lives. So, we definitely need classes . . . to be educated on the positive side of technology and the negative side of technology and how to use technology to positively impact our lives. (Ana, Iganga, January 2020)*

Without educational direction, users like Ana may not know how to distinguish between fake sites, fake bloggers, and of course fake messages directed to them. That is the reason why they are constantly falling prey to anonymous mobile money (M-Pesa) scammers in East Africa because no one had ever been schooled on detecting fraud online (Buku and Mazer, 2017). In an African culture where identity formation is a socio-cultural byproduct of a child socialization process from birth, the issue of anonymity is foreign. Children are schooled to be like their forebears, their parents, and to embody the traditional and cultural mores of the land. Pre-primary traditional African education is focused on producing and cultivating individuals whose identity will mirror that of the community. This is the reason why Africa had oral culture before written culture. With written culture, there was also the emergence of digital culture that started with Kemetian hieroglyphics as stated by Bangura (2020). To him digital communication had its genesis in *seshu nu per ankh,* which translates into English as "hieroglyphic writing" and "copyist of hieroglyphics texts" (7). From an Afrocentric perspective, this kind of writing from Africa was intended to be a replica of the African traditional and cultural cosmologies and authors of such writings would certainly emerge from the community reflecting what the reality is and not distort them as we see today with anonymities and fake messages. To show that digital communication today has mimicked, and at the same time, not accurately reflected the community of context such that users and readers can ascertain meaning and associate them with the source, Abdul Karim Bangura presents the assertions of Ananthakrishnan and Siri (2018) below:

> in the modern digital age, the route the Kemetian hieroglyphs took has been mimicked via emojis which now permeates all Internet and network applications such as Facebook, WhatsApp, Twitter, etc. Like some hieroglyphs, modern emojis are practically an amalgamation of emotions and other images of objects that represent various denotations within the milieu in which they are employed. (48)

The key takeaway from the above testimony is that messages represented the "milieu" (context) for which they should acquire meaning and be used by those for whom they are intended and not be distorted as is often the case with some modern/Western digital message transfer from sources and authorship that could be deciphered. Since Western digitalization has spread its wings on the entire planet, users on the continent of Africa cannot be immune to its positive and negative effects. Even though this "new" form of communication has its genesis in Kemetian (Egyptian) tradition as already discussed, the mushrooming effect has been unprecedented and the negative underpinnings associated with it cannot be underestimated.

Chapter 5

Cyberfeminists and Black Gendered Voices

In an apparent self-conscious mood of thinking, Bell (2001) opines that the Internet is a sphere of disembodiment. Body politics (anatomy) in the offline world do not hold leverage in the virtual realm because interactants are in another universe of thought. That aspiration does not go further, especially if we ponder on Anthony Gidden's structuration theory of yoking in-person cultural realities with online experiences. In short, cultural transplantation, especially within the virtual interpersonal communicative frame, is possible. It is with the later view that gender seems to still play a pivotal role in cyberspace, especially when seen through the lens of some women in Africa who have been silenced in the in-person universe of political communicative discourse. Cyberspace appears to have unlocked the chains in the feet of some women in Africa who, until now, have not had active presence in the political public sphere. The unfolding events of "Tahrir Square" in Egypt, where men and, more importantly, women stormed the city center to publicly seek the ouster of their longtime leader Hosni Mubarak, will go down in the annals of history as the launching pad for social media revolution in Africa. What was more news-breaking was the onslaught of supposedly silent women who ventured to cross-gender cultural lines to march with men on the street (Tufekci and Wilson, 2012). In fact, by doing that they circumvented harsh gender separation lines in the Arab world (Hamdy and Conlin, 2013).

According to Bury (2005) in her book titled "Cyberspace of their own: Female fandoms online," female-only online communities started forming in the early nineties. This was a subtle form of disarming the male gender of complete control of cyberspace. Gajjala (2000) confirms this by emphasizing the role of cyberfeminists:

"Cyberfeminists" attempt to work towards the empowerment of women through technology while resisting various male-dominated discourses that surround the use of technology. Cyberfeminists attempt to design web sites and other electronic synchronous and asynchronous spaces online that will resist dominant constructions of gender while empowering women all over the world. (120)

So, resistance to "male-dominated discourses" and "empowering women" as stated above seems to be the ultimate goal of cyberfeminism in the world. Rai (2017) also strongly believes that "in cyberfeminism women themselves make content, raise viewers and participants, channelize discussion and this virtual world givens [*sic*] them a tool to give and take their own definitions of cyberfeminism" (5), but what about African, Black, or women of color cyberfeminists, or is there such a thing? Be that as it may, the essentialization of the Internet as a liberating terrain for all women is a myth. Before the advent of Internet communication, "some" women, whether affluent White or colored, have had a certain edge in traditional communication media by dint of their educational and economic statuses. Those in the fringes like the agriculturally prone South Asian women or the drought-stricken African women in Eastern deserts of Africa never shared the same communication spaces and that is true with the Internet communicative age. One has to have a certain social, political, and economic clout to sway communicative agendas on the mediascape to influence policies that cater to the plight of the above-mentioned women. Without that, the same epistemological, ontological, and axiological battle between first, second, and third wave of feminism and Black feminism as well as womanism will continue to be transplanted into the cyberspace. Now to the complication raised by Bury (2005) about cyberfeminist using the Internet for the "empowerment of women through technology while resisting various male-dominated discourses that surround the use of technology" (5). One can quickly visualize where resistance to male dominance with respect to the volume and content of messages that are posted online attacking women's this or that, but what about anonymity, trolling or Facebook wall posts from someone purported to be male when in actual fact it is female? How can we quickly decipher this without the aid of some encryption engineer gurus? But she is against Bell (2001) disembodiment argument.

In her argument against David Bell's disembodiment position, she states that "rather than dismiss the 'dream of disembodiment' as outdated, I wish to historicize it in order to come to a more complex understanding of the body in cyberspace" (5). By historicizing she takes us back to Socrates and Michel Foucault who all believe that we cannot separate the body from the soul and identity of the person and in this case men and women will continue to see things differently, act differently, think differently, and write differently regardless of the setting or medium and in this case CMC. As far back as the early 2000s, Shade (2002) confirmed this allegation by underscoring that

> Although many access barriers to the Internet exist (*especially in Africa*, emphasis and addition mine) for women and women's group, the Internet has, without a doubt, been seized by women and women's groups as a relatively inexpensive and fairly flexible tool with which to communicate interpersonally and between women's groups and sympathetic NGO groups. (34)

The barriers are numerous and extend to the developed world where African American women, according to Alexa Harris, find solace at the workplace, which seems foreign to her, to concentrate in her corner browsing social media and blogosphere in search of what she calls "digital sistas" (Harris, 2015, 87) who share similar lines of Black fashion world with her. It becomes the virtual sphere of comfort because Harris (2015) also agrees that "women of Africa descent" (138) have, according to her, been "denigrated" in the past. The present dispensation wherein women can participate in the non-discriminatory virtual public sphere with men has provided an enormous leverage to them that they have not experienced in the past as already discussed. This is where gender equity from the communicative point of view can be agreed upon.

AFRICAN WOMEN AND DIGITAL COMMUNICATION SPACES/CHALLENGES

Given that this new seamless mediated communication platform called social media have provided voice to the voiceless women especially in some rural parts of Africa, there are still insurmountable obstacles for them to claim digital equilibrium with their male counterparts. Hilbert (2011) joins the voice of this gender inequality, especially in developing countries, with other authors by citing cases where some scholars are of the opinion that the gender balance with respect to Internet content favor men than women. Be that as it may, African women resident in the urban cities in Africa with ICTs readily accessible and educational facilities available are likely to compete with male users, thereby fighting to close the gender digital gap. But a sizeable majority of them live in the rural areas with relatively little affinity with the Western language that powers ICTs. They are married off at an early age and sometimes their education is cut short as a result of that or early pregnancies and HIV AIDs also contributing to the panoply of problems for them. In a continent where polygamy is allowed and women till the soil and bring up children and take care of their husbands, there is ample evidence to suggest that gender digital inequality is bound to be present.

Despite the challenges facing equal Internet space between male and female users in Africa, women have been able to gainfully maintain a significant presence on the net to fight issues like sexual harassment that are prevalent in the offline sphere. Skalli (2013) explores and examines this vexing situation on African women's psycho-social malaise in her article *Young women and social media against sexual harassment in North Africa.* Her work is centered on the activities of Egyptian and Moroccan all-exclusive female digital spaces called *Harassmap* and *Women-Shoufouch.* These are activists' sites that empower women to speak up against these ills and to collectively seek solutions to combat them. With such virtual presence by North African women, the tendency to broaden strategies becomes primordial, given that many others online would have the benefit of counseling that would have been remotely impossible in the offline world because of the stigma that is often attached to victims. The fact that they can even divulge stories using anonymous tags on any given social media platform and receive consolatory as well as techniques from those in similar situation is laudable, thanks to social media spaces. This is where combatting male dominance in digital spaces can inevitably gain currency in North Africa. It should be noted that sexual harassment differs from place to place in Africa, but that of North Africa could be peculiar given the strict adherence to Arabic religious canons as opposed to Tropical Africa where Christianity predominates. Additionally, Islamic traditions permit polygamy, whereas Christianity prohibits it. But those who are polygamous in Tropical Africa are hardly Christians. They are Muslims as well as African religious believers. Cummings and O'Neil (2015) noted this about the attitude of men when they are aware that their women are online:

> By taking advantage of new technology, women and girls may be seen as transgressing gender norms, threatening men's position and power in the family or society. Where ICTs give women access to means of private communication, they may lead to men's control and surveillance over women. (10)

It was precisely due to the prevailing scenario recounted above by Claire Cummings and Tam O'Neil that these North African women took to creating these exclusive sites for female gender empowerment. With this state of male cognitive inertia where change of mindset is hard to come by, these women have no option but to seek for relief sometimes at the cost of their freedom. Similarly, studies carried out by Hafkin and Huyer (2017) in the francophone African countries of Benin, Burkina Faso, Cameroon, Mali, Mauritania, and Senegal found male rigidity to allow their girls and wives online for fear of being exposed to indecent acts like pornography, and so on. To the men allowing these women to access the Internet on an Internet cybercafé was wasteful investment. In fact, Cummings and O'Neil (2015) say men would "feel threatened" (10). This is what often create digitalization gender imbalance in Tropical Africa. In fact, studies upon studies have shown not only increase in traffic on the Internet by minorities like African American women, especially in the United States, it has also shown how their health has witnessed significant improvement just by signing on to sites in cyberspace that enhance their well-being. A study by Joseph et al. (2016) on increased physical activities for overweight or obese African American women by subscribing to Internet-based websites saw an overall increase. Such a study goes to demonstrate how certain activities, especially women that are deemed by the society as "less acceptable" like being obese or overweight, can receive positive results in a virtual setting like the online sphere.

In a WhatsApp open-ended survey posted to an all-Muslim women site in North Africa, eight women responded in the affirmative as to how they have 100 percent freedom when they are on social media as can be seen on the pie chart below. The open-ended survey also produced another interesting finding: 74 percent say they spent four hours or more per day on their smart

DO YOU OWN A SMART PHONE?

■ Yes ⚒ No ▦ Maybe

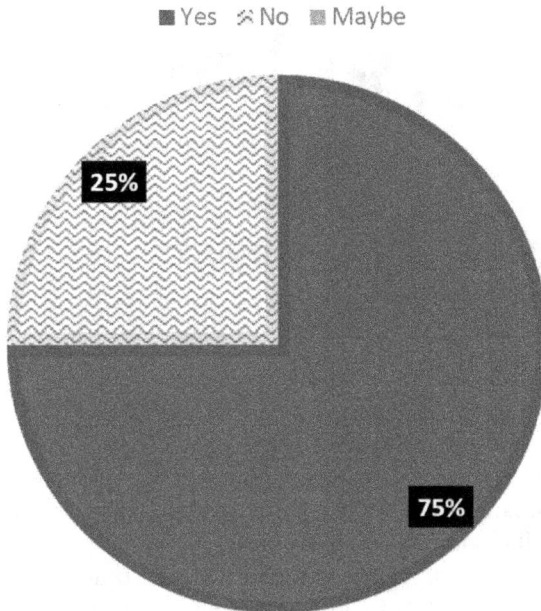

Figure 5.1 North Africa female digital presence. Created by Author.

If yes, how many hours per day do you spend on your phone?

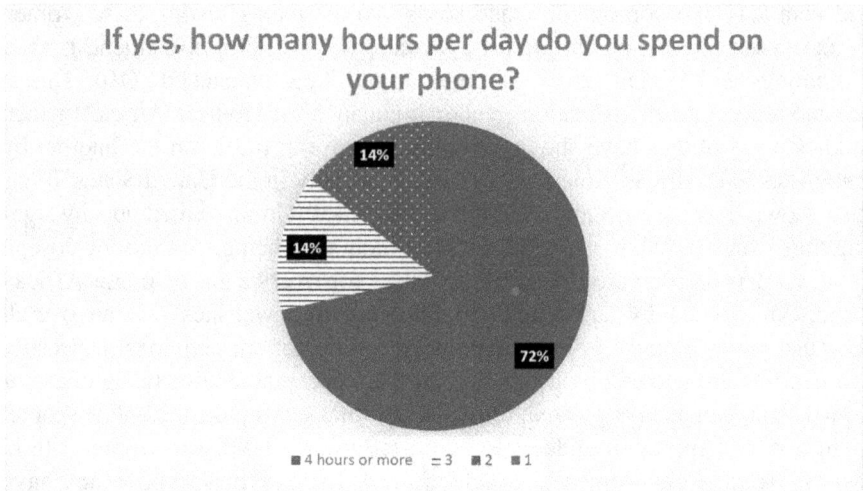

14%

14%

72%

■ 4 hours or more   ═ 3   ■ 2   ■ 1

Figure 5.2   Created by Author.

What do you mostly do while you are online on your phone?

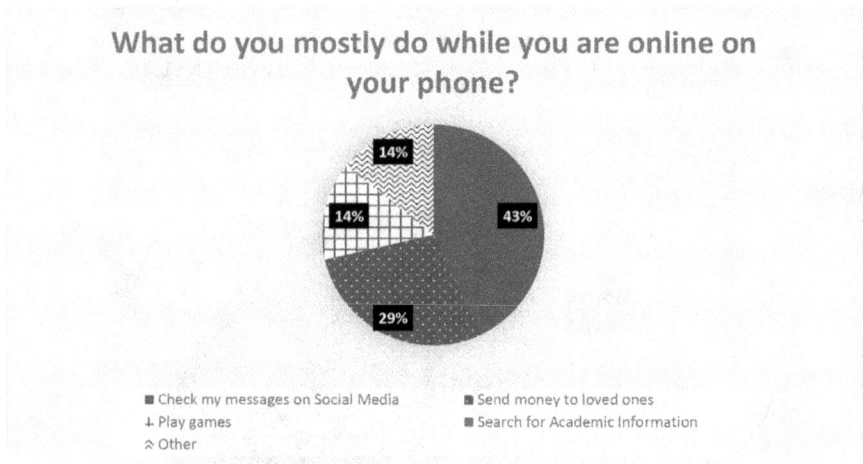

14%

14%   43%

29%

■ Check my messages on Social Media   ■ Send money to loved ones
⊥ Play games   ■ Search for Academic Information
≈ Other

Figure 5.3   Created by Author.

phones and according to question 3, they do this by spending 43 percent of their smartphone activities by checking on their social media posts. None of them use their smartphones to check on academic information as seen on that same chart. On the contrary, they use their smartphones also to send money to loved ones. This accounts for 29 percent of their time spent on this device. What is intriguing about this finding is the fact that the Internet has come with a new cultural shift especially in the lives of young Muslim women who can

Do you have freedom to do whatever you like when you are on your phone?

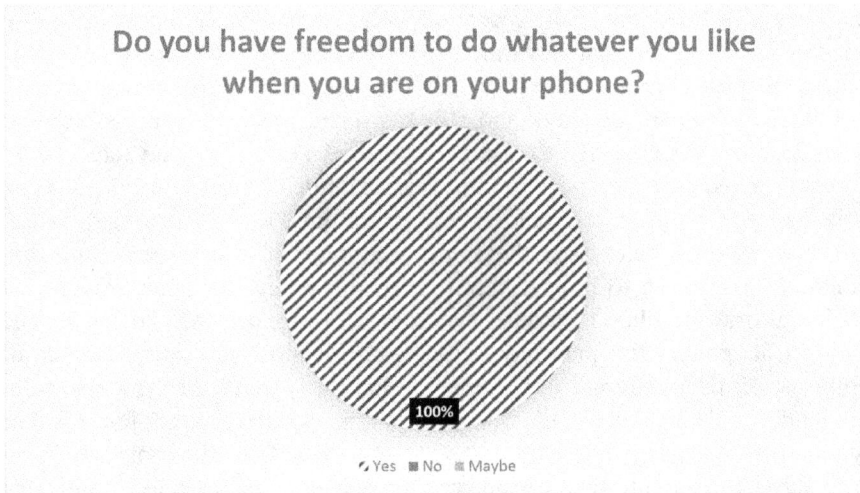

⟋ Yes ■ No ▥ Maybe

Figure 5.4   Created by Author.

now have an avenue to proactively communicate with 100 percent freedom as opposed to the strict in-person religious and cultural restrictions like wearing hijab that they must adhere to in Morocco.

BLACK CYBERFEMINISM

Whether one is referring to the first- or the second-wave feminism, there is broad agreement as to the fact that the term is a movement against male dominance, whether White or Black. But worthy of note is that women are not a monolithic group and so when there is discrepancy as to who should speak for which group and why, there is bound to be friction and that is the case for the birth of Black feminism with authors like Patricia Phil Collins and Sojourner Truth who stand for the Black feminist movement. That was pre-cybernetic revolution. Today virtual Black feminist individuals like Mikki Kendall have risen to the forefront. This is the kind of write-up by a White feminist on blogs on the Internet that spurred people like her to rise up. "Going To Africa. Hope I don't get AIDS. Just kidding. I'm White!" (Daniel, 2016, 42). Jessie states that this statement came from a White woman who apparently was fired for this kind of tweet. Even though she calls it "Stupid tweet" (42), it is in fact a true reflection of what she has nursed for a long time about Africa. It is not surprising that a lot of people think that worse things are only found in Africa simply because the media have not only denigrated livelihood of millions of residents in that continent of more than fifty-four countries, the media have made most White think that Africa is a country and not a continent in dire need of salvation and that salvation can only come from the West.

Digital spaces seem to have provided leverage for outspoken, mostly urban city African women dwellers and Black women in developed countries to have a voice. Gray (2012b) outlines African American female fate of racism and sexism with respect to confused identities by other users in Xbox Live interactive online sessions. These are not limited to African Americans. Other women of color face the same dilemma because there is apparent cognitive assonance to believe that interactants share the same universe of socio-cultural livelihood because everyone is a woman and writing in one Western language. But that may be far fetch for mostly all other women of color who expect nothing short of equality having suffered the same fate from all gender inclusive sites. This is what often gives birth to other feminism or womanism among diverse women on the net. "Black women-only-site" also face some form of discrimination or what Sawyer (2017) calls "politics of respectability" (83). She discloses how *memes* posts and reactions by members play a huge role in making the originator feel inward satisfaction. In her interview with one of the participants, she recounts how her natural black hair *meme* post did not return immediately with a huge number of likes and so made her feel disrespected because others were having over 3000 likes on their own memes. But she recovered afterwards when the likes started trickling in slowly. This is what happens, especially on specialized sites like Black Twitter all-female Facebook pages. Black feminists use digital spaces for activist discourses as well as promote Black ideologies that seem to be controversially examined in the mainstream media. Another issue worthy of note that transpires within the cyberfeminist site is that these Black women like Latoya Lynda Sawyer points out in her work, have other concerns. These spaces are used by Black women stars like Nicki Minaj to square off with Miley Cyrus on issues about their stardom that go on offline as well as online. It is worthy of note that when Black women occupy a safe space where psychologically they appear free from male gazes, they vent and open up about their sexuality and their role in a male ideologically dominated society. African American women in the United States of America have the luxury of occupying those spaces and acting in manners that is not detrimental to their relationship dynamics with their significant others. But as already mentioned that is not the case with African women who face the silent war with their husbands, should the message be released by a third party about their actions online as already discussed in the work of Cummings and O'Neil (2015). All in all, women from developing countries and those immigrant women in the United States seem to be "restricted" due to some unwritten cultural rule that makes them to "tone" down their rhetoric when they are still mothers or daughters and their male relatives still exert a certain amount of power on their well-being irrespective of setting. The kind of liberation that African American women feel while interacting online may not be the same as with African women on the continent of Africa experiencing polygamy and having a large number of family members to take care of. But the digital spaces could be a safe place for them if they could, at least, read what is written about them from time to time.

In as much as African American women occupy a space on the digital virtual world due to their offline citizenry opportunity within the confines of the United States (Advanced world) as many would attest, they seem to avail themselves with Internet freedom that African women, especially those living in rural Africa, do not have. African American women living and working in or out of the United States are imbued with certain innate opportunities like capital to enable them enjoy the Internet presence as opposed to an African woman living in the rural part of Africa overwhelmed by a lack of economic wherewithal and "freedom" to be subscribed to group chat about women on Twitter. A study by Jackson and Banaszaczyk (2016) examines contributions from all women using the hashtag #YesAllWomen and #YesAllWhitewomen on topics that focus primarily on violence perpetuated on women by men. Since this is a cry by all women, those women who decry such malfeasance use the all-inclusive hashtag to debate these issues, but at the same time, another counterpublic space triggered by the marginalized groups that would rather not characterized all men as violent would use another hashtag like #YesAllWhitewomen to discuss those matters giving the Twitter space another public sphere for women voices to reach the public realm. The resurgence of counterpublics especially with the dawn of online communication triggered by the birth of the World Wide Web and the Internet has brought plurality of human interactions: online and offline on similar and divergent topics. The onslaught of online interactions has magnified the sense of urgency to pinpoint an issue or to galvanize stakeholders to pertinent issues, say of rape, domestic violence, and female marginality that could hardly go through the halls of power. The culmination of street protest and online protests using several platforms have brought about the multidimensionality of voices of victims. At the same time, the virtual sphere has dichotomized these women to create what they see as counterpublics. Black women, for instance, have differences in the approach on certain gender issues regarding marginalization of their communities by both White men and White women. They would like to debate among themselves in a forum that brings them together like Black Twitter or uses other hashtags that would involve only Black women. At the same time, womanists would analyze the same hashtag "Me Too" movements differently from mainstream White and Black women. In short, many Twitter hashtags can be created and many opposing/divergent views on issues that affect women in general can be approached from different angles. This is what the new mediated forms of communication has come to signify. The counterpublics that the issue of men's violence on women can create would provide other viewpoints that may not be quite evident on street protests that seem to bring everyone under the same group concerns.

Feminist authors like Kylie Jarrett question the commodification of human labor on digital media through what she calls "digital housewife" (Jarrett, 2016) omnipresence on the digital platforms. From a Marxist point of view, she believes that "women still spend more time on unpaid work than men on average, 2 hours and 28 minutes more per day" (4). This unpaid labor by women as opposed to men goes to demonstrate disproportionality between sexes in the labor force with the onslaught of digital media communication. The digital media communication has come to signify another arena of discrimination where corporate media, through what most scholars would gladly refer to as the political economy of the new media, continues to be the enabler of human exploitation of labor and this time women pay the heavier price. The two hours that she has mentioned above that they are not being paid for their labor, somebody is benefiting and compared to men this imbalance has to be addressed. The "stay-at-home" mother uses platforms like Facebook to connect with friends, well-wishers, and relatives, but at the same time whether she is on Facebook or Twitter, she is subject to have the advertising window pop up on her screen and if she chooses to follow through, the corporate media will reap the benefit and her unpaid labor will continue to be a cause for concern. Still, with respect to Facebook participation by women, Kylie Jarrett makes the observation that while she is using this platform for activism, some other women are using it as a bridge to expand and optimize their friendship with others through increased likes, and other comments that can gladden one's day. But the user-generated content by the consumer continues to expand the bank account of the digital commercial enterprises, whether it is with Tumblr, YouTube, Instagram, and so on. The constant upload of information by the user swells the content of the site creator, who in turn does not economically satisfy the needs of the user and this is exploitation. This is what Jarret (2016, 93), referring to the views of Smythe (2014), says on commodification of the online user:

> The commodification of the non-work, reproductive viewing time was an extension of the alienation of workers from the means of production. Time outside of the work, and therefore outside of capitalist exchange-relations, that workers would otherwise use to produce and consume use-values important for the creation of individual and social identity is colonized by the requirement to continue adding value to commercial goods through the act of watching and consuming. (Jarret, 2016, 93)

So, the act of watching and consuming benefits the commercial entities at the expense of the social and economic growth of the user. The aim of the commercial site is for the consumer to watch, consume, and add content, and the aim of the producer of the site is to reap economic benefit from the non-paid activity (Casili, 2017) of the consumer and that is exploitation at its worse stage because neither the user who is a content creator nor the producer of the site is liable and so the psychological and socio-economic exploitation continue unabated. Fortunati (2007) buttresses this view below regarding women's labor material contributions that has

> completely ignored the material labor of the domestic sphere (cleaning the house, cooking, shopping, washing and ironing clothes) and above all, ignored the labor done in order to produce individuals (sex, pregnancy, childbirth, breastfeeding and care), as well as the other fundamental parts of the immaterial sphere (affect, care, love, education, socialization, communication, information, entertainment, organization, planning, coordination, logistics). (Fortunati, 2007, 144)

These are women activities in addition to what Jarrett (2016) has referred to as the work of the digital housewife. When these two labor-intensive activities are combined, there is no gainsaying the fact that women's offline and online labor activities are grossly under-assessed, underappreciated, under-valued, and exploited. This is again because "the digital housewife does the very particular relationship to capitalism as domestic workers for s/he generates products that contribute economic value by providing free content and user data" (Jarrett, 2016, 71). The free content that these women provide to the capitalist machinery goes to provide wealth to the economy and the private companies. Unfortunately, the women voice has been echoed and reechoed about pay equity, but their cries have gone unheeded for decades and the onslaught of digital communication has made their contributions to triple, yet they are never rewarded or compensated for user-generated contents that they provide to online digital platforms in addition to their offline household chores and marketing contributions.

INTERNET AND AFRICAN WOMEN EMPOWERMENT

The African woman is an embodiment of strength, fortitude, resilience, and courage in the face of mounting socio-economic challenges that she faces on the continent of Africa. When discussing issues affecting the African woman, care must be taken not to mix the activities of the rural African women with that of the urban ones. Urban resident African women have the luxury of educational facilities, cybercafé availability, transportation convenience as opposed to rural women who have difficulties getting such services at affordable rates. It is in this light that several studies including Wafula-Kwake and Ocholla (2009) highlighted the role of traditional media like radio and television still gaining more attraction and weight in the information communicative technology lives of rural women in Kenya and South Africa even with the plethora of ICTs enabled activities in the two countries. But needless to say the emergence of ICT related activities have provided ample weapon of communicative latitudes to African women on the continent to own and operate their own cell phones for which they receive and send SMS to friends, relatives and loved ones across the world. With the presence of mobile money like M-Pesa especially in East Africa as already discussed, these women have been able to receive text messages indicating that money has been sent to them which they can receive at a nearby M-Pesa kiosk in the village centers without necessarily traveling long distances to the city.

ARAB AFRICAN WOMEN AND THE "ARAB SPRING" CYBER ACTIVISM

The African woman has been upheld by Western standard as subservient to the all-powerful African male (Oyewumi, 1997; Omotoso, 2017). This conceptualization was triggered and enforced by the infiltration of Arab and Christian religions into Africa starting in the sixth century BC with Arab presence in Africa. The conception of the subordinating role of the African woman has not ceased from being perpetuated. It is no surprise, therefore, that with the omnipresence of new media technologies in Africa, that mentality continues to prevail and sometimes it is aided by research that portrays more male active participation in cyberspace than women. Wyche and Olson (2018) have beautifully placed the blame where it should be when studies after studies have portrayed that African men are more participatory on the Internet than African women. It is always ill-advised to place all African women in one basket for analysis because there exist rural and urban African women, mothers and pre-mothers, single and married, urbanized and ruralized African woman. The rural African woman, as argued by Wyche and Olson (2018), is faced with poor electricity supply in the village and limited ownership of the cell phone that is more often than not ill-powered by the Internet. Of course, these problems are central to the married motherly African woman of eight or more children in the village and whose husband has traveled to the urban city in search for jobs. In fact, in most African cities, men have populated the urban centers in search for employment and left their married wives back in the village. Those women that are in the city centers are educated urbanized women who compete equally with men, especially within the educational setting on the cyber activities (Langmia and Hammond, 2018). This is the backdrop for which the North African women protested alongside their male counterparts during the Arab Spring uprising in Tunisia, Egypt, and Libya as confirmed below by Radsch (2012):

> Several of the women who participated in and led the Arab uprisings were cyberactivists prior to the convulsions of 2011, but many more were inspired to become activists by the events happening around them. Although women young and old took part, it was the younger generation that led the way online. They helped organize virtual protests as well as street demonstrations and played bridging roles with the mainstream media, helping to ensure that the 24-hour news cycle always had a source at the ready. Twitter became a real-time news-feed, connecting journalists directly with activists and becoming a key tool in the battle to frame the protests and set the news agenda. (Radsch, 2012, 4)

The courageous action by these women goes to discount the a priori assumptions that African women are less active in cyberspace. Here they are not only present, but they are cyberactively present and their action with that of the men in North Africa helped toppled longstanding autocratic regimes like Hosni Mubarak of Egypt, Ben Ali of Tunisia, and Colonel Muammar Gadaffi of Libya. So, gender equity with respect to online cyberactivities, especially in Africa is debatable.

BLACK WOMEN AND ONLINE GENDER EQUITY

Khannaous's (2011) extensive and significant study on the role of Moroccan and Saudi women's "feminists" activities on various platforms like blogs, Facebook, Twitter, and so on can be viewed as a liberating phenomenon. Liberating, not from the Western one-dimensional conceptualization of feminism that is rooted in materialism but liberating for themselves because as she contends, the Moroccan society while citing Nadine Yassine, one of the famous Moroccan feminist is "autocratic, chauvinistic and traditional" (361). Their overall push and advocacy on the Internet is not to strive for equality with their male counterpart as the Western notion may portent, but rather to be released from the old traditional shackles of conservative mindset that keeps women to their so-called gender roles. She calls this "Islamic feminists" (361).

> Data from postings on Facebook and blogs in English, French and Arabic shows what Arab Muslim women want to communicate to each other, as well as their

desire for reform of family law, greater freedom in public space, fuller participation in the economy, and stronger representation in their nations' political life.
(359)

So, judging from the citation above, there is clear indication that the Islamic
feminist as characterized in this study by Touria Khannous is nothing similar
to the demands of the first, second or third wave feminist demands in most
Western countries. It should always strike a cord to all and sundry that women
are not a homogenous group and there cannot be a situation where hot-button
issues can be generalized to include all women in general. Moroccan women
are Black women, but they are African Black women and their socio-political
and cultural telescopic view of women's desires and demands are different.
We should also be mindful of the fact that these issues are similar to the different opinions of American feminists and Black feminist. Black feminists
like Sojourner Truth have created another term alongside feminism that
needs to be carefully scrutinized when dealing with this issue of women's
empowerment and rights. She came up with "Womanism" and that provoked
another debate within feminists to examine the concept of feminism using
another third eye that points to another direction to indicate that all women
may share common characteristics but when it comes to the issues of White
women and Black women the latter maybe dealing with the issue of racism
from both White men and women that need to be addressed. Consequently,
women all over the world are witnessing different kinds of restrictions and
limitations that may not necessarily be related to what other women are facing. Take, for instance, the issue that Black women face in the United States,
Europe, and Canada may be dissimilar to the ones faced by rural and urban
women in Morocco. The issues that Islamic women are facing in the Middle
East and Africa may also be different and that is why as stated by Touria
Khannous, their approach may be different when they engage in a dialogue
on Facebook, Twitter, Instagram, or Snapchat. By calling themselves Islamic
feminists, that is already another ideological path from that mainstream feminist in the developed world. On the other hand, there are traditional issues as
already insinuated that are not presently being covered in these studies. Some
of these issues include those of offline cultural manners that are also brought
to the public sphere by these women. Ethnic affinities, authentication, and
identification are other attributes for Internet verification on given sites for
group uniformity. Anyone can pose as a female in an all-female group chat.

Chapter 6

Black Cybernetizens and Inequalities

The Internet revolutionary "surreptitious" storm on everyone's communicative live has precipitated the rush to have everyone online, thereby making it possible for governments and stakeholders to work toward closing the digital divide gap. That attempt has propelled all and sundry to get on the virtual locomotive that now defines all facets of human life regardless of race, gender, age, class, creed, ethnicity, or political affiliations. In fact, without the World Wide Web or the Internet, human communication can "almost" grind to a halt, especially during COVID-19 where time and space have all merged seamlessly. Even though human communication exchange and content creation have mushroomed, there are still vulnerable populations that find themselves on the periphery or the fringes due, in part, to insufficient technical know-how and affordability. Those living in the subaltern, poor neighborhoods in most economically developing countries are not only grappling with know-how but also with access. Affluent communities, including some members of the Black race in Africa, North America, the Caribbean, Asia, Latin America, and some parts of Middle East and Europe, find themselves in this category. Nevertheless, though they are on this virtual ride with all other races on planet earth, instances of inequality are still exhibited. Inequality is as old as humanity itself, but the fact that every new dispensation, revolution, or innovation starting with the industrial revolution continue to perpetuate, in one form or the other, inequality means that humankind will continue to wrestle with this phenomenon because it is fundamental to growth and progress of life in general. On the digital public sphere, there are cybernetizens, cybercitizens, cyberneophites, and cyberimmigrants. The latter are those gradually making in-roots into the systems to meet the veterans who are already established. These are folks who need a helping hand like our seniors and elders who did not have such training during their educational upbringing. When they can manage to navigate the World Wide Web and adapt to some of the mobile applications downloaded on their phones, they become digitalneophites. Most of the digitalneophites are in the developing countries like Africa, where they use the services on the Internet to receive mobile money from loved ones, watch and play videos on popular social media sites like WhatsApp on their phones. When they make the next move to sit on a laptop and use voice over Internet protocol (VOIP), for instance, and pay bills online and acquire email accounts and social media accounts on platforms like Facebook, that will enable them to have access to loved ones' photographs and watch videos on YouTube. This will make them cybercitizens. They would be unable to become cybernetizens unless they master the gimmicks of the platforms, upload and download applications, use memes, configure their setting features appropriately on all their social media accounts. They can distinguish between spams, trolls, phishing etc and how to handle them appropriately. Members of the Black race in all parts of the world as aforementioned belong to all these categories and it is intriguing to ascertain how and what specific activities are carried out by this race and what are the challenges and progress made so far, especially in the era of digitalization.

AFROCENTRICITY AND NEW MEDIA

African communication scholars have continued to borrow Western-driven theories to resolve issues in Africa. Since they were trained by Western scholars or scholars knee-deep in Westernization, they've tended, in the past, to appropriate theories like Uses and Gratification, Magic Bullet, Spiral of Silence, Diffusion of Innovation, and Agenda Setting to test communication challenges in Africa and among African immigrants abroad. In the era of digital communication, Africa is witnessing a rapid increase in the rate of social media communication use on the continent. Social media communicative platforms like Facebook, Twitter, and YouTube have invaded the continent significantly, re-shaping mass communication as we knew it (Langmia and Mpande, 2014). They are among the most popular and the fastest growing media of use by urban youths in a plethora of cities on the continent. As a result, interpersonal, group, and mass communication have undergone a significant shift from the traditional forms of communication that Africa has been accustomed to. This shift has impacted life in the rural and urban cities, thereby dividing the communication audience into three: Those who still adhere to traditional forms of communication, those that are hybrid, and those that have embraced new media forms of communication. African communication scholarship is now on the crossroad. They can either appropriate Western communicative theories to examine and test inter-human communication dynamics in Africa or inculcate non-communication African-centered theories like Asante's (2015) Afrocentricity or Rabaka's (2009) Africana critical theory as frameworks. For issues affecting the continent and the people of Africa, including communication, Afrocentricity as a theory maintains that Africa has to be centered in any given discourse. The conscious mind frame of interpersonal communication between Africans must contain elements that include the culture, values, and world views of Africa. But with the omnipresence of new digital communication ravaging the continent, it is quite glaring that this is not often the case and this is a problem.

There are no easy answers to this problem, given that African scholarship, be it in Communication, Philosophy, Sociology, Anthropology, or Education, has relied heavily and, sometimes, too heavily on Western concepts, thereby privileging foreign epistemologies over indigenous ones (Nyamjoh, 2012). The search for African-driven communication theories to examine cross-cultural polemics on a large continent like Africa has become a daunting task for African scholars. African Communication scholars have, in their various research projects in and out of the continent, been using Western conceptual frameworks to examine issues that have little-or-no direct correlation with Western thoughts. Colonial educational forces that still have a firm grip on the continent are largely to blame.

This chapter uses dependency theory as the lens through which media globalization, that has affected communicative patterns for Blacks on the continent and those abroad, can be examined. It may help us understand African communicative themes that have so far been forced to be examined using Western lenses, what Francis Nyamjoh calls "imported thinking and things in their European greenhouses under African skies" (Nyamjoh, 2012, 133). Afrocentricity theory, as already discussed, seeks to place Africa in the center of any given perceptual analysis. It seeks to provide warm feelings to the fears of prior African scholars like Cheikh Anta Diop, who believes that assimilation is as worse as death (Babou, 2004). By constantly using Western-driven theories to research and examine communication problems in Africa, we are falling victim to Thomas Sankara's dictum that "he who feeds you controls you" (Akomolafe, 2014, 66–67). Dependency theory, from the viewpoint of one of its proponent Ghosh (2019), affirms that there is a developmental imbalance between the developed countries (DCs) and the least developed countries (LDCs), where the latter are subservient to the external determinants of indices of development from the former. This causes dependency. The dominant multinational economies dictate the pace, form, and content of what should constitute development. This has plunged developing countries in Africa, Latin America, and South East Asia to be totally under the control of Europe, the United States, and China. They are at the center and the others are at the peripheries. So the concept of inequality is quite broad.

Africans who only speak non-colonial languages do not have access to the Internet let alone participating in the cybercultural public sphere. The Internet brings together an amalgamation of all classes and subgroups of human beings on one communication pipe sending and receiving messages without discrimination and racism. But somehow message contents display inequality with respect to message intent or motive. With everyone on the Internet race track, some groping to observe what is going on while others compete for attention under the guise of cybernetizens, equality and human dignity is supposed to prevail. However, the subaltern, ie those on the fringes are just seeking to be recognized or be counted in, what Franklin (2013) calls "digital inclusion" (96). They are always underlooked by Internet hegemonic forces of capitalism. Black Internet users, especially on the continent of Africa, constitute one of those groups that find themselves on the fringes due to the overwhelming forces of the digital divide that impede the overwhelming majority of rural and urban de-Westernized educational folks from active participation. Across the Atlantic Ocean in the United States, the situation can equally be abysmal as captured by Sholz (2013) while pondering on technocultural politics by stating that "Victims of Hurricane Katrina, for example, couldn't register for federal emergency help *unless they use the Internet Explorer* (my emphasis) browser" (4). This is demonstratively disingenuous marginalization of the have-nots and in this case the poor African Americans that constitute the majority of users. By limiting only one browser for Internet access only, it means users of Mozilla Firefox, Google Chrome, and Safari have to be re-schooled in order to be registered to a compulsory database in case of unforeseen help. The few "lucky" ones with availability and access equally find themselves teaching themselves as they navigate the electronic universe that constantly changes with advanced Western technological updates. Since they find it hard to keep up with the flow, they tend to spend their hard-earned incomes purchasing expensive Western-made gadgets like iPhone, iPads, Android Phones, Tablets, Mac Laptops, and so on, so as to keep abreast with those changes. But the cost to them, especially without governmental support, is burdensome. Being cybernetic is one thing, but being a Black cybernetic means hopping into a realm with disadvantages that range from the cost of access to the quality of access. Then comes the content of messages to be transmitted through a tube which subconsciously, the Black or African user knows he/she can be quickly defined through the lens of Eurocentricity.

The result, therefore, becomes aggressive behavior to assert one's personality and presence in a seemingly volatile and hostile environment. Since the cost of owning an Internet-driven laptop, Mac and desktop PC can be prohibitive to an average user on the continent of Africa, time spent in an Internet café/home is very limited compared to an average user in Europe or the United States. This is inequality in all its dimensions. The money spent at an Internet café in Africa or in the Caribbean is compared to how much the user would spend for food before a decision is made to log on and send an urgent email to a loved one abroad, let alone chat online. That is why mobile telephony is mushrooming on the continent because users with a small amount of money can credit their phones and be able to WhatsApp friends, relatives, and loved ones quickly and conveniently. But when they have to upload or download bigger files for one reason or the other, they would be forced to pay a fee at a nearby Internet café to have access to computers with printers, and so on. These are some of the manifold challenges confronting the African Internet user, especially outside the borders of Western countries. Take, for instance, the issue of language use in cyberspace. Once an elderly mother or father in a remote village in Africa receive a new phone sent to them by a relative in the city or from the Western world, the next thing they have to do is adapt. This adaptation is in two phases: first they have to change the sim card if it is not an iPhone and second, be given a local number. This process is carried out for the elderly mother or father by an educated son or daughter. Then the next process of receiving and sending messages is another daunting task. Take note these elderly personalities grew up during the colonial era in Africa. They are not generation X, let alone Gen Zs. They have to rely on a third party to help them through. Granted, we are assuming that they have readily someone educated to undertake this process, but what happens when there is no one to help with this process? It means the task of adaptation is even more daunting. When the phone is fully adapted, the user then has to communicate in local languages but may not send text in local languages because of the limitation with the keyboard since the manufactured keyboard was Westernized. The user receives calls and could send messages. So, the user is limited to receiving and sending phone messages and in some instances receive mobile money from loved ones. The question that now arises is why such inequities, when the user was supposed to be at ease with using the mobile phone that was made for everyone.

The problem that non-Western language users of the mobile phones is confronted with has not been created by the user. In the age of electronic and digital communication, this user ought not to rely on a third party in order to swim like the rest of mankind on the ocean of digital technology. This user ought to have a mobile phone made and adapted for them by the manufacturer or better still those countries in the subaltern could liaise with companies that manufacture mobile phones to respond to the exigencies of all groups, classes, age, race, and literacy levels of users in a given community. The problem that users in Africa have is that they have relied for far too long on Western manufacturers for their daily utilities and that has come with a cost. Another factor to consider when dealing with the user of the digital phone eager to actively participate in the public sphere with all others in the community that they find themselves is that there are features provided on the same phone they possess that they have not been able to utilize. Imagine the insurmountable hurdles an elderly person faces when s/he is provided with a smartphone with all the foreign applications installed on it. This user would need another class session to understand and utilize the emojis, the camera, downloading, and editing photographs taken at events in their community on YouTube, getting music from Spotify, iTunes, obtaining a Twitter account, sending email, blogging, and searching websites. These are activities that require advanced educational talents that the villager in a remote part of Africa may not have, and the question is: was that supposed to be the case? Why are some left behind and others allowed to move faster on the superhighway when we are all being looked upon as consumers of the mobile phone gadgets and are always being included in the statistics of users. These are disturbing issues that need further examination and introspection. The solution could be that centers for adult mobile phone education are established all over the world and expatriates train advanced users to cater to the needs of the downtrodden as depicted above. Mobile phone companies should be able to fund these centers, and this could help with rate of return or increase turnover for the companies. These centers are created to take charge of needs of cultural exigencies, including languages that can be adapted to suit the needs of these users. There is no gain in pushing one Western agenda when in the long run only a certain sector of the population is benefiting. It should be borne in mind that the larger population of people in the continent of Africa are non-Western literate and reside mostly in the rural parts of the continent. What we have at this juncture is that neo-colonial tendencies continue to sow their seeds on the minds of people. An elderly non-Western literate person in Africa knows more about Beyoncé that a local artist in his/her area. They are more familiar with Bill Gates, Oprah Winfrey, Donald Trump, and so on, than their local folks because of foreign media consumption. So, with new media, the circle of dependency continues, and local African issues are relegated to the background.

BLACKS AND CYBERNETIC INEQUALITIES

With respect to Black cyberneticism, levels of expertise on any given issue demonstrate the chasm of unequal plain field on the Internet. If the term "digital divide" as already argued captures the technological disparities between the haves and the have-nots (Eubanks, 2011), then cybernetic divide should go beyond that because "the divide is actually a product of social structure and institutionalized inequalities" (Eubanks, 2011, 39). Blacks, like most other non-Western individuals on the face of the earth, suffer from institutionalized marginalization marked by various unpalatable forms of human indignities inflicted on them prior to the launching of the superhighway technology. It would, thenceforth, be equivalent to pushing a huge boulder up the mountain if the gulf of that inequities between the haves and the have-nots could automatically disappear with the advent of technology. Even though Internet penetration on the continent has risen since 2019 to 40 percent according to ITU on www.internationalworldstats.com/stats1.htm, most African Internet users reside in the urban centers and in the universities. But the majority of African populations live in the rural part of the countries.

This is a tragedy that should raise eyebrows, yet there are no palpable decisions that are being taken to resolve the growing digital divide that has left some people unable to be present online. In fact, those unable to read and write Western languages and resident in the rural settings do not have their digital footprints (Robinson et al., 2015, 570) felt in the global world. How can the footprints be seen and felt when according to Fuchs and Hovak (2008), "digital apartheid" (104) has been practiced on the continent? Certain regions are privileged over others based on criteria determined by the internal agencies and organizations charged with implementing governmental and private investments. It is no secret that rural Africa has been affected most because no one would want to invest where returns on profits are poor or nonexistent. That is why the government needs to include citizens in the rural settings through educational programs that can slowly bring them to join the information superhighway like those in the urban areas. Fuchs et al. (2008) also discussed various forms of divide that exist within the world of Internet usage and participation. The one that is most important for us in this chapter is "usage access" (100) which implies the tendency to use the Internet meaningfully so that encoding and decoding skills do not constitute an impediment. That is where cyberspatial discrimination hurts the most. For someone gaining access to the superhighway where everyone is treated as an equal and where availability of online materials is there for use is daunting. Even with access, some users do not have the requisite skills and knowledge on how to navigate and engage with the content. This is where the concept of digital apartheid gains currency.

This new form of apartheid can also cause "digital civil wars" (Doueihi, 2011, 34) among Internet browsers. Though Milad Doueihi focuses more on browsers, we think the plethora of Apps that are available on mobile phones gadgets that are shipped to Africa have the tendency to cause digital civil wars. Facebook, Twitter, Instagram, Snapchat, and YouTube are all competing for attention on the African virtual space. Unlike China, South Korea, and many other Arabic-speaking countries that have dominant Apps that function like the Western form of Facebook or Twitter or YouTube (Hammededeen, 2017), Africa has not yet come up with its own domineering ones in the likes of Facebook, Twitter, or YouTube that is pushing Western users to subscribe to when dealing with Africa and African digital spaces. These Western conceived Apps are all competing for attention in Africa to the extent that Facebook deemed it necessary through the pressure from Kishwahili scholars in California to create Facebook Swahili in 2009. But this has, in no way resolved the issue of digital civil wars for African digital consumers. They are forced to play by the rules by following the dictates of the West when using these platforms and that includes reading and writing in English or French on them because they control them. Franklin (2013) makes the case by stating that

> the corporations who now own the codes and control access to today's web-based media, namely proprietary software platforms that make up the social networking sites and (micro)blogs officially accessed and used by billions as well as personal computing, reside in the west, the United States in particular. (183)

This is the problem of inequalities, especially with respect to African consumers. The fact that other users reside outside the United States makes it a duty for manufacturers to configure platforms that respond to needs of African users in Africa. The fact that Facebook created the Swahili version was not due to their volition but done after the pressure group pushed them to. The Nigerian Facebook users have resorted to using the same tactics to push for the creation of Facebook office in Nigeria especially after the visit of its founder Mark Zuckerberg on August 30, 2016. To ship PDAs to Africa without enough research on their socio-cultural needs that could be inculcated into the machine is irresponsible and an act of conscious marginalization and consumer subjugation. The same argument can be made with respect to what Nakaruma (2002) says about Western-driven advertisement on the Internet that is skewed to favor Western taste. This is her reaction:

> It proposes an ideal world of virtual social and cultural reality base on specific methods of "othering" a project that I would call the globalizing Coca-colonization of cyberspace and the media complex within which it is embedded. (99)

The process of embedding materials in mobile phones, laptop computers, and other portable accessories destined for Africans without due regard to their cherished socio-cultural facets of life is a travesty. This makes the process of adaptation difficult to be implemented. African consumers are commodified citizens, put simply "pawns in the chess board of European games" (White, 1973, XII). Alzouma (2012) has strongly hammered home this issue by asking rhetorical questions as to "how a device designed or invented in one cultural context is used in another, particularly the effect of that use on the relationship among members of extended family based on differential meaning attached to the device and its use" (193). This further buttresses the argument we have made about outside-in flow of manufacturing media gadgets flooding the African market without prior inside-out research carried out to ascertain their functionalities in given settings. The Coca-colonization insinuated above by Nakaruma (2002) coupled with Fuchs and Hovak (2008), "digital apartheid" (104), clearly demonstrate the imbalance relation between Africa and the West. Electronic and digital technologies seem to flow from the West to the rest of the world, from north to south and this creates a fertile group for the top-bottom process that is reminiscent of colonization. This time it is no longer physical in-person domination and annexation through Coca-colonization or McDonalization, it is through what McPhail (2006) as beautifully described as Electronic Colonization Theory (ECT). To him " ECT looks at how to capture the minds and to some extent the consumer habits of others. ECT focuses on the global media influence on how people think and act" (23). This is the height of inequality where those that have in abundance take advantage of the have-nots and by so doing continue the process of mind colonization. It is this mind colonization that is responsible for the lack of imaginative inspiration and dormant curiosity to cater to the needs of future African generations by those on the continent and abroad. The future, according to them, seems to be the prerogative of the colonial master who continues to chart the pathways of technological progress. The effect of mind colonization is partly responsible for the half-baked independence that most African countries have arrogated for themselves since the departure of imperial Europe but are now faced with neo-colonial realities. Most forms of modern material advancement for Africans still come from overseas. This is the reason why Asante (2020) has given this warning to Africa that "sometimes Africans carry the wood of others to build their fires only to discover that the smoke from such fires suffocate us" (22). The African consumer's mind has been captured, thereby altering his/her consumer habits to believe that technology that emanates from the north is by far superior to any, if at all there is one that is created in Africa. ECT now constitutes the death-knell of dependency. Thomas McPhail continues by supporting this thesis by stating that

> examples of media systems that attract heavy users are MTV, ESPN, soap operas, CNN, The Internet, or video games. These systems tend to be the output of global communication giants, such as Time Warner, Disney, Viacom, SONY, and the News Corp. Collectively, they have the potential to displace or alter *previous cultural values, habits, activities or family rituals* (Emphasis, mine). (McPhail, 2006, 23)

The alteration of existing cultures and habits as insinuated by this author clings of mind domination and subjugation at the subconscious level. Most consumers and users of digital importations from the industrial nations have no clue that they are being culturally raped and suppressed because their erstwhile cultural norms and practices have been swept away and replaced by a foreign dominant force that has subjugated their sensibilities and sensitivities. There is no natural law that stipulates that the technology have-nots will perpetually continue to suffer under the huge heavy burden of scarcity. Their economic material lives that always classify them under the poverty bandwidth should not compel them to lick the empty bottle of technology at a time when bridging the technology gap between the poor and the rich is the goal of the International Telecommunication Union (ITU). The digital apartheid, as already discussed, has had a different unfolding in South Africa, where they had toiled under the White regime of unequal and separate rulership for years. With the arrival of new digital technology, this inequality has assumed a different significance. "This has created a situation where young White people enjoy a duel advantage over their black and coloured peers, being exposed to rich technological environments both at school and in their home" (Pritchard and Vines, 2013, 2538). These two authors have captured it below with respect to broadband and electricity:

> Issues surrounding access are not just limited to high-end technologies enabling music recording and production. Black townships have poor landline telephone provision and many homes are not connected to mains electricity. Although mobile ownership is relatively high in South Africa, many of our samples found making regular phone calls prohibitively expensive. The lack of electricity provision compounds this further by creating a situation where even if someone has credit, they might not be able to charge their phone's battery. (Pritchard and Vines, 2013, 2544)

So, it is not just participating actively in cyberspace and having equal cultural space and technology mutual exchange and understanding without one culture dominating the other, it is the question of availability, affordability, and access. For those that do have access, knowledge, and affordability, it is important to delineate their online public and counterpublic activities.

CYBERNETIZENRY AND COUNTERPUBLICS

The Internet culture has created a gulf between the real public and virtual publics. Those cybercitizens that have now become cybernetizens are further divided by online and offline interests making way for counterpublics to exist concurrently in cyberspace. The tendency for the subaltern in Africa or India or any other parts of the world where people live on the fringes and managing their day-to-day life in the real in-person world, those who can afford to go online (wealthy literate subalterns) create a counter culture/public of pushing an agenda or concerns that further their erstwhile in-person cry. This cry has consistently been against the mainstream dominant hegemonic cultures and politicians like the bourgeois Blacks and Africans on the seat of power in the continent and abroad. The parallel cultures and publics that exist on the Internet create room for the perpetuation of what Marcus Breen calls "Internet Proletarianisation" (Breen, 2011, 53). The domination that prevails in the real world has been transplanted onto the virtual world. Case in point, the net neutrality saga in the United States in November 2017, where the FCC chairman Ajit Pai went ahead to dismantle (www.fcc.gov) the equality data transmission sharing between large corporations, SMEs, and consumers. The fact that more leverage was given to powerful companies against that of the smaller entities shows that the political economy of the cyberspace will continuously shift to benefit wealthy capitalists. Most users especially the subaltern will have to pay heavily to have some of their data transmitted to a certain group of people. In essence, this ruling has created digital apartheid in cyberspace. Black-owned media companies and many other infant companies representing subaltern groups in the developing, medium developing world will find it hard to compete with larger conglomerates like AT&T, Verizon, Comcast, Netflix, Amazon, and Google, who dominate data traffic flow on the Internet. With this FCC ruling, users will have little bandwidth on the Internet tube as opposed to these media moguls. This, therefore, reinforces the stereotypical media-driven notion that Black users in almost all spheres of life are playing catch-up all the time with domineering, mostly Western oligarchs for a seat at the table of power and decision making.

BLACK COUNTERPUBLICS ON CYBERSPACE (AFROSPHERE)

The mere existence of a counterpublic presupposes that there is a public and the counterpublic that is there as ancillary or a parallel forms meant to cater to the needs of those whose voices are either mute or absent from the public sphere usually powered by the government and big media companies, think tanks, and pressure groups like the Koch Brothers in the United states. It is often as a result of inequality and marginalization that other groups decide to form another sphere to advance a cause or criticize public policy. Jurgen Habermass, the German philosopher, is credited to have conceptualized the theory of public sphere that was limited to citizenry discourse at public salons and coffee shops during the pre-Internet era. Not everyone felt welcome in those spheres, and that is where the issue of inequality started to rear its head. But with the omnipresence of online universe, where humanity has taken cover from the COVID-19 pandemic that has enveloped the planet, there now exists public and counterpublic spheres on the cybernetic universe and this time the same discrimination, segregation, marginalization, and inequality still looms due to restrictions from password limitations and account login ID blockages. There now exist Blackstopia where Blacks in the Diaspora converge to discuss issues relevant to their culture and value systems. The same is true of Black Twitter, LGBTQ sites, blogs, and listservs. These sites have all mushroomed as a counterpublic sphere as opined by Nancy Fraser who is credited for theorizing about the counterpublic sphere. What takes place in the counterpublic sphere is often the antithesis of what dominates in the general mainstream public sphere, mostly with the dominant White race. Boutros (2015) justifies the reason for the presence of a Black counterpublic because "prevalence of elements of Black national and Pan-African ideology and discourse that make bids for a unified Black diaspora" (322) are discussed. Pan Africanism is an ideology that the Blacks in the Diaspora and the continent have been fomenting and discussing ever since they were coercively made slaves to the Whiteman in a foreign land and so they have been longing to have a counterpublic with the emergence of the Internet to push that agenda through. This is an agenda to seek collective unity, and that is why no one is surprised with the birth of the Black Lives Matter (BLM) movement as a consequence of years of online counterpublic galvanizing effort to unite Blacks in the Diaspora. Alexander Boutros continues to buttress the role of the Afrosphere as a counterpublic site on the dominant Internet platform as an arena where those that have suffered from years of marginalization through the Jim Crow laws in the South of the United States of America and the lynching of slaves can now assemble and decry similar tragedies on their race like the brutal killings of Black men by White police officers. The aim of the counterpublic as argued by Alexander Boutrous is to make the Black Diaspora visible. Invisibility creates inequality and imbalance.

CYBERSPACE AND INTERNATIONAL INEQUITIES

Manifold documents, papers, and books have resurfaced tackling the "globaletics" (wa Thiongo, 2012) of the cybernetic inequities for developing and near-developed countries. The gulf between what Ragnadda and Muschert (2016) call "information rich" and "information poor" (23) or what Lister et al. (2003) call "technology rich" and "technology poor" (180) continues to deepen within the electronic communication sphere as well as digital communicative sphere. And what has not been adequately addressed is the issue of online activity equity between those in the north or Western countries and those in the south or non-Western countries. But one can easily argue that equity cannot be possible between these two groups of users because the former has the wherewithal in terms of infrastructure, systems in place, and user productivity, whereas the latter are still wrestling with accessing online data from their mobile devices that more often than not have limited or no Internet connection. Recently, Southern Cameroonians who have been fighting to restore their statehood from La Republique du Cameroon were deprived of Internet access for over 100 days because of political struggle with the regime in place. If the International telecommunication Union spends over 500 billion US dollars to reduce the digital divide gap with African countries, this tendency to block a certain region of the country from having Internet should raise alarm but it isn't. This is where the West is failing to fight for equality in the use and dispensation of the Internet to all and sundry. Since these new forms of communications are foreign and considered a new culture within the African cultural space, it goes without saying that the body charged with dissemination and regulation should bring pressure to bear on regimes that crack down on it as a weapon to stop message transmissions. Another issue is with the slow speed in regions that have cybernetic facilities in Africa. This is another cause for concern. When those users in the developing countries in Africa are deprived of the Internet oxygen as exemplified with the Cameroonian Government shutting down the Internet in the southern parts, users who were already engaged in a kind of Habemassian public sphere dialogue with folks online have no possibility to continue that dialogue. That dialogue will be skewed in favor of those Southern Cameroonians residents in Western countries. As seen with the Arab Spring of 2011, those using Facebook, Twitter, and YouTube were both local Egyptians and those abroad. The line of communication between these two groups blurred the territorial physical boundaries giving way to seamless communication that galvanized folks on the ground to rally at the "Tahrir Square" to demand the ouster of their longtime dictator. Equity in public sphere dialogue on say WhatsApp and Facebook between Cameroonians at home and abroad is being stymied by the brutal crack down by the powers that be as it deprived the local citizens from active participation. Within Cameroon itself, citizens residing in the north, east, and central parts of the countries are not affected by the Internet blackout, but students in universities, private and public schools, businesses, and other entities that rely on the Internet for international transaction in the southern parts are affected. The result is massive migration to these regions that have Internet access and cybersnetic activities and other transactions.

CYBERSPACE AND THE DISABLED

Psycho-cognitively speaking, we unconsciously wish to satisfy the hunger and quench the thirst of the critical mass in our society. The tendency to plan for the masses is an "acceptable" unconscious bias that human beings practice on a daily basis, especially when introducing new products in the market. The American Disability Act (ADA) makes provision for all public service organizations to respond to the needs of those with some form of disability. This can be seen in most spheres of life in the United States, including tele-communication facilities. But this cannot be said about institutions in some developing countries including Africa where not only resources are scarce to meet the needs of the disabled in our communities, but the will to enact and execute laws that will benefit the disabled is difficult to quantify. With the mushrooming of electronic and digital services, lots of people with some forms of disabilities that prevent them from participating in cyberspace are losing out and the governments are more concerned with political survivals than the well-being of the citizenry. Borchert (1998) citing his study with Calabrese in 1996 agrees with this statement:

> Technological advances in communication, however, have not always benefited persons with disabilities. Individuals who are deaf or hearing-impaired, for example, were quickly cut off from mainstream American culture, occupational opportunities, and access to goods and services when sound films and the telephone were developed. As a new communication market place emerges, policy making will play a role in determining the emancipatory potential of the technology. (52)

This new communicative marketplace called digital modes of communication have forcefully penetrated the telecommunication world of Africans and their disabled populations are still in the dark as to how to cope in this digital communicative universe with no specially designed keyboards or sound system to meet their needs. When we look back at traditional or conventional media (radio and television), most African countries have been lagging behind. In Cameroon the Head of State, President Paul Biya has never had a sign language interpreter of his nationally televised or non-televised speech to the nation for the thirty-five years that he has been in power. So long as the disenfranchised are left in the dark in the knowledge and skill economy, inequality will continue to exist in our society. A 2016 study by Bornman, Bryen, Moolman, and Morris (2016) in South Africa indicates that people with severe forms of disabilities but who use Augmentative Alternative Communication (AAC) devices on their mobile phone registered higher media interactivity because they are able to download Apps and use their devices properly. But this may not be the case with others in other parts of Africa that are not fortunate to have AAC devices installed on their mobile devices. A much more recent study in 2020 carried out in the same South Africa indicate another area of concern with respect to other forms of disability that are not being catered to especially when it comes to health and information dissemination.

> Lack of health information and campaigns tailored for the deaf community is a form of discrimination termed as audism and it is unjust. Deafness and other disabilities warrant a fair chance for such persons to access health information and support to overcome their limitations. (Kubheka, Carter and Mwaura, 2020, 4)

The Deaf and other people with disabilities in the larger African community are not to be neglected, especially as African governments embark on media to be available to all and sundry. When imports of electronic and digital gadgets are being brought into the shores of the continent or in the case where some African countries like Uganda have begun making their own cell phones and cars, the need to inculcate the needs of all people including those with all forms of disabilities is of prime importance. Since the year 2000, mobile phones have made serious in-roots into Africa, to the extent that Africa is being ranged as one of the countries with geometrical growth in mobile phone ownership in the world (Bornman, Bryen, Moolman and Morris, 2016). The rate at which more people are acquiring mobile technology has by far outpaced the landline phone ownership in Africa. The reason being the cost of landlines is more prohibitive as compared to mobile phones. But as the rate of ownership is skyrocketing, there is need to not create an internal digital divide debacle by not including amenities to include all sectors of the population in the distribution and access. True access has often been recognized as impediments related to costs and affordability, but that of the people with disabilities is far beyond the issue of affordability because they are not, for any reason whatsoever, to be left out in the periphery. Even if it means governments have to subsidize internal and external manufacturing companies to include provisions for those with all forms of human impairments to be counted as also benefiting from mobile phones technology regardless of their physical and mental handicaps, these African governments are by moral duty oblige to make that sacrifice so they can all be counted as belonging to the pool of those technologically advanced users just like that some of their counterparts of South Africa who are benefiting the AAC technologies as users with disabilities (Bornman, Bryen, Moolman, and Morris, 2016)

Chapter 7

Digi-Culture and Racism

Virtual and in-person bi-directional communication are the two ways of interaction among the Black race on the continent of Africa and abroad. The two media of communication are diametrically opposed to each other with respect to modes, ethics, and context of communication. Cyberculturally speaking, those who transmit information through the various application lines are aware of the limitations of virtual communication as well as the risks involved. They are equally proficient with ways to effectively transmit messages with the knowledge and skill necessary for the encoding and decoding processes of communication.

The emergence of online communication and interaction with unknown individuals who post messages filled with vitriolic and hatred directed at certain groups of people has a direct repercussion on human communicative growth. Anonymities have found refuge in cyberspace. They have created a crater lake of hate speech that could take a generation of right-thinking mindset to resolve. The two personalities that carry out communication (offline and online) are diametrically opposed because some users find Internet freedom as the means to unload years of grudges on certain group of people under the pretext of non-existing regulatory framework to track them down. White supremacist groups (Charlottesville incidents in the United States) have websites like *stormfront, KKK,* and other listservs that are meant to champion their cause and promote bigotry, racism, and anti-immigrants' sentiments. Minorities from various racial backgrounds have become victims of Internet racism. Joe Feagan in the citation below sees racism as an age-old fundamental problem, especially in the U.S. context that does not leave new media immune to it:

This framing of society goes back to at least the 1600s. It is nearly four centuries old now. This nation was founded in extensive slavery, and those whites that founded it soon rationalized that racial oppression (enslavement of Africans and killing of Indians) with this well-developed white racial frame. That frame, then and now, is full of racist stereotypes (such as lazy and dumb African Americans, uncivilized Indians, white culture is civilized and superior, etc), prejudices, and emotions that have been perpetuated by all forms of mass media since the first century of slavery. (We had 246 years of slavery in our first 258 years after the founding of Jamestown. VA in 1607; this was followed by nearly 100 years of legal segregation from 1870s to late 1960s). Thus, we have only been an officially "free" country that is free of legal racial apartheid, since the last civil rights law went into effect in 1969. About 90 percent of our history has been one of overt and extreme racial oppression. Ten percent has been free. The early mass media spreading the white racist frame (which was and is white suprema-cist in many ways) included ministers Race, Civil Rights, and Hate Speech in the Digital Era 131 speaking from pulpits and early pamphlets and newspapers. Later on in the 1900s many new magazines came in, then radio in the 1920s, and television by the 1950s. Then, the email system and the Internet [emerged] in the 1990s. Each new technology has mostly just extended the ability of those, mostly whites, interested in spreading that white racist frame to more people. It has not changed the white racist frame itself. (Joe Feagin, cited in Daniels, 2008, 130–31)

The quotation above from Joe Feagin demonstrates the depth and breadth of racism in the United States that is so pervasive that the Internet cannot be immune to. There are sites on the Internet that promote hatred, prejudice, and xenophobia for certain racial groups. In the following website, the Australian authorities way back in 2002 outlined some of the cyber threat that they termed "cyber racism" where racists as well as antiracist messages are dis-tributed to the world as indicated below:

- "Ideology: to spread ideas and propaganda;
- Communication: via e-mail, Usenet (news groups), chat rooms;
- Commerce: mail orders for material such as racist music, games, T-shirts etc." Source: (http://www.humanrights.gov.au/racial_discrimination/cyber-racism/index.html)

Since the World Wide Web is a free-for-all public sphere to send both posi-tive and negative messages to targeted groups, it has become the most power-ful medium for racist ideologies. According to this site above, the majority of racist messages in cyberspace are from the United States. But there seems to be a veil of discomfort when the issue of race is brought up in any discussion with the Americans (Bonilla-Silva, 2001). Inequality of digital access creates a fertile atmosphere for racism in cyberspace as buttressed by Nakamura and Chow-White (2013). They state inter alia that "access to digital technologies is unevenly distributed and that the people of color and other groups are still denied equal opportunities in relation to digital media" (5). Redd (1988) noted in an argument on this issue in the *Journal of Black Studies* that disparity in cyberspace between White and Black is tied to economic viability. The latter group is not only facing economic disempowerment with accessing the latest technology on the Internet, it is also facing technology illiteracy. As a result, according to Koch and Schockman (1998) in their paper focusing on Internet access for Lesbian, Gay, and the Bisexual communities "people will gravitate to comfortable 'cyberghettos' to find strength in numbers" (182). Human communication transition to electronic spheres as predicted in the 1960s by Marshall McLuhan has not resolved the ever-haunting inequality between the haves and the have-nots. The breeding ground for disparity between races started with the notion of inferiority and superiority complex from an economic standpoint, where Europe saw the rest of the world as beckoning and submitting to them as they sought to create empires. That mindset continues today even in the virtual realm of communication unabated. However, Mark Hansen has seen it differently. To him

the suspension of the social category of visibility in online environments transforms the experience of race in what is, potentially a fundamental way: by suspending the automatic ascription of racial signifiers according to visible traits, online environments can, in a certain sense, be said to subject everyone to what I shall call a "zero degree" of racial difference. (Hansen, 2006, 141)

To him the online world of communication is equitable. All races should neutralize their erstwhile offline racial bigotry and unite for a common cause, and that cause should be to establish a zone of what he calls "zero degree." That is, there should be no tolerance of racism in cyberspace. This is a wish that is far from reality as the virtual sphere still exhibits racial intolerance to those who "infringe" or dare to challenge the dominant power, especially if they are of a different race. The emergence of online communication has not stopped the spread of racial smirks as it is an age-old phenomenon as opined by Kolko (2000) with the following rhetorical questions:

Does race "disappear" in cyberspace? How is race visually represented in popular film and advertisements about cyberspace? Do narratives that depict racial and ethnic minorities in cyberspace simply recapitulated the old racist stereotypes, do they challenge them, do they use the medium to sketch out new virtual realities of race. (Kolko et al., 2000, 11)

The response is in the affirmative. Take for instance, the #CrimingWhileWhite on Twitter exposed the wounds of how some Whites felt about police senseless brutality on innocent Blacks:

"White people rioted because if you see a black family, they're looting. If you see a white family they're looking for food." #CrimingWhileWhite

"#CrimingWhileWhite and White privilege are the reason domestic terrorists keep growing" #CrimingWhileWhite.

"You keep the poor people of all races uneducated and make them fight each other while you hoard the wealth" #CrimingWhileWhite.

In some site on the Internet, if you do not speak, act, and write like Whites, you are ghettoized or excluded "Black and Latino gamers in particular reveal that they are constantly harassed when the default gamer hears how they sound. They are told that they sound 'too black' or that they use 'too much Spanglish for the space'" (Gray, 2017, 114). He continues to say that "even in a quasi-liberation space such as the Internet, racial and ethnic minorities are still marginalized" (Gray, 2017, 107). The hashtag from #CrimingWhileWhite is again demonstrated below:

"Played with realistic toy gun my entire childhood, wherever we wanted." #CrimingWhileWhite

"My 13yo [*sic*] son and his friend were loitering at Walgreens recently. Only his black friend got searched for shoplifting." #CrimingWhileWhite

"Ticket for going 120. No license. Judge let me off. You go to too good a school to be dumb so I assume you aren't." #CrimingWhileWhite

"Exhaled blunt smoke in a cop's face as I opened my door and then told him he couldn't come in without a warrant. He left." #CrimingWhileWhite (Gray, 2017, 108)

Most automated voices on GPS, video games, credit card calling machines, media companies like Verizon, Comcast, and so on, are largely White. The Internet, therefore, continues to be the online theatrical stage where hate speech and other derogatory practices abound, as evidenced by the quote below from Jessie Daniels:

The presence of white supremacy online reinforces this epistemology of white supremacy offline by allowing whites to retreat from civic engagement and into a whites-only chimera. Thus, the early emergence and persistent presence of white supremacy online calls for multiple literacies: a literacy of digital media and new literacies not merely of "tolerance," but literacies of social justice that offer a depth of understanding about race, racism, and multiple intersecting forms of oppression. (Daniels, 2008, 130)

Later in another publication, Daniels (2016) demonstrates how Sheryl Sandberg in her quest to empower women to fight for equality in a male-dominated world failed to mention African American women and other women of color who are also disproportionately disenfranchised. This, therefore, begs the question as to the conscientiousness and consciousness of those who perpetuate racial tendencies online. If race or racialism is proportionately tied to experience and socialization at one's prime age, then it could quite easily be understood that there is a direct correlation between exhibiting racialized tendencies in both attitude and behaviors online and offline with parenting and socio-cultural upbringing. To extricate oneself from this cocoon of blindness to sensitivities of those affected by posts and direct offline messages that are directly aimed at hurting someone's racial makeup or ethnicity, education of the mind is the key.

The casual web user browsing the Internet for information on any given topical issue is, therefore, forced to wear two lenses: one for ignoring the distractions of pop-ups with messages from say ultra-right groups seeking new recruits or expounding on their ideological stances. The other lens is to fight back by articulating the stance of the "other" who are economically disenfranchised or victim of digital divides with no pixelized weapons to provide alternative views. These are some of the binary positions that most non-followers of extremist sites on digital media adopt but if they are Blacks for obvious reasons as aforementioned stated then White hegemony from the ideological standpoint will continue to dominate the digital airwaves for the foreseeable future. Gray (2017) makes this observation: "There are discursive realities of technology of the self that are both objectifying and subjectifying as racial and ethnic identity are approached discursive terms constituted in the margins of objectivity/subjectivity, outsider/insider, and domination/liberation" (Gray, 2017, 109). The case of Jacob Blake, George Floyd, Trayvon Martin in Florida, Michael Brown in St. Louis, Eric Gardner in New York, and Freddie Gray in Baltimore brought Black people and their sympathizers to collectively vent about police brutality on Black Twitter giving birth to the #BlackLivesMatter that has continued unabated till today.

CYBERBULLYING

The tendency to berate or send taunting images to someone or to a group with the intention of causing psycho-mental harm through the digital media is what is referred to as cyberbullying.

Cyberbullying is the transplantation of in-person bullying onto the cyber-netic space with the overall intention not far removed from the in-person psychological harm to the target person or persons. The extent to which this damage can have on the targeted individual has been analyzed and discussed by most scholars to include mental health challenges, low self-esteem, depression, and suicide tendencies (Edwards, Kontostathis, Fisher, 2016; Stone and Carlisle, 2015). Findings from the study of Edwards et al. indicate that Blacks perpetuate acts of cyberbullying more than Whites as seen below:

> Youth of color report lower levels of cyber-victimization than their white peers; indeed, black and Hispanic youth are more likely to be cyber-bullies and offline bullies than victims of bullying. Black and Hispanic teens report levels of cyberbullying victimiza-tion similar to the national average (from 16% to 30%). (Edward et al., (2016), 74)

The findings from this study demonstrate the intricacies of tackling and studying racism on cyberspace. It is not inconceivable to think that Blacks would be the victim as it is most often presented offline. Nevertheless, find-ings from such a study turn the table on some minorities who equally display tendencies of racism most often associated with the domineering class. What this study purports to signify is that racism is color prejudice and it must not always be the Black who is victimized. In this example, the Black race is perpetuating instances of cyberbullying. In this same study, Blacks carry out more in-person bullying than cyberbullying and the reason given is that Internet penetration to Black household is less compared to Whites. Chetty and Alathur (2018) introduce the element of online hate speech, and when it targets race it plays the same deleterious role of demeaning the opponent as less valuable or appreciative by the other race. The online form of cyberbul-lying can take various forms, ranging from textization to emojification. One of the potent effects of this, especially on the self-esteem of an individual, is through video postings, memes, and trolling. Given that only a few people can distinguish between photoshopped images/videos that are posted online, the mere consumption of these posts directed to oneself can be detrimental even before the consumer has the cognitive effrontery to question its authen-ticity. That is probably why teens are the most affected group of people who face insurmountable obstacles dealing with the effects of cyberbullying and hate speech. What also makes it daunting is because senders of such messages hide behind anonymity and fake ids to disseminate them, and the receiver may not know that multiple users may have been targeted so as not to bare the sole burden of the pain.

#BLACKLIVESMATTER AND RACISM

Vogels, Perrin, Rainie, and Anderson (2020) report on Pew research.org that by May 28, 2020, there were over 8.8 million tweets using the hashtag #BlackLivesMatter and this was by far more than the regular 2 million since the acquittal of George Zimmerman on July 13, 2013, after he shot and killed Trayvon Martin. Since then this hashtag has continued to grow and since it is mainly discussing matters related to White police officer's brutality and killing of Black men and women, the debate over racism has resurfaced. Racism is a social construct as most scholars seem to agree. But suffice it to say that it is imperative to include the socio-cultural aspect of racism because one of the ingredients that forms the menu for characterizing racism is culture.

The way Whites and Black Americans are culturally brought up can be a contributory factor to stroking the concept of racism. Culturally, Blacks who originated from Africa were culturally brought up to be custodians of traditions and customs, and so even though much of African culture was stripped from them when they reached the shores of Virginia in 1619, they still had vestiges of internal African culture in them. Though their African names and languages were taken away from them, their psycho-cognitive mindset and cultural mores for the land of Africa that they left behind have remained intact. Their spiritual belief system has equally remained intact, which is the reason why congregating and singing praise to the most High God was always ever present in the negro spirituals in the South. So, they kept their customs. One of those customs was communal livelihood. Where Blacks have resided during and after slavery that they experienced after the emancipation proclamation in 1865 by Abraham Lincoln has been a cause for concern for them. Most Blacks congregated and communed together to look for safety valves to weather the storm of survival that was now becoming thorny because they were no longer under the control of their master's whip. That cultural-inbuilt consciousness in them was quite different from what White America experienced. Whites who were of European descent practiced individualism, capitalistic modes of production, and communal livelihood, which was nothing they were accustomed to and still do today. So, when these two races confront situations where ideologies can clash, this historical–cultural perceptual lens rares its ugly head and the resultant effect is racists' behaviors because they have not interpreted/perceived the same situation from the same lenses.

This is also quite evident in their online interrelated discourses. Another contentious issue related to race, racism, and racialism is in the subconscious. The extent to which one can comfortable say "an act" is racist is open to several interpretations. Take for instance, when Darren Wilson, the

White police officer who killed Michael Brown and his fellow cops abandoned his body on the road for hours before it was attended to, was interpreted by interactants on #BlackTwitter as racist. They said a dead White person would not have been abandoned on the road for that long. A similar thing happened when George Floyd was mercilessly murdered intentionally by Derek Chauvin in Minneapolis. He and his fellow police officers refused to perform CPR when they saw that he was giving up the ghost. They stood there watching him to die and this too was perceived by online and offline interactants as racist. The Black users who have perceived this as racist are responding to their cultural–ideological upbringing that has drilled unto them to respect and honor the death because the dead are not dead, and their African ancestors would not respond kindly to anyone or group that have maltreated a dead person. This is why funeral ceremonies are accompanied with all sorts of rituals and prayers. The same racist view was echoed by all the Black media outlets when Garrett Rolfe, another White police officer shot and killed Rayshard Brooks and kicked his dead body. When the video camera footage was released and shown on TV and on other new media outlets like Facebook and Twitter, especially during this COVID-19 pandemic period where most Americans are hunkered down at home, everyone was stunned. By kicking the body of a dead Black person, he was displaying racism.

These are all incidences that have prepared the fertile ground for the birth of BLM (Black Lives Matter) movements. The BLM movement that had begun after the death of Trayvon Martin and Michael Brown has gained international exposure this year, 2020, after the brutal callous killing, especially of George Floyd. The gruesome video that circulated on the digital media spaces brought all races in the world to condemn the action. There were messages of condemnation as well as demonstrations in major cities of the world including Africa. The gruesome manner with which he was killed did not leave the world indifferent to the race problems that America has faced in decades. Republicans and Democrats in the House of Representative and Senate all condemned the inhumane murder though the Republicans did not go as far as some Democrats to call for police reforms and others went as far as calling for the police to be defunded. The issue related to racist attacks on Blacks and other minorities in the United States had begun years ago and had been the topics of numerous books that have been written. Poets and musicians have also made their voices heard, yet with online virtual spaces today, and especially while the rest of mankind have been confined at home due to the COVID-19, pandemic, social media posts on issues like this have mushroomed. Black celebrities like W. E. B Du Bois who earned his PhD at Harvard University in the late nineteenth century published a classic titled "Souls of Black Folks" and in it he has pointed to the fact that the Black person in America does not have similar conscious self-perceptual lens to view and interpret the world like the rest of the human race. The Black person is suffering from a term that has become universally known today as "double consciousness"—meaning that the Black person, due to years of enslavement, years of dehumanization in the hands of White slave masters in the South, has been rendered subhuman. With the loss of human dignity, love, and respect from the White community because the latter arrogates to itself the title of supremacy, the Black man sees the rest of the world through the White's lens. The education s/he has acquired has been devoid of anything related to Africa. After all his/her African name, language, culture, history had been stripped away since 1619.

The appellation "African American is a misnomer and an attempt to de-recognize the origin of the Black person" Mazrui (1986) puts it quite convincingly when he describes succinctly what happened to the slaves from Africa when they were received as captives in the new world, "forget you are African, remember you are Black . . . forget you are African remember you are black" (110). These are soundbites that remind one of the great book and movie *Konta Kinte*! There is no other way to depersonalize, de-culturalize, de-humanize another human creature than this. With this psycho-demoralizing effect on the mind of the Black person in the United States after more than 400 years of their lives in this country, Du Boisian caption of double consciousness may be an understatement today. With the recent police brutality as already discussed, the Black person now suffers from multiple consciousnesses. The Black person is unlike an Irish American, Italian American, British American, French American, Indian American, Chinese American, or Korean American. The Black American cannot arrogate to himself or herself similar titles like Kenyan American, Nigerian American, Moroccan American, Ugandan American, Ghanaian American, and so on, like their counterparts in Europe and Asia but has been lumped into the title "African American." A continent of more than fifty-six states. How can one Black person be a citizen of all the countries in Africa from north to south and from east to west? This was clearly an attempt to uproot their origins and lump them under one category so they could never be exposed to their identities as people who were originally taken away from slave ports of Senegal, Benin, Ghana, Cameroon, Angola, Congo, and so on. This is a classic example of racism! This was an act of denigration of a human species by another species that believe in the doctrine of supremacy and inferiority of another race. As Ali Mazrui has portrayed above, the Black person has to forget they are Africans but to remember they are Black! Blackness was synonymous to being at the lowest rung on human classification. Frances Cress Welsing has captured it well in her Isis papers publications where she elaborately discusses her color confrontation theory: "the goal of the white supremacy system is none other than the establishment, maintenance, expansion and refinement of world domination by members of a group that classifies itself as the white 'race'" (Welsing, 1991, 3). The idea for them to forget they are Africans is an attempt to deny them dignity as people with a culture, memorable history, and value like other human beings from other parts of the world. This was not only an insultingly racialized categorizations, it was blatant debasement of another human creature on planet earth.

This has been in the mind of the freed slaves from the South after the 1860 slave emancipation proclamation by Abraham Lincoln. Today most African Americans are still struggling to search for their roots in Africa. No doubt a huge number have decided to get through the ancestry site on the Internet in an attempt to search for the national origins of their Great-Great parents in the continent of Africa so as to restore some sense of dignity to their humanity. The protests march across cities all over the world and the online hashtags after yet another killing of an unarmed Black person has resurfaced the debate on reparations for the Black Race in the United States.

> Reparations for the African American community are an appeal that America undertakes, for the first time in its history, a politics of love. Reparations require acknowledging America's shameful past and its continuing failure to recognize Black individuality. The politics of repair, of love, constitutes a rethinking of the American community shorn of its antihuman principle of White supremacy. Such a politics includes making available provisions for those who have, thus far, been denied capacity to live fully and freely in the nation. It is to extend the resources available in the United States according to principles that defy White supremacist thinking. (Prager, 2020, 648)

Prager is insinuating that the politics of love through some form of reparations to the sins of the past committed on the Black race can atone for the shameful acts of the White race in the past to the sons and daughters of the Black race who, due to no fault of theirs, have been living with this pain on their personhood for years. With reparations they may have reasons to consciously and peaceably cast the White sins of the past when narrating the story of the Black struggle to their children. Maybe this can start with the recognition of the Black Lives Matter anthem that has been forced down the throats of conservative racist Whites who have still not yet comes to terms with the fact that racism had existed, still exists, and would continue to exist if it is not honestly confronted with all our political, social, cultural, and most importantly economic might.

#ALLLIVESMATTER VS. #BLACKLIVESMATTER?

When the online and offline public sphere was inundated with the slogan Black Lives Matter after the death of Trayvon Martin, other parallel movements were also given birth to. *All Lives Matter* has emerged as one of those movements that have emerged as the counterpublic to BLM. It is no coincidence that these issues are seemingly at odds at this moment in time in American history of Black and White relations. It is no longer a matter of semantics with the content of what they all stand for but rather an attempt to draw attention to other issues of equal weight that are plaguing or not plaguing the American society. The chants from the BLM followers on all the platforms on digital media and on electronic media like radio, and television, to respect and recognize Black Lives as integral members of the planet earth with equal rights legally as one looks up to the U.S. constitution that "We the people" . . . and also that "All men are created equal." There has emerged an ALM (All Lives Matter) movements born under the supposition that it is wrong to only single out one race as victims in the American society. All lives indeed matter because in as much as Blacks are being killed by White police officers, Whites too are being killed, Native Americans are being killed, Asian and Hispanic Americans are also suffering under the same yoke so it is better we do not practice another segregation by focusing only on one race, the Black race. Proponents of ALM, especially on the Twitter handle #AllLivesMatter, have consistently believed that Blacks are not proportionately murdered more than Whites. But statistics from Pew research on August 2020 indicates democratic congressional members have mentioned #BLM on social media platforms more than their Republican counterparts.

> Mentions of "Black lives matter" on social media are highly correlated with party affiliation. A majority (76%) of Democrats in the current Congress have used the phrase "Black lives matter" or the #BlackLivesMatter hashtag on social media dating back to 2015, with roughly half of these members mentioning the phrase for the first time during this three-week period. In contrast, very few currently serving Republicans (10%) have explicitly mentioned "Black lives matter" on social media in the last five years—either before or after George Floyd's killing. (Shah and Widjaya, 2020)

The statistics is quite evident that Republicans in Congress have not bordered to discuss the BLM uprising even after the death of George Floyd on social media. This is where the taproots of racism start to emerge on online and offline public spheres. The death of George Floyd was decried by the entire world and no one, including the Republicans on the U.S. Congress, supported Derek Chauvin in the inhuman murder of the unarmed Black man. Yet, the muted responses on social media platform from a majority of White Republican members of the U.S. Congress can only point to some kind of racist gestures that cannot be denied. Since 2015 when the BLM movement has invaded the mediascape of the world, mostly people of color, and of course, Democrats that are made up of Whites and Blacks have condemned the police officer's action. This is not surprising even as one witnessed the diverse number of races and ethnicities that marched on the streets mostly in Democratic cities in the United States. But a study by Legewie and Fagan (2016) indicate that Blacks are murdered at a higher rate than Whites in the United States. If that be the case, then the issue of racism has further been complicated. For police officers to target more Blacks than Whites in minor and severe infractions recalls to mind the historical past of lynchings and past brutal killings even when it involves minor crimes like that of Emmet Till who was brutally murdered by the Ku Klux Klan for whistling at a White woman in the South.

This is why racism becomes an irrefutable terminology because that same crime cannot be met with the same brutal killing of a White kid whistling at a Black woman. This notwithstanding, followers of #All Lives Matter on Twitter have singled out the fate of a five-year-old baby called Cannon Hinnant brutally gunned down by a Black neighbor called Darius Sessoms (Karimi, 2020). Sessoms is an African American who, it is reported, had dined with the family few days ago before brutally shooting the five-year old who was riding a bike in the neighborhood. This is racism too. The suspect has been arrested and charged with first-degree murder.

CYBER RACISM AND REGULATION

The U.S. Congress passed the Active Cyber Defense Act in 2017 sponsored by Representative Tom Graves as a measure to safeguard and protect the United States from increasing cyber criminalities at home and abroad. This bill was introduced because cyber criminality was posing a threat to national security. Crimes like this needed to be checked and persecuted even though they also recognized that cyber defense practices could, in fact, help in reducing cybercrimes and fraud. With the proliferation of international cyber negative activities that range from overt racism, cyberbullying and cyber sexting, the boundaries to be drawn between what constitute first amendment rights of a citizen to exercise rights of posting self-protected messages and targeting the "other" with the intention of causing pain of unmeasurable proportion is still open to debate. New media are still nascent and an uncharted territory that humankind is still seeking to understand and appreciate. As already discussed, if Blacks and Hispanics as seen in the study of Edwards et al. (2016) exhibit low levels of cyber racism but high levels of offline racism because they are less frequent on cyberspace because of the multiplier effects of digital divide, then it gives ample room for Whites who have the leverage as seen with the Charlottesville, VA, nationalist march to continue their online racists rhetoric against other minorities or people of color. How is regulation going to handle this? The Active Cyber Defense Act cannot be used in this case because the security of the United States is not threatened, but racism is a crime if overtly stated.

Chapter 8

Cyberculture/Capitalism and Digital Colonization

There are two classes of users navigating, consuming, and producing cybernetic contents in cyberspace. The first group are the digital netizenry who have mastered cybercultural politics of exploitations of the have-nots and the digital citizenry who are the savvy-nots. The savvy-nots are digital citizens with novice political knowledge on how they are being used or exploited on the net; they are unaware of the surreptitious work of cookies and other malicious updates installed on their gadgets. They quickly click on their mouse and digitally sign the terms and conditions of "everlastingly" long messages for access to certain contents without reading through all the subtexts of messages. Of course, the producers of such contents, "cyberhawks" have mastered the psycho-cultural limitations of the user who is only quick to click and have no patience to read the fine lines and reject the manipulations. They only browse the digital space for a brief period in search of quick information or to satisfy their ambiguous anxieties. The digital netizenry have mastered the tricks of exploitations and manipulations of the consumer-user on the digital road trip. It is this manipulation that has brought in the term digital colonization of the Internet.

DIGITAL COLONIZATION

The term "digital colonization" has been ascribed by other scholars in different phenomena and circumstances. According to Casili (2017), Casati (2013) describes it as "automatic normativity" (3944). This is limited to the internal pasteurization of data driven by self-inflicted policies that users must abide by before riding the ship of virtuality. This is seen when users are confronted with, say, long terms and condition documents almost as long as the pages of a nation's constitution for which they have to read before clicking the submit button. Nonetheless, digital communication in this context of Africa is a combination of what Casati (2013) believes and the added layer of content availability on sites that are taken for granted that users in developing countries like Africa would ride along. A case in point is the configuration of most commercial websites for email messaging like Yahoo and Google that are globalized and where some local contents have been configured but are limited to certain economically advanced countries. You will hardly find those configurations from the point of view of language and culture in most Tropical African countries, but users in these countries continuously log on and create accounts to enable them send email messages across the world or read business news, world affairs, and weather forecasts. This is a transplantation of foreign cultural influence unto another culture. The intrusion or incursion of foreign communication media into developing countries like Africa for the purposes of expansion was the fear expressed by James Carey and Harold Innis about the destruction it may cause on indigenous cultures (Langmia, 2016). This is digital colonization at best.

The traumatic cultural shifts that Africa experienced with her contact with the Western world in the form of religious indoctrination and educational conquests have complicated her journey of self-discovery. Faced with a volcanic wave of bowing to Western ways of worship and imposition of foreign languages in schools and political corridors of power in almost all 50 states of Africa for close to 300 years before independence, Africa has seen crippling socio-political and cultural growth. For a continent imbued with God-given natural resources to be on her knees and waiting for innovations from Europe and North America to be created so that they can find their ways in Africa, is nothing short of a tragedy. The culture of dependence has crippled the hopes of Africans in the face of capitalistic and vulturistic commercialization of digital technology on the continent. It is not uncommon to find cybercafés littered in every street corner in major cities in Africa in similar ways as one would find liquor stores on some 90 degrees corners of Black suburban neighborhood ghettoes in the United States. The people have mortgaged their lives within the confines of these Telecenters. They send user-generated data with little-or-no knowledge about the politics of international surveillance initiated by NASA since the Bin Ladin psychological fear created by George W. Bush era, especially during the Iraq conquest that prompted him to tell the rest of the world that "you are either with us or against us" during the 2003 State of the Union address. Since then, monitoring of digital data from most parts of the world has become the norm and as Internet users all over the world send sensitive data through the airwaves they may be deemed "terroristic" and that by itself crosses the boundaries of privacy as any soul on this planet earth knows. But those innocent users in most African countries are unaware that their data are being monitored, screened, and archived in the cloud to be accessed by a privileged few in some ivory tower in a Western capital with-out consent from the user-generator or content creator in a far-off land called Africa. The painful part of it is that they pay the Telecenters to send messages to loved ones across the globe.

The intrusion on civil liberties and the "taken-for-granted" mindset that people in the Western world have adopted as posture when exporting elec-tronic and digital manufactured gadgets to these developing non-Western parts of the world has resulted in capitalistic hunting expeditions. This is what Bowers (2014) has aptly termed the "colonizing agenda" (71), and he goes on to explain that "the colonizing agenda also includes promoting Western-style democracy, individual freedom, and a greater reliance upon Western technology and science" (71). The reliance on Western technology has been imposed on the people because that is the only prism of progress that they have been indoctrinated during and after the colonial experiment in Africa. Western digital and electronic technology have taken the Whiteman to the moon and back and so the Black person sitting in a remote village in Africa will only have his/her hopes pinned on conquering the mind of the Whiteman because s/he has been able to use technology to conquer the moon and the Blackman has not. This mindset is difficult to erase, especially as the educational and political systems of the continent are all tied to what pertains in Europe and the United States. There is no other reality that matters to the people. Dependency is the cankerworm that is eating developmental initia-tives in Africa and the only way to resolve it so people can rethink strategies to achieve wholesome happiness and mind awareness is to resist as Bowers (2014) concurs:

> Contrary to our way of thinking, the promotion of our highest values will be viewed in many non-Western cultures as examples of colonization and thus the destruction of their taken-for-granted world. Faced with the loss of traditions that are the basis of their identity, their core values, and patterns of mutual sup-port, the only appropriate response is to resist—which we would do if a foreign power were to impose its basic values and social institutions upon us. (Bowers, 2014, 71)

The irretrievable loss of traditions, customs, and cultures of Africa as a result of the people's contact with the West after 136 years since the Berlin confer-ence of 1884/1885 has had a devastating effect on the mind and psyche of the people. They can only boost pseudo-cultural norms because they have been mixed with those of the West with the latter holding the upper edge in the name of superior values because it is the "standard" in the economic advanced Western world. Today media globalization has spearheaded a rebirth of that colonial experiment but in the form of what Thomas McPhail calls "electronic colonization"; but which in hindsight, today is actually digital colonization since electronic media (radio, TV, and satellite) have been taken over by the digital media. So, for Africa and Africans, this has been excruciating to say the least because their bourgeoning socio-cultural, political, and economic growth rooted from their unique contexts and circumstances in this geographical planet earth has not been given the freedom to flower and spread her wings to the rest of the world. Imagine what Africans could have achieved had she been given the freedom and rights to exploit her mineral resources like coltan in the Republic of Congo that is being stolen from her and made to power cell phones in the world. The wealth that could have flowed to the continent from such exports when over billions of the world population now own cell phones is unimaginable. This has been extremely painful. So according to Bowers (2014), resistance is the only way out. To resist means to decolonize and de-westernize political, economic, and cultural systems of life that seek to uproot the African from his/her cosmological sphere of life by putting him or her as an appendage of the West and that anything that is contrary to the West is unacceptable. This colonial mindset by the West has put our digital communication consumer on a collision course of striving to succeed in a capitalist's fast pace world where success is only measured by the accumulation of the American dollar. This is what continues to push Africans to die in the Mediterranean Sea in search of greener pastures in Europe. The Black person has become the laughing stock of the West especially as Donald Trump has not only banned some countries in Africa from visiting the United States, he and his government has deported Africans at the Mexican borders running from war-torn countries in Africa.

DE-WESTERNIZING DIGITAL CULTURES

Domain names or the universal resource locator (URL) are designed by the West for Africa and the rest of the other non-developed world. This means, therefore, that data uploads and downloads are controlled by a third party who literally does not grasp the subaltern cultures or the developing cultures and most especially the domestic and international digital divides that these developing countries are experiencing. The fact of the matter is that an international organization-apportioned domain name to a given country in Africa does not culturally demarcate it from its neighbor. The knowledge of artificial colonial boundaries set up by the colonial masters after the Berlin conference is not factored in, say, by the International telecommunication union (ITU) that is responsible for regulating international telecommunications. A newly graduated tech guru in Silicon Valley in California who is uploading emojis on social media platforms like Facebook that is viewed in the entire world works on intuition to allocate emojis about global sadness and happiness from the Eurocentric lens. This technician has no clue that there is no global definition of happiness and sadness and that there are contextual differences. Cities on opposite sides of most African countries share various cultural traits like non-verbal display of happiness and verbal expression of sadness that one would find it vexing to think that they belong to two countries and, therefore, two cultures and customs. This happens as a result of the artificialization of boundaries that were arbitrarily carved out to respond to the voracious appetite of the colonial masters of Britain, France, Belgium, Spain, Portugal, and Italy after the Berlin conference. Africa was seen as a basket of gold and silver that they would quench their material thirst. Now with the prevalence of digitalization of media communications, it has become an arduous task for Africans in cyberspace to carve a niche for themselves. It is still a daunting task for them to have a domain name or URL that is purely in any African language like Zulu, Swahili, Yoruba, Wolof, Amharic, and Hausa. Majority of the sites in Africa are predominantly in Western imported languages, and these foreign languages can hardly reflect the concrete customs, cultures, and traditions of the people within a regional setting. To de-westernize means site owners need to upload materials on sites that can be read and reacted upon by the citizens using their own languages and emojis. Miller (2011) echoed this in his discussion on how digital communications have helped Africa leaped frogged into the twenty-first century without the difficulties of fixed-line telecommunication that has become a disaster in most African countries. Nonetheless he cautions:

> But it is also clear that they will gain most not by mimicking what advanced economies have done so far, but by taking advantage of the adaptable nature of digital technologies, such as mobile communications infrastructure, to engage with the information society in a way that meets their *specific needs and circumstances* [emphasis mine]. (Miller, 2011, 109)

The suggestions by Vincent Miller for Africa to adapt Western digital technologies in Africa according to what he terms "specific needs and circumstances" (109) correlates well with the bottom-up process of the de-westernization procedure that I have belabored all along. But the question that hangs on one's lips and reechoes at a distance when one is done discussing this vexing issue is why Africa must only adapt from West. What is the West adapting from Africa? Why must a continent of over 1 billion people subscribe to the anthem of recycling and adapting Western digital communications to fit her unique circumstances. Has the continent become the dustbin of adaptability? When will Africa lead in electronic or digital technologies so that other Western nations can mimic or adapt to their own circumstances. The culture of dependence continues to rear its ugly head on Africa's quest for economic and cultural development, and there seems to be no solution in sight if Africa continues to embrace material and digital adaptations. Thussu (2007, 21) made this revelation back then that "media content and services being tailored to specific cultural consumers not so much because of any particular regard for national cultures but as a commercial imperative." This revelation still rings true today. National African cultures do not occupy a central place in the cognitive sphere of manufacturers in the West who, by and large, are driven by how much profit margins are made than by the Western cultural suffocation that the people are facing. With digital media, their only safety valve is adaptations. But adaptation comes with its own associated costs like importing expert engineers, maintenance technologies, and training crews to prepare African network engineers on how to troubleshoot seen and unforeseen problems that do crop up time and again with digital technologies. To de-westernize means starting digital educations for primary and secondary kids in Africa and teaching them about the importance of promoting African cultures, customs, traditions, and history. This way when they do study in the continent or abroad, they can Africanize their research initiatives. But this can only happen if Africans themselves are mentally ready to preserve and honor their cultural heritage. Sansone (2017) accuses Africans for not honoring their traditional heritage unlike the West:

> Another aspect that is relevant in terms of memory and heritage—and central to the purpose of this text—is the storage of knowledge about the past and its accessibility. Generally speaking, Africa scores low in both. Libraries and archives are comparatively poor. In spite of the efforts of librarians and archivists in many countries, public funding is insufficient. (Sansone, 2017, 13)

Africa cannot de-westernize without strong willpower to come to grips with the reality that certain core issues need to be dealt with. These issues affect the progress of the continent like the idea of the government not investing in libraries and museums. These are institutions that preserve the cultures and traditions of a people. They provide archival data for the next generation so they can freely appreciate the efforts of their forebears to preserve the continent for posterity. So de-westernization and decolonization should come with a price tag. Africa can start by digitizing and de-colonizing their library systems.

AFRICAN LANGUAGES AND DIGITAL DE/ NEO-COLONIZATION/WESTERNIZATION

There is, of course, an apparent difference between de-westernizing digital cultures and communication in Africa and decolonization. To decolonize is to be mindful of Afrocentricity, which is the conscious display of African values, systems, philosophies, and culture as prominent when centering anything on the continent. Right now, digital communication has created an omnipresence on the continent and the need to embrace it without decolonizing the African mind, without placing Afrocentric values as front and center, is an affront to the ancestors of Africa. It will create chaos in any given communication enactments on the continent between the various generations of consumers. By chaos, we mean the tendency to make listeners, readers, viewers, and all the consumers of those communicative acts translate all those facets into their African world view and when there are no associative elements that can be found in the community, miscommunication and misunderstanding can be the outcome. Take for instance, what can an African cyberspace user equate/ relate dropbox, avatar on YouTube, robots, Artificial intelligence, or algorithm with? It can be appropriated, but how effective can that be to an average person not quite exposed to Western education? The user on the African continent is faced with difficult translation and interpretation, and this can cause lots of misunderstanding and miscommunication. The African educational curricula that some of the countries have been using had not included these complex concepts, but now they have to be included and have teachers well trained, not by the West, but by Africans to handle this and it is not often easy. To de-westernize has some commonalities with decolonization, but the difference is that while the former is a way not to import all the mores and behaviors associated with Western culture into Africa, the latter is not to be subjected again to the horrors of colonization that was brutal suppression of African ways of life through direct and indirect rule by the colonial masters. This time, it is no longer colonial tendencies but neo-colonial tendencies whereby some of those rules that were shunned at before African countries gained their independence in the 1960s are slowly creeping through political and economic structures like democratic principles that Africa is being subjected to at the moment in the twenty-first century. Given that digital media communication is mostly an economic tool because they form an integral part of the economy as most people rely on it for employment, there is every reason to suppose that Afrocentric principles are also needed to completely make digital tools and communication platforms meaningful entities within the African cultural systems. One cannot refer to African culture without navigating the thorny issue of the African language. Right now, sixty years after independence of most states in Africa, the official language of interaction at the African Union (AU) remain English and French. Even though according to the website of the AU, "Article 11 of the Protocol on Amendments to the Constitutive Act of the African Union states that the official languages of the Union and all its institutions shall be Arabic, English, French, Portuguese, Spanish, Kiswahili and any other African language," problems still abound. Of all the six languages listed, only one is African, Kiswahili. The remaining five, Arabic, English, French, Portuguese, and Spanish, are all foreign or colonial master's languages. This is why the neo-colonial project on the continent is still very strong. To make matters worse, the last phrase says "*and other African language*" (my emphasis). This is not only sickening but nauseating for Africans to learn that the main organization that brings together all the independent states of Africa is still hooking up with and married to the same colonial languages that were meant to depart with the train that carried away colonial rule from the continent when it ended in 1957 with Ghana being the first country in Africa to declare independence from Britain. The casual reference to other African languages shows the callous disregard to more than 1000 languages beside Kiswahili that are spoken on the continent. The African languages have been given a passive pad on the backs of Africans through this disrespectful position at the AU and this is beyond humiliation and shame. This organization should use the popular African languages like Kiswahili, Wolof, Zulu, Yoruba, Hausa followed by a translation into the Western languages as the case maybe. How then can digital technologies emanating from Europe, the United States, and China not code their programs in any of their own languages? The manufacturers know for sure that there will face no resistance whatsoever on the continent. The cavalier nature that our main organization has treated African languages and given that the educational curricula of a large majority of African countries are either in French, English, Spanish, Portuguese, or Arabic, the Western countries have come to understand that the language barriers are nonexistent on the continent, from a commercial point of view. Since Chinese is not listed on the website by the AU, China as one of the biggest investors in Africa has begun instituting Mandarins in the educational curricula in Africa. Right now, South Africa is taking the lead with Chinese-language institutes in Africa. Qi and Lemmer (2013) have revealed the following information related to the embrace of Mandarin, the Chinese language being taught in tertiary educational settings in South Africa:

> The introduction of Mandarin as a foreign language on a tertiary level was pioneered by the University of South Africa (Unisa) in 1993. Since then, three other South African universities have followed suit, teaching Mandarin in some format and at some level: The University of Stellenbosch (US) in 2002, Rhodes University (RU) in 2009, and The University of Cape Town (UCT) in 2010. In the ensuing sections, Mandarin tuition at these universities is discussed according to the chronological sequence in which it was introduced at the respective institutions. (Qi and Lemmer, 2013, 37)

So, way back in 1993, barely thirty-three years after most countries gained independence in Africa to arrogate to themselves greater autonomy to manage their own affairs, South Africa adopts the teaching of Mandarin to its citizens? South Africa could not see the long-lasting importance of disseminating her indigenous languages like Zulu, Afrikaans, and IsiXhosa in order to gain greater prominence on the world stage. This is why the AU would not find it ridiculous to officiate its affairs in purely Western languages and allocate passive importance to the so-called African languages for Africans in Africa. This is as humiliating as it can get, and no one should be surprised at the position of Africa on the world digital communication stage today.

The other countries with heavy Chinese investment have begun to follow suit like Ghana, Zambia, Kenya, Uganda, Nigeria, and so on. The dominant languages ever since it was called the Organization of African Unity (OAU) before it was changed to AU in 2002 have been English and French. The African languages have been undergoing extinction as a result of the organization not paying particular attention to it and given that schools in Africa are instrumental in promoting and upholding Western languages. Brenzinger, Heine, and Sommer (1991) have confirmed from their study titled "language death in Africa" way back in 1991 that 222 African languages have either died or are in the process of dying.

African writers and scholars saw the need to salvage it and that is why they organized the Asmara, Eritrea conference in January 2001. So, according to the Asmara Conference on African languages and literature, there were ten declarations put forward by African scholars at the end of the conference:

1. *African languages must take on the duty, the responsibility, and the challenge of speaking for the continent.*
2. *The vitality and equality of African languages must be recognized as a basis for the future empowerment of African peoples.*
3. *The diversity of African languages reflects the rich cultural heritage of Africa and must be used as an instrument of African unity.*
4. *Dialogue among African languages is essential: African languages must use the instrument of translation to advance communication among all people, including the disabled.*
5. *All African children have the unalienable right to attend school and learn in their mother tongues. Every effort should be made to develop African languages at all levels of education.*
6. *Promoting research on African languages is vital for their development, while the advancement of African research and documentation will be best served by the use of African languages.*
7. *The effective and rapid development of science and technology in Africa depends on the use of African languages and modern technology must be used for the development of African languages.*

8. *Democracy is essential for the equal development of African languages and African languages are vital for the development of democracy based on equality and social justice.*
9. *African languages, like all languages, contain gender bias. The role of African languages in development must overcome this gender bias and achieve gender equality.*
10. *African languages are essential for the decolonization of African minds and for the African Renaissance.*

(African Cultural Quarterly Magazine, 2000)

Source: https://www.culturalsurvival.org/publications/cultural-sur-vival-quarterly/asmara-declaration-african-languages-and-literatures

It is now twenty years since this declaration was made in Asmara, Eritrea. There has not been any visible movement geared toward implementing the recommendations from this conference. Item 7 is so explicit: *"The effective and rapid development of science and technology in Africa depends on the use of African languages and modern technology must be used for the development of African languages"* (Asmara Conference, 2001). Digital communication is the rapid scientific development on the continent. The same is true of the subsequent statement that modern technology ought to use African languages for its developmental goals, aims, and purposes in Africa. Dominant Western social media platforms like Facebook, Twitter, Instagram, WhatsApp, and Snapchat are not making use of African languages. These are multinational corporations owned and managed in the West. Facebook bought WhatsApp from the founders in 2018, and since then Africans have flooded that platform using it for interpersonal communication, international communication, video chats with loved ones at home and abroad. Texting and emojifications with groups of people in the rural and urban centers of Africa, money transfer details including pin numbers and password are being exchanged on WhatsApp. College students are using it for research to record interviews and upload data in the field to each other. In the era of the COVID-19 unprecedented pandemic, primary and secondary schools including some colleges in Africa have turned to WhatsApp for knowledge dispensation because the costs of LMS, Learning Management Systems like Blackboard, Canvas, Webex, and other video conferencing technologies are expensive for some schools in Africa to afford. Given that at least one family in Africa has access to one device like a smartphone that can have WhatsApp software downloaded on it, students who have been left idle at home because schools have been shut down are now using these platforms for educational purposes. The problem is that this can effectively be done using either one of those Western languages that have been listed on the webpage of the

AU. But the Asmara Conference stressed the need for inculcating African languages into any modern technology geared toward Africa and African people. This is modern technology and there are no inbuilt African languages like Wolof, Yoruba, Hausa, Fulani, Zulu, Kikuyu, and so on, factored in the dispensation and dissemination of this knowledge, especially to the kids in primary schools who are the future leaders of the continent of Africa. Item 10 is equally crucial: "*African languages are essential for the decolonization of African minds and for the African Renaissance*" (Asmara Conference, 2001). It is twenty years since this declaration was made known by the African scholars and in the era of digital modes of communication, we are emphasizing again what they had agreed upon and that is the process of decolonization. The reason why language is extremely crucial in the era of decolonization is because Africa cannot be chanting the hymn of independence and celebrating self-rule yet still bestows ontological, epistemological, and axiological ideologies to the West through the use of language. Language is the carrier of culture, customs, and traditions of a people. If these languages are not used on social media platforms to indicate the level of decolonization of the mind of the African, then it will be a fallacy to state that Africa has acquired independence from her colonial masters. There are some sites that are being developed and created by a few digital gurus on the continent where some of the African languages can be used. A classic example is the *Lenali App* created and patented by Mamadou Guro of Mali that has inbuilt audio features where users can record messages in their local languages and it is translated in a given official language of French in Mali (see Langmia, 2020). But this is limited to Mali. However, there are other indigenous social media platforms that are beginning to make in-roots into the communication public sphere in Africa like *Chomi*, in South Africa, *Esoka* or e-Soko (e-market) (Langmia, 2020), *Naijapals* in Nigeria, *Yookos*, and so on. The problem with these African-driven applications is that Africans are not rushing in to embrace them as their own unique platforms that need visibility. A continent of over 1 billion people, there is apparently no logical reason to convince any sensible human creature born on planet earth that Africans should rather subscribe more to Facebook, Twitter, Instagram, Snapchat, and so on, than *Chomi, Lenali App, e-Soko* and so on, that are owned, operated, and managed by Africans for Africans. If China, South Korea, India, and most Middle Eastern countries have their own unique digital social media platforms where they are using their own language and they have been configured to welcome those languages and emojis are formed and produced to accommodate the cultural uniqueness of those countries, why not in Africa? If there are Arabic keyboards on most computers in Africa including English and French in North, East, West and South Africa, how can that help improve and promote the African languages and culture? The Asmara Conference that focused on decolonization had exactly this in mind. Africa cannot be seen to take steps to become independent yet at the same time flooding her airwaves (electronically) and Internet (digitally) with non-African languages on platforms that are universal and not meant to advance the Afrocentric agenda. This focus on Western languages is also affecting e-health dispensation on the continent since health issues are also being discussed on digital media (Onwumechili and Amulega, 2020). It appears after independence Africa has remained the junior brother of Europe, waiting to be served or better still waiting for crumbs from the dinner table of world dinner.

With respect to the very first declaration from the Asmara Conference in defense of the African language, there is already the looming danger: *"African languages must take on the duty, the responsibility, and the challenge of speaking for the continent"* (Asmara Conference, 2001). With digital communication seen on all the computers in Africa, all the laptops, tablets, and smartphones in Africa, Africans are encouraged to use African languages as a responsibility and duty to speak for the continent. On the contrary, Africans have sacrificed themselves on the altar of foreign language pride and imprisoned themselves in the classroom of Western ways of writing and speaking. Mind you, there are most Africans on the continent unable to write their own languages and mother tongues because they were taught only the Western languages in the colonial and post-colonial schools.

DIGI-CULTURAL CONUNDRUMS

It has often been said that if knowledge is the key, we need to show those interested where to find its rightful padlock. Africa needs economic uplift, and this uplift can surely come through taking several indices and politico-cultural context into account. The information economy now pioneers the engine for economic growth in the world today, but Africa needs relevant and adaptable engine oil that will spin the wheel of growth for her to compete meaningfully with the rest of the world. The slippery slope that a continent like Africa finds herself at the moment is the "curse" or better still the "blessing" of colonialism that exposed the continent to outside influences and inspiration. Critics of Afrocentricity argue that Africa cannot afford any form of isolationism at this time of global race for dominance and influence in the world. If Africa retreats, then the rest of the world will be matching to the moon while she, in the words of Ali Mazrui, will be moving to the village. Those critics have their reasons, and they should be allowed to air their arguments, but Afrocentricity is the cultural springboard and lens to forge ahead with issues that concern the continent. Africans are still hoodwinked to the economic systems, socio-cultural systems, and political systems of their former colonial masters. It is still that same colonial master that has exported democracy to Africans even if the soil recoils in a whimper to echo Ali Mazrui. The colonial masters have exported digital communication platforms that African must use in order to be competitive and gain the much-needed jobs and education for her people. Yes, fine and good, but so do the, Indians, Koreans, Singaporeans, Brazilians, and most other countries who also experienced some form of colonization from China, Japan and other European countries. They are putting their countries' socio-cultural, economic, and political realities first before embracing what comes from the West or their colonial masters. And this starts with language and culture. The digital communicative sphere of human interaction for these aforementioned countries starts with their languages, cultural traits, and traditions. The influences of the West are there but not predominant as one will find with Africa. We visited a McDonald food store in Chennai, India, in 2013 and were shocked to find that they have "Indianized" the menu even though they still keep the format and structure of serving the customers the same as one would find in the United States. But Chinese restaurants in Africa have not Africanized their menu. We have never eaten "fufu corn" or "Eru" (west Cameroonian stable foodstuff) in any Chinese restaurants in Yaounde, the capital city of Cameroon. In any Chinese restaurant that we have visited in any part of the world, the structure and architecture of their buildings is Chinese. They will have chopsticks on their tables. Most Western restaurants in Africa are purely westernized in form and menu. So, the dilemma that Africa finds herself in the match to globalization and media representation and recognition is whether to adapt or innovate. Blogging has been a good example for some on the continent to raise their voices on issues of national concern. Another is the use of hashtagism. The #Bringbackourgirls on Twitter helped to bring attention to the kidnapping saga of 120 Muslim girls in Northern Nigeria by the Boko Haram terrorist groups. That attention galvanized international forces of Nigeria, Cameroon, and Chad with the help of Western supplied artillery to hunt down most of the terrorist group in the Northern part of Nigeria and the Lake Chad Basin. Even though the issue has not been completely resolved, some of the girls were released but others are still in captivity. But it was thanks to Western technology that international awareness was brought to bear on this heinous crime. So, the dilemma that Africa continuously faces is either to request technological help in the form of technical expertise and sophisticated hi-tech equipment to help them resolve pressing issues like road, rail, and airport constructions, landslides, earthquakes, mudslides, plan crashes, and so on, or relyon their trained engineers. The same routine of begging from the West has begun with COVID-19 vaccines. These issues continue to haunt self-reliance and development in the continent and that will make the thorny debate over dependence difficult to resolve anytime soon until the continent becomes self-sufficient and be able to export other skills besides manpower to the west.

UNTAPPED RESOURCES

Africa is home to all the world minerals that can render her self-sufficient. But the problem is that Africa has allowed foreign countries like Europe and the United States and recently China to exploit her resources with impunity. Most of the resources that are used to power the Internet and other telecommunication infrastructure on planet earth are from Africa. Coltan, Uranium, platinum, iron ore, manganese are all found in Africa. To decolonize means to maximise the use of these resources.

DIGITAL LABOR EXPLOITATION

Casilli (2017) argues that digital labor exploitation, especially in developing countries, has reached an alarming rate. Most transnational companies located in Western capitals have resorted to exploit the labor skills of users resident in Africa and especially in India. These agents provide minimally paid services to these Western companies on their online services that would have been economically burdensome for them to hire local labor. In the in-person parlance, this is often referred to as outsourcing, but in this case where the Internet communication is boundary-less and workers for services that are virtually demanded with no restricted spatiotemporal locations, it is easy to violate national labor laws and pay the workers "under the table." Granted, the level of economic poverty in most countries in Africa has reached an unmanageable proportion that has triggered emigration on an astronomical proportion leading to tragic deaths at sea crossings between North Africa and Europe. But that does not in any way provide latitudes for global media companies to practice "unfair" practices (Casilli, 2017). The fate of migrant workers in Western countries is similar to what multinational companies are practicing with those labor residents, say in Africa or India or any other developing country. Digital labor exploitation is a form of digitized capitalism that needs scrutiny, such that those who provide synchronous and asynchronous services to billion-dollar companies in the Western world should reward this digital labor fairly and lawfully. With the level of ignorance of labor laws across state boundaries, it becomes increasingly daunting to ascertain what is true and what is fiction, especially as these individuals are simply in dire need to survive and fend for their families. We thought that digital revolution was a blessing to most people who find themselves at the bottom ladder of economic achievements since cyberspace is free and democratic. What most scholars have termed "media globalization," Hardy (2014) aptly calls it "cultural imperialism" (157). He says "in the conventional version told, crude, neo-Marxist accounts of cultural impositions, American hegemony and 'one-way' cultural flows."

Figure 8.1   Photo by Gwaivu Azed.

(157) seem to dominate. As a result of the World Wide Web and the influence of the Internet, the influx of American cultural service goods has swamped the African mediascape. The MTV shows are transmitted live from YouTube unto private TV sets in popular musical centers, five-star hotels, restaurants, and bars all across Africa. African youths have changed their taste to embrace Western style of dressing, speaking, emojificating on Facebook, Twitter, Instagram, WhatsApp, Snapchat, and YouTube. The culture of amassing tons of likes on one's Facebook selfies and Snapchat sites has become fashionable. These youths are oblivious of the automated algorithmic bots that sometimes self-populate these likes for commercial purposes. They are unaware of the political economy of user-generated uploaded content that they have initiated on their social media accounts that advertisers in the Western world are taking advantage of. These are some of the vexing issues of digital labor exploitation that have gone unattended by international law enforcement so that those who feed the multinational digital companies are themselves handsomely compensated. Andrejevic (2013) quotes Steve Lohr article in New York Times discussing an initiative by the United Nations that "will conduct so-called sentiment analysis of messages in social networks and text messages—using natural—language deciphering software—to help predict job losses, spending reductions or disease outbreaks in a given region" (Lohr, 2012). Maybe this could be the barometer for successful hybridization of our electronic and digital communications (figure 8.1).

Chapter 9

Blacks and Artificial Intelligence

The underprivileged and the downtrodden are, more often than not, the target of the hegemonic and dominant elite critical mass in any given society to fashion out their economic and political fate. The political economy of the media avers that market forces are generally tilted to benefit capitalist hawks bent on maximizing profits and minimizing losses. The emergence of Artificial Intelligence, algorithm, and big data discourse has resurrected the debate over who is targeted on the digital public sphere and who is not. Blacks, Hispanics, and other people of color in the United States have decried the bias nature of these technologies, especially on the issue of facial recognition that has wrongly been applied (see details in chapter 11).

The intersection of digital technology and human privacy rights and freedom has been plunged into a huge bottomless hole of controversies. The transfer of human cognitive intelligence into robotic and algorithmic machineries is now proving to be the future. By future, according to the Chinese Artificial Intelligence legend, Kai-Fu Lee dubbed the oracle of AI by 60 minutes weekly CBS TV show in the United States, AI is something that will prove to be more powerful than electricity. Thomas Edison, one of the fathers of electricity, saw electricity as a conduit to revolutionize human progress like the improvement in mass communication and industrial productivity. Electricity was not meant to discriminate nor dominate. Artificial Intelligence, henceforth, referred to as AI has started on the bad footing, whereby only the materially rich advanced countries seem to be reaping the benefits even when it has not fully taken off yet. China and the United States are fighting to dominate with the creation of smart cities and self-driven cars. GPS and other algorithmic facilities seem to be dominated by these two countries including Europe and Canada. The issue of dominance is just one of a plethora of criticism that AI and algorithm are facing in this postmodern world. Sonia Katyal writing on the UCLA law review in 2019 states:

> While algorithmic decision making may initially seem more reliable because it appears free from the irrational biases of human judgment and prejudice, algorithmic models are also the product of their fallible creators, who may miss evidence of systemic bias or structural discrimination in data or may simply make mistakes. These errors of omission—innocent by nature—risk reifying past prejudices, thereby reproducing an image of an infinitely unjust world. (66 UCLA L. Rev. 54, 2019)

Like any new invention and experiment, there are bound to be limitless and forgivable errors of the machine but a deliberate attempt by that same machine to constantly, and on a consistent basis, misrepresent, miss-identify, and miss-classify people, especially people of color and other races, is unpardonable:

> It turns out, some analysts argue, that big data has failed to include marginalized communities, including African American, Latino, Native American populations, people of a lower socioeconomic status, LGBT individuals, and immigrants. Not only are these people disproportionately missing from sources like internet histories, social media, and credit card usage, but they are also missing from electronic health records and genomic databases. (66 UCLA L. REV. 54, 2019)

This is unfortunate. At the turn of the twenty-first century when we need to pull all creative forces toward positive growth of all mankind regardless of creed, culture, and race, another invention is starting at the wrong foot to categorize certain groups as substandard. The age of massive data often dubbed "big data" has given ample room for technology-driven companies to use all sorts of mechanisms to collect data from online users as well as credit card owners and users on Uber and Lyft. Kim (2018) has equally noticed a pattern, especially with Facebook and advertisement. People who are the so-called 'the look-alikes' are targeted for promoting items for sale. Since users' private travels, friends they associate with and their favorite spot to visit, algorithm is being used to aggregate their likes and dislikes and targeted randomly by commercial companies. Most of the times, the method they employ to reach optimum benefit is questionable. This is what Kim (2018) concludes with respect to people of color:

> Race is a bit more complicated. In theory, an employer cannot select a Facebook audience based on race, but some interest categories are closely identified with

race—such as the attribute of "African American affinity group." Selecting or screening out an audience using this attribute would probably come pretty close to selecting on the basis of race. Even without using ethnic affinity, employment ads might target or exclude along racial or ethnic lines by using proxies, such as "interested in BlackNews.com" or "interested in Nuestro Diario." (Kim, 2018, 319)

This is what AI has come to represent. Machinic communication has come to replace human-to human communication and this system could predict a rough relation between humans and machines with respect to communication and exchange of messages. Increasingly, AI has come under intense scrutiny for bias facial recognition, especially with respect to people of color. This of course does not only raise the issue of racial bias it equally brings into question the issue of ethics, and Weber (2019) addresses this in his most recent article:

At the other end of the spectrum, however, is the ethically challenged use of AI as the basis for facial recognition technology to track (and subsequently incarcerate) religious minorities in China. This is presumably the first largescale deployment of "a government intentionally using artificial intelligence for racial profiling." (Weber, 2019, 47)

Racial minorities in China have become victims of government use of AI to track down "renegades" and these happen to be religious minorities. Most developing countries have continuously been at the receiving end of technology and AI is certainly not going to be different. While Blacks in the United States and other impoverished people in the world are concerned about putting food on the table and fighting the psycho-mental effects of poverty that has affected them disproportionately, those with advanced knowledge and capital are paving a new future for mankind based on their lived experience. This lived experience has and will continue to be with Europe and America calling the shots as they did with the industrial revolution and expanding their empire beyond their territorial boundaries. China is now competing with them with respect to AI but looking at the quotation from Weber (2019), it would appear they will use it to monitor and control the actions of religious minorities that are under their control.

AI by itself has lots of positive effects, but as in any new endeavor that seeks to improve the life of humans on planet earth, scholars from all parts of the globe examine the advantages and disadvantages in order to call to wit those responsible for implementation and execution that there has to be a cost to human lives when such initiatives are undertaken. Unfortunately, the costs, more often than not always involve the downtrodden, those on the fringes who struggle to get by in this tumultuous world of capitalist greed and disregard for those who bear the pain of economic poverty. One of the advantages of AI and algorithm, as pointed out by Mckenzie (2018), is that they do predict at the same time provide amenities for "abused children" (530). When data is collected and assembled, they use analytics to predict what can and cannot happen ten years from today on children that are being abused or cyberbullied. It is this same data that can be used by the forces of law and order worldwide. But the cry is that that data should be objectively used and not subject other children of color or of other ethnicity, creed, and race under undue circumstances of discrimination where they become targets for law officers. Another important point raised by Mckensie (2018) is that AI and algorithm are being used for hiring by employers and the fear especially those people of color that with this advancement in technology, they are being subjected to additional scrutiny. According to him:

> If employers wish to take advantage of the potential efficiency benefits of using artificial intelligence in hiring, they should use caution in selecting a program, encourage the use of responsible algorithms, and push for long term changes in the lack of racial and gender diversity in the technology industry. (530)

The question that often arises is what constitutes "responsible algorithms"? What should constitute a responsible algorithm is that it is void of bais. It should not have machine error and it should be bias-free. But to achieve all these, the role and input of human intelligence is required because "artificial" means "artificial" regardless of the circumstances. That is why since some minorities and many people of color are hardly consulted and may not be in the board room of decision making by top executives, their voices are decided by others that would impact their lives. They are subjected to discriminatory practices that affect their psycho-cultural, economic, and moral systems that are often overlooked by the powers that be. This brings in the issue of diversity that has recently become the buzz word for all agencies and organization the world over struggling to bring people who not only look different but have different lenses to perceive the world. It is now customary to see companies hiring to diversify. But what does that really mean in actuality? Diversity and multiculturalism are the two concepts especially in this era of new media that gets confused. When people from other parts of the world are hired (for whatever reason) to form what is referred to as equality at workplace, they call that diversity. When men have a few women added to their midst in whatever high-end companies in the world, they still call that diversity. But these two scenarios cannot be the same. The former is what should be referred to as multiculturalism and the latter diversity. People from other parts of the world or other regions within the same country can be hired to constitute equality at the workplace because they bring different types of cultural practices unknown by those that already had homogenous forms of culture.

We have once visited a bank in the suburb of Washington DC that uses AI for its teller services. There is no human being on the counter that one can talk to, let alone touch. You slide in your card and enter the pin number and behold, a human being from another part of the world appears on your screen and asks a few questions to ascertain your identity and after that is concluded, the transaction is processed and if you need cash, the cash dispenser will deliver your cash. But what we noticed was that before the arrival of this machine, those who were on teller services that knew some of our names and could chat with us and make banking more pleasurable were gone. The bank was now like a ghost town and when we inquired from the bank manager, he confirmed that machines have now replaced human beings. This is the downside of AI and those who will feel the pains more are those on the fringes and they are mostly immigrants, people of color, and those with low educational acumen. What is to be done with this type of situation has not yet been factored in this saga of AI. If as Michel Foucault enunciated in his book *The technology of self* that human bodies seem to be objectified with technological expansion it equally goes to strengthen the argument that Marshall McLuhan began making in the 1960s about electronic technology being the extension of man. If part of our intelligence has been transferred for machinic computation, with little-or-no control from us, it means man is empty or can only function in dual capacity when working in tandem with, say, the computer. But what about those who cannot afford the computer, let alone having access. Who makes the decision for them when they struggle and get online, say at a library and when they cannot keep pace with updated software developments? Are they shut off? This is what Schradie (2019) has recently stated in her book *the Revolution that wasn't: How digital activism favors conservatives* when discussing the role of the Internet in our lives. She says

> The reality is that throughout history, communications tools that seemed to offer new voices are eventually owned or controlled by those with more resources. They eventually are used to consolidate power, rather than to smash it into pieces and redistribute it. (Schradie, 2019, 25)

So, the binary relationships are skewed in favor of the haves and not the have-nots and this goes to emphasize the role of AI and algorithm in the life of humankind if only a privileged few are in control. Blacks and other minorities will continue to be at the receiving end and not participants in the whole schematic journey to new self-discoveries for humanity as demonstrated by the quotation above. The Internet has not yet become the space where inequality is smashed according to Jen Schradie; rather, it has become the space for rich conservative Westerners to excel and exercise their tech muscles.

CHALLENGES FOR DEVELOPING COUNTRIES

> To create the model, the algorithm is trained to behave in a specific way by the data it is fed. (McKenzie, 2018, 533) (figure 9.1)

This quotation from Mckenzie is definitely where the problem lies in the not too distant future with respect to AI and algorithm. With the plethora of big data accumulating on a daily basis on the entire planet on various sites and devices, there is bound to be mistakes made just as the drones in Afghanistan make mistakes and civilian lives are in danger and all we get is apologies from, say the United States and the coalition forces charged with rooting out the Taliban "terrorists." If the algorithm is given tasks to perform by humans, the likelihood that the task can be faulty is greater given that no human presence is there to operate as we can do with an aircraft or ship. The issue with digitalization is that they have been programmed and no one can alter especially as the likes and dislikes on Facebook can affect an entire organization who make take literally to mean that their organization is doing fantastic or dismal as the case maybe and this can affect policy decision.

Figure 9.1   Photo by Gwaivu Azed.

Most countries in Africa are yet to handle the challenges with AI and algorithm as they are to handle digital divide that has continued to create a gulf between those who are educated and can afford the luxury of being online and those that cannot. In the economically advanced countries like Europe and the United States, data archiving, data mining, and data analytics and interpretation can be daunting, especially in this era of big data but imagine the developing economies like in Africa when this is still a novelty and where data archiving can be problematic, given the state of technological advancement. This observation by Kshetri (2016) speaks to a larger challenge that some countries are facing in Africa when it comes to big data politics. He states inter alia when dealing with poor data quality in Africa that

there has been a proliferation of data sources in Africa. However, compelling evidence exists of manipulation, misreporting and misrepresentation of data from some sources. For instance, a comparison of maize yield estimates for Malawi for 2006-2007 from three available sources (a routine data system from the Ministry of Agriculture; the National Census of Agriculture and Livestock conducted by the National Statistics Office; and the FAO) indicated that there were significant inter-source differences. (Kshetri, 2016, 37)

The differences in data reports can have significant impact on policy and future planning initiatives. The data flaws, especially in the medical field, can equally have a long-lasting effect on those targeted and this is just one of the manifold problems that big data can have for Africa. A system with checks and balances can help resolve such issues, but with governments that can sometimes be autocratic with strict bureaucratic systems, change can hardly be swift and that is the issue with big data and AI. If private companies have to come in from overseas as it is often the case to perform tasks like data mining, analytics, computation, and interpretation, it can cost a fortune for some countries. These are just a tiny fraction of myriad challenges that big data, AI, and algorithm can have for developing countries. These challenges, as Everett (2009) contends, are mostly due to the fact that "high-cost Internet access fees, difficult computing operating systems and chronically underfunded public education in minority communities" (150), have compounded the challenges for a foreseeable future for Africa. In Africa, the cost alone to access the Internet from mobile phones has pushed users to instead go and pay a one-time fee at some cybercafe Internet stores on streets of cities for a short period of time, mostly to send an email and other large datasets with attachments. Also, given the fact that the Wi-Fi connections are often slow and power supply are not often regular, users find themselves waiting for an untold number of hours to upload data to sites on the Internet. This is why in some communities with no access users hardly go on Twitter, Facebook,

Instagram, LinkedIn, and YouTube except where one is in a five-star hotel or with the government of private companies that have powerful Internet connections. Now that AI is gradually making in-roots in developing countries, there are bound to be challenges. The country that is leading this initiative for Africa, according to Kshetri (2016), is China: "The Beijing Municipal Environmental Protection Bureau and IBM signed a 10-year US$ 160 billion deal known as Green Horizon, which provides a high-profile example of the deployment of machine learning and AI" (63). Like the undersea Cable initiative that was carried on installing broadband network to Africa with no African taking part in the decision-making process, this is what could happen with the deal already signed between this Chinese company and IBM. Since AI is already heavily biased with people of color as already discussed with such an initiative coming to Africa, there are bound to be questions raised as the accuracy of the report that the AI data will be sending to Africans and to the rest of the world about environmental pollution or any other related issues about the continent.

ARTIFICIAL INTELLIGENCE, ROBOTICS, AND DIGI-CULTURALISM

The concept of digital technology creeping into the livelihood of Africans presupposes that for them to optimize their use, their electronical and in-person technological knowledge is congruent to digital imperatives. The last issue regarding in-person technological know-how can be understood by simply believing that the term "technology" means learning new ways to do old things. Technology must not and should not be equated, as it is often the case, with only electronic and digital know-how. This is a misleading concept that has consumed the cognitive mindset of most people in developing countries. We seem to believe that the word "technology" or being "tech-savvy" is synonymous to being conversant with and having the skills for computer hardware and software technologies. It also presupposes that someone is proficient with the requirements of the World Wide Web and the Internet. This erroneous concept of technology has affected the approach for new technologies on the continent, especially digital technologies. The influx of social media, Internet, googlizations, the robotics, drones, and various forms of nanotechnologies have arrived with cultural imperatives that people in Africa have to abide by. They have changed the culture and are forced to become what Marcus Breen calls "technologized everybodies" (Breen, 2011, 7). This is the thrust of his fundamental argument in his book title "*Uprising*: *The Internet Unintended Consequences.*" His views that we now have created a folksonomy class by expanding Karl

Marx's proletarianization into the plain field of the Internet has once again reignited the debate of labor exploitation by the dominant class. This time on the Internet as cultures have shifted and labor, in this case the African Internet labor force is working to satisfy the thirst of the greedy Westerner whose hidden agenda to make everyone "little Europeans" through language and content is invincible yet visible. Breen (2011) sees the contrary because according to him,

> the values, ideas, possibilities, forces and trajectories of the underclass, the swarm, the masses, the subaltern and the abject are now before us, with us, altering our landscapes of meaning, replacing *good language* (emphasis mine) with bad as the unregulated offers itself, no rational responsibilities required. (5)

What Marcus Breen calls "good language" is problematic, to say the least. According to him, users in the non-developed world are distorting the beautiful "Queen's language," the European colonizing language that was pushed down the throats of the colonized by the colonizer without regard to their own language growth is now being "replaced with bad" (5) ones. And since regulation of the Internet has become a far cry, anything goes, and the subaltern seemed to have found its voice in this new reality of communication. But the subaltern is still heavily limited with respect to encryption politics, cookies, surveillance, keyboarding, alphabetization, and emojifications that have heavily tilted to the West in most part. When they do have the opportunity, they infused their local realities using symbolizations and iconizations best known to their cultural milieu for expression, but they are few and sometimes limited because digital divide is still real. Not everyone is on board yet. But for those already on the train ride, for those already speeding on the superhighway, their African ways are not often the right way, so they cannot alter the culture as aforementioned. The concept of Western digi-culturalism for it to have a symbiotic relationship with local African digi-culturalism, commonalities in language use, effective and efficient translatory technology, ownership and control must be shared with creators and manufacturers, where rules and regulations of some sort are established. Right now, the regulations for some use of digital technologies by the West have been problematized.

It is these rules and regulations, as already discussed including curricula changes, that have provoked the concept of decolonization of the mind. If these new technologies are to help revolutionize health facilities in Africa, it is also possible to include traditional African health imperatives in the equation. With the introduction of Western new ways of operation either in the health, educational, economic, and political sector, it presupposes that African ways of operation are redundant and archaic. In order to show how inculcating new technologies have changed the culture of how life used to be like, the legal impediments have to be in place for a smooth functioning of the new technologies.

In a 2018 article Cisse (2018), titled "Look to Africa to advance artificial intelligence," the author has called on the African government to play a significant role in the growth and development of AI by setting frameworks that include legal structures and standards to accommodate the demands of AI. This is laudable, but the question is whether governments in Africa can work in tandem with their Justice departments to carry out such an initiative. If history is something to go by, there has continuously been a travesty of justice, especially when actions don't favor the interest of the government. The manifold human right abuses, mass arrests, trials, and sentences in court without due process as a result of bribery and corruption (Mazrui, 1986; Fanon, 1967), it is quite possible to believe that when standards are set by the European Union Commission on AI, as reported in Cisse (2018) article, the same practices will prevail. From an Afrocentric perspective, Africa needs to reckon with the fact of law and order with public interest in mind and not law and order that are meant to extend the rulership of the incumbent ruler for eternity. This is why the challenges for AI on the continent are huge. By the way this is another classic example of outside-in initiative and not inside-out intended to force it down the throat of Africa and Africans. The paradox is that Africa cannot be indifferent to the forces of digital development on the global stage. But how the continent manages internal dynamics like this legal issues is paramount. It, therefore, goes without saying that before Europe, the United States, and China impose new initiatives for the entire world including Africa, feasibility studies, long-term research initiatives need to be undertaken to factor in challenges that can be overcome. This is the same with digital technology that took the continent unawares. Vernon (2019) makes a case for the positive and negative ramifications for AI in Africa:

> There is an increasing awareness of the positive impact that AI will have on developing countries, including sub-Saharan Africa, in sectors such as agriculture, health care, and public and financial services. AI has the potential to drive economic growth, development, and democratization, thereby reducing poverty, increasing education, supporting healthcare delivery, increasing food production, expanding the capacity of the existing road infrastructure by increasing traffic flows, improving public services, and bettering the quality of life for people with disabilities. AI can empower workers at all skill levels to be more competitive. Specifically, it can be used to augment and enhance human skills—not to replace or displace humans—and to do so at all levels, enabling average and low-skill workers to fit better in high-performance environments and take on more complex responsibilities. Africa's biggest economic challenge is to equip large sections of its economy with average workers who are primed

to perform tasks far better than most employees are currently managing to do. In South Africa, approximately 31% of employers cannot fill their vacancies. (Vernon, 2019, 131)

No doubt, there are huge benefits that can accrue with AI technologies on the continent of Africa. There are advantages from AI, including self-services in banks, restaurants, movie theaters, and so on, in the developed world due to the AI technological advances. The case of South Africa, as clearly indicated above, is what this cause for concern is all about. In as much as Africa gains economically from AI through poverty reduction as indicated above, it is also possible to factor in the issue raised in the last sentence where employers are finding in difficult to get requisite talents to fill positions that required basic tech knowledge in that field. It is often easy to place the blame on the citizens when in all honesty, they are far from the problem at hand. The educational system that they were forcefully subjected to due to foreign infiltrations into their culture made it possible for them to imbibe Western forms of education in South Africa. They have been learning more about the political, economic, cultural, and social lives in Europe and mentally thinking about life in that part of the world and looking at their own part of the world as substandard to Europe and the United States. Today, they are not able to fill vacancies in the slot that needs advance skills-based Western educational standards while living in South Africa. Also, no one reflects on the toll that Apartheid South Africa had on the average Black person in South Africa for all the years that the regime cracked down on the people who were exercising their human God-given right to yearn for freedom and respect for human rights. Millions were killed and Nelson Mandela, their leader, sat in the Robin Island prison for twenty-five years. In 1990 when he was released and took power in 1994, four years was not enough to reverse the toll of years of discrimination and racism by the minority White domineering population and the majority Black subordinated populations. Consequently, when 31 percent employers are finding it difficult to fill open slots, their natural God instincts will be to look for outside skills for help and that is what will continue to fan the flame of internal violence that has been rocking South Africa between Blacks in the country and other Blacks who have migrated from neighboring countries like Zimbabwe and others from West Africa like in Nigeria. This is why Afrocentricity remains the foundational principle and theory to be employed when dealing with issues affecting the continent of Africa. New technologies are appreciated and welcomed, but they too must be under rigorous adaptation and re-adaptation process to fit into the epistemological, ontological, and axiological backdrop of the community in question. After the defeat of the Apartheid regime in South Africa, focus should be placed on re-education, reformation, re-habilitation, and reconfiguration of economic, political, social, and cultural elements that contribute to meaningful development of a people. Development of a people, especially people who have been traumatized, subjugated, and made to feel inferior about themselves, cannot be transformed overnight with the introduction of AI technology that will revamp their entire lives. AI as a new digital communicative technology demands far more from the government, the private sector and the people for which it will serve. The need to handle it with fundamental principles that put the people of Africa at the center and not make them imitators of Europe and the rest of the technologically advanced world is primordial. As Vernon (2019) highlights in the article, drones are being used for surveillance in Africa and the sophisticated technology in them could be a blessing for Africa. They could be used for getting information that will help in agricultural innovations. At the same time, drones can scare the cattle, goats, and chicken who are peacefully grazing in the landfills and mountains and there has not been any psychological infrastructure in place to educate the cattle rarer and goat keepers to handle this new form of communication with the animals. As a new form of communication, it is an intruder force, a new element in their lives and that has to be a cause for concern. The sound of the drones can frighten as well as traumatize the animals and when humans feed on them the effect can be far reaching. The truth is that no study has been carried out on the extent of drone's technology on the holistic life of living things on that part of the world. When drones are not well controlled from a robotic philosophical standpoint or from a social standpoint, the consequences can be grave and that is what can result from a new technology that has not been carefully researched with respect to the terrain that it will operate. Drones can also be used as a weapon to suppress voices of dissent against powerful governmental establishments in Africa. The opposition rallies and gatherings can be eavesdropped using drones by the incumbent government for what is often referred to as reconnaissance mission for information gathering. When Amazon tested drones in the United States to deliver packages for customers, it was a disaster and so they had to shelve the technology and nothing like that occurred. The media discussed all the social and cultural implications of having several drones flying above houses to deliver millions of packages to citizens in almost fifty states and since the negative results outweighed the positive ones, they could not continue the technology. This is what the African community needs to do when they find drones flying all over their country for reasons only best known to the government. The issue of oversight and clear communication channel to let citizens know in advance what is on the pipeline is what accounts for the dependency status of Africa since the colonial experiments in Berlin between 1884 and 1885. Others decide for the continent and Africa consumes and the consequences are borne by Africans.

ARTIFICIAL INTELLIGENCE AND COVID-19 IN AFRICA

It is no longer a secret that the rest of the economically advanced countries of Europe, the United States, Canada, the Middle East, and China have accused Africa of having a weak health system. This was evident during the Ebola outbreak, where the rest of the world had to come to the aid of Africa because African virologists were never there to answer present to respond to the Ebola virus outbreak. So, laboratories in Europe had to quickly send experts to Liberia, Sierra Leone, and Congo, the epicenters to stop the spread of the virus to other parts of Africa. It was not uncommon for a lot of us to fly into airports in Africa where lines were formed for temperatures and those suspected with the virus were singled out and other measures taken for them. Experts came to Africa with gears, gloves, stethoscopes, and other PPEs (personal protective equipments) to help nurses and others dealing with patients. Before their arrival, those who were caring for the patients were dying from the virus because they did not have the PPEs. There was no African country producing and distributing PPEs in millions to these countries. Europe was the answer, and with this other novel virus called COVID-19, Africa was still not prepared and so according to Mashamba-Thompson and Crayton (2020), the health problems of Africa still persists. "There is a growing concern about a failure to find and report cases, especially given weak health systems, inadequate surveillance, insufficient laboratory capacity and limited public health infrastructure in African countries" (Mashamba-Thompson and Crayton 2020, 1). Africa's healthcare infrastructure is still dismal. The surveillance systems to quickly detect hot spots and growing needy areas is very lacking in Africa. With many African countries reporting rising cases of COVID-19, the need for rapid intervention cannot be overemphasized. According to the Africa CDC website (https://africacdc.org/covid-19/), South Africa leads the continent with confirmed cases of 592,000, Egypt, 96,753; Nigeria, 49,895; Ghana, 42,993; and Ethiopia, 32,722 infected individuals. As Mashamba-Thompson and Crayton (2020) have emphasized, "this calls for the rapid development and deployment of health innovations for accurate diagnosis and electronic surveillance of COVID-19 in underserved populations" (1). The question is whether ears are listening to this outcry if the same ears became deaf during and after the Ebola epidemic. If Africa had learned her lessons well, the continent could have emerged from the Ebola pandemic with hope and glee, especially as lots of countries are dealing with mobile Health (Mhealth) facilities that they have found ways to avoid future ailments of that nature and not totally rely on Europe, the United States, and China even for masks and other PPEs. Factually and psychologically speaking, Europe and the United States and now China have learned that with matters of life and death on health and military-related issues, Africa has continued to stretch a hand to them for help. Again, this is done when the continent has invested in health education producing medical doctors and engineers that are unable to help resolve issues of this magnitude for the people. Given that most of Africa's medical doctors are educated and trained abroad in the Western countries that had accorded independence to Africa, their experiences in both worlds (Africa and Europe) could be a boon to the continent of Africa. But that is not often the case because they are migrating out of the continent in search of greener pastures.

Chapter 10

Digi-Culturalism and Black Politics

WHERE ARE WE?

Aristotle said way back in the fourth century BC that "every man is either a political animal or an outcast like a bird which flies alone." So, we are all political creatures because there is not one single human creature who flies alone without external help. Not one! Why then has political quests become an anathema, especially in regions where leaders have taken an oath with the "devil" to stay in power till their end of day on planet earth. Political quest is the yearning for change, yearning for another phase in human growth and development. In the past, campaigns and canvassing for votes from the electorates have been through in-person door-to-door contacts. No more, at least for now due to the fear from the invisible airborne virus call COVID-19 that has invaded the planet earth. The ballots are either shipped to the electorates or for those who can brave it, to wear masks and go to the polls to cast their ballots. With masks also come the challenges of identification, especially in the era of virtual modes of human interactions. Virtualization of human activities has drastically altered the political tapestry in the world, especially during this COVID-19 pandemic. With virtual communication comes identity certification, true citizen participation, and message over-load, which sometimes can overwhelm the system and plunge the entire activity on another collision course. Massive outpouring of online petitions, social media wall posts, memes mushrooming on Twitter and Instagram as well as caricatures of political activists on the Internet are issues of big data that have casts doubts on this new dispensation of having our political activities manifesting itself on our tiny desktop screens at home. It has become difficult to ascertain the veracity of incumbent Twitter messages and Facebook posts in the era of fake news. The incumbent party eager to remain in power all over the world is quick to deny any virtual misrepresentation of their goals and platforms by referring to them as fake news. The age of Donald Trump, where factcheck.org has become the site to fact check what politicians have electronically or digitally posted on the World Wide Web or the Internet, is almost a norm that is not going to go away any time soon. Also, at the time when the two main parties in the United States, the Democrats and the Republicans, have largely held their conventions virtually as a result of the pandemic, the effervescence and exuberating atmosphere that often characterize and accompany these festivities have all been muted. This can create political doubts as to the magnitude of the event, especially as popularity of the candidates and their speeches is no longer measured by large crowd attendance but by relying on Nielson's ratings to ascertain the millions that have watched on regular TV and those that watched on their mobile devices. The challenge is counting robots or relying on algorithms that sometimes can be misleading as to who watched on digital media and those who merely gloss over and did not pay any attention to what was said. This is quite different from in-person participation when just crowd size is often enough to sow the seeds of fear on the other candidates who may psychologically be affected by such scenarios. It was thanks to the traditional in-person crowd attendance in addition to online participation that catapulted President Barack Obama to the helm of the American presidency. We all recall the argument between Donald Trump and the media about the crowd size during his own inauguration. With virtual campaigns, and perhaps virtual inauguration of the new American president on January 20, 2021, there were no crowd allowed to attend because the COVID-19 cases in the United States continued to rise. Already mail-in ballot for the November 2020 presidential election in the United States was shrouded in doubts as the notion of fraud was being floated around, especially by the Donald Trump supporters who preferred in-person voting. For centuries, humankind has practiced in-person voting system, but in the age of the pandemic that has spurred virtual communications, most political participation will henceforth be carried out on the digital public sphere.

AFRICA/BLACK DIGI-POLITICS

There has been lots of literature that have endorsed as well as unendorsed the digital space as having promoted the Arab Spring of late 2010 and early 2011 in Egypt, Tunisia, and Libya (Eltantawy and Wiest, 2011; Khondker, 2011; Howard and Hussain, 2013; Bruns, Highfield and Burgess, 2014).

Critics of digital space argue that the depth of digital divide and the apparent lack of proximity to the capital cities by the large majority of the population of these countries could not have allowed the revolution to be triggered and fostered by the digital modes of communication. Still others argue that in an authoritarian country like those three already mentioned, digital media were the only invisible free safety nets for the revolutionists to wade through and get their messages disseminated to the larger population who could have online access. The call for people to gather say at the "Tahrir Square" in the case of Egypt where campers installed their tents and stayed there for weeks before Hosni Mubarak, the then president resigned was mostly done through this media since traditional media (Radio, TV, and Newspapers) were largely controlled by the state. In the age of media censorship, especially with respect to dictatorial regimes in Africa, the arrival of digital communication platforms that can galvanize youths to rally, comment, and forward human rights abuses in their various countries is certainly a welcome relief. True, every human being is potentially a political being regardless of context. In other words, where communication is possible, especially between human species of any hue and creed, politics is manifested. Consequently, the internal and external interactive communication that have gripped the online media platforms since the late 1990s and early 2000s have opened another door for silent voices to be heard and that is helpful in itself. On the other hand, the Internet and more importantly social media platforms have experienced not-so-positive appraisal in some parts of Africa as already discussed. Be that as it may, the Internet has now become another political escape route for those seeking anonymity to send provocative messages to rally support for a cause or course and trigger consternation and condemnation for another.

Before the advent of digital communicative space, electronic and in-person communication channels constituted the space for dialogic interactions. This was the space for propagandistic speeches from dictators, progressives, and conservatives the world over. Those in the Advanced world (Europe and North America) who, as a result of the industrial revolution, continued to economically progress in the manufacturing of steel and iron, created electronic forms of communications like the radio and television. The birth of the television in the 1950s, coming after the expansion of radio communication, gave room for visual forms of communication that saw an unprecedented flow and dissemination of Western political systems to the non-Western worlds like Latin America, South East Asia, the Caribbean, and Africa. Since most of these Western countries also contributed in no small way in the colonizing mission of these continents, there was no doubt that these countries were to emulate the political lifestyles of these former colonial masters as they watched them on TV. Television stations just like radio stations started mushrooming on these continents and political leaders who had assumed power after the departure of the colonialists exploited these media to spread their own propagandistic political messages to solidify their hold on power. When Keane (2013) underscoring the effects of what he termed "media decadence" states that "technologies of communication are neither intrinsically demo-cratic nor intrinsically authoritarian" (110), he is emphasizing the neutral role that technology plays in our daily lives, but Marshall McLuhan, the Canadian media scholar, will fundamentally disagree with this assertion as he stated in his dictum in the 1960s that "the medium is the message" as already dis-cussed in the previous chapters. Whether one is sending a political pamphlet or uploading a flyer announcing the door-to-door, get-the-voters-out message in America or in Africa, one is actively using a medium of communication that is attributed to fostering a political agenda in the case of the United States or is the arm of the government in the case of Africa. Digital communication has ushered in a new dispensation to the extent that e-democracy, e-voting, and e-campaigns have now become the new vocabularies. These vocabularies were nowhere near the central discussion table, even as early as the 1960s. Today, this new dispensation has changed the face of politics as we knew it.

So, the vast potential of the Internet has made it possible for all sorts of stakeholders to take to the digital communicative realm to target politically charged messages with the intent of influencing public opinion. With the ubiquitous nature of interactive communication on platforms like Twitter and Facebook that can galvanize support from millions of readers, politi-cal pundits, and people running for office have taken to these platforms to disseminate messages and receive likes and comments that can help them reformulate their slogans. The same is true of Black politicians and African politicians. President Barack Hussein Obama will go down in the annals of American political history as the first Black president who used social media as a technique to reach his supporters during the 2008 United States Presidential election. According to Strahler and Flynn (2013), Obama effec-tively used social media in an unprecedented way that enabled him to win the Democratic primary against Hilary Clinton and the Presidential run against the Republican challenger John McCain.

Political figures all over the world have adopted memes and logos to pro-mote their campaign slogans on popular sites like Snapchat and Instagram in order to draw young people to their sides. At the same time that the Internet has become the new public sphere for inter-human dialogue and news dis-semination for political gains, a plethora of so-called " fake news" syndrome has engulfed that space making truth and reality complex and difficult to unravel (Schapals, 2018). This has produced significant problems that would be difficult to easily discipher in the coming years as we've become more and more prone to politicking on digital spaces. The spread of propagan-distic messages either from the top brass of the government or powerful corporations that have wielded considerable power can become the way life would be from now henceforth since we are all hooked to receiving, uploading, and downloading messages through this media. A lot of this cannot be limited to the Western world. Users who create content and download content off the World Wide Web and the Internet have to grapple with this because truth has become illusive. Those who can have control have decided to spin facts to their favor.

DIGITAL VS. CITIZENS POLITICS

Political candidates in any given country, especially in Africa, have the challenge of confronting two electorates: digital natives, mostly young followers on social media, or the senior/elderly baby boomers who are not using cyberspace and do not intend to ride that ship. A candidate running for office, say in any given African country, will have staff that would cater to the needs of the offline citizenry and another staff that would devote more time and energy channeling messages of appeal to the electorate through billboards and electronic messaging on radio, television, and newspaper. The problem is the instantaneous feedback that the candidate would get from those following the speeches, say on YouTube, and comments would not be readily available and it will have to take the candidates more time to travel to where they live to deliver messages and answer questions. Smyth and Best (2013) have demonstrated how social media are now becoming an important instrument for elections in Tropical Africa, especially as they act as alternative media supplying more information to the electorate that they wouldn't have had with traditional media that act sometimes like armchairs of those in power. They studied the 2011 political elections in Liberia and Nigeria. But increasingly, I dare say, deep cesspool of have-nots (technical and literary non-savvy ones), who cannot afford or let alone understand digital communication, will continue to create headache to politicians in developing countries who are torn between relying on in-person communication with electorate and using digital modes of communications. Before digital communication, literacy was encouraged. Western literacy was encouraged as Africans flogged to Western schools of learning. So the transplantation of offline literary knowledge unto the virtual platforms like social media or the general Internet portals has created another group of people who will never ride the same train with the digital natives and that should be a cause for concern for political junkies and those planning to consolidate power by means of coercion. The young people who have bought expensive smartphones may be less inclined to follow politics since, by and large, they are more prone to following Daimond Platznum, Flavor, Jay Z, Shakira, Jennifer Lopez, or Beyoncé on Snapchat, Tiktok and Instagram than to read a long text on Facebook about incumbent Y or opponent X politician vying for power. When such an imagined scenario is actualized, then we are compelled to question the role of politics in the age of globalization and new media. Should politicians target offline electorates with a different kind of messages, especially as they are likely to be seniors and elders speaking different languages and mostly resident in the rural part of the nations as opposed to urban youths who have flogged the cities and slums with or without advance knowledge of the digital communication. Even though the latter may be disinterested in politics, when messages are tilted to their favor like #RhodesMust Fall and #FeesMustFall are used as a slogan by student activists during their 2018 protest on decolo-nization of the curricula in the University of Cape Town, South Africa, on Twitter. But when they know that dictators are able to use any means at their disposal to remain in power, including shutting the Internet as has been the case in Tropical Africa, apathy sets in, and no matter how attractive a politician platform message and blog posts are on cyberspace, the turnout at the polls will continue to be dismal. Therefore, online channels for political messages may target those that are conversant with the new technological tool but to determine that could be an uphill task given that political figures are always in the quest for maximum coverage and interests. But with the case of Tropical Africa, the example of Arab Spring in the Northern part of the country could be the learning curve. But in 2011, when this uprising was taking place, the military did not intervene brutally to suppress the revolution as has been the case in Sudan before the fall of President Niemeri or in Cote D'Ivoire before the fall of Laurent Gbagbo. Similar online push was used to oust Blaise Campaore of Burkina Faso but only after a bloody struggle between the civilians and the military. The present case of Cameroon and Togo is proving to be different in the sense that Internet communications have witnessed intermittent shut down by the regime and the military crack-down, especially in the English-speaking regions of Cameroon, has contin-ued unabated. This is where the nexus between in-person communication and online communication in the arena of what Habermas calls "public sphere" is often not an ordained marriage. To begin with, machinic communication has the help of a device to channel communication called the third party, whereas in-person communication is organic. And as Jim Morrison is reputed to have said that he who can effectively control the media has the power to control the mind of the listeners, it is analogous to the saying of Thomas Sankara, the late Burkina Faso president who equally said that "He who feeds you controls you" (Akomolafe, 2014, 66–67), referring to the Frenchification of Frances' colonial enterprise in that poor African country. Politics in the age of the Internet revolution has experienced a rather nuanced reaction. It is minimal in some parts of the world, especially the developing countries and robust in the developed countries like the United States with the break-through from the era of Barack Hussein Obama.

BLACK WOMEN AND DIGITAL POLITICS

Byerly and Valentin (2017) have observed even within the electronic media landscape that women in general do not have equal representation with men within the broadcast industry. It is not only the ratio that is heavily in favor of men with respect to ownership, the same unequal representation is seen with news coverage. According to them, women in general are reduced to covering only "soft news stories such as health and entertainment" (268). This means that hard political news that covers the activities of the president, Congress, and the opposition parties are left in the hands of men. Black women who do not even possess the apparent soft power with electronic news outlets resort to the digital media realm to advocate their cause for fairness with other women on issues that sometimes do not get attention from the mainstream media. Williams (2015) notes that the #SayHerName was coined by Kimberly Crenshaw, an African American woman, in response to the muteness she observed by the mainstream media refusing to bring attention to police brutality that caused the death of some Black transgender women in the United States. The use of alternative media by Black women to further such an important political cause for the Black race underscores some of the basic and fundamental assumptions about leverage. When leverage is lacking and other minority groups like the Black women have to rely on Twitter to send messages to politicians to take action on something of such a magnitude for national security, we are now left with the presumption that ownership of media and power really matters. Part of the issue is the positioning of Black female scholars within the discourse of politics and their vocal representative-ness. Party politics is the mirror of one's personality in the larger community. Evelyn Hammonds is quoted in Williams (2015) as saying that the politics of articulation is what should define the role of the Black woman in a given soci-ety like the United States where there are various counter-narratives within the larger society. For Black women to be respected, "iterations of certain black feminists need to stop talking about twerking and pleasure and turn their attention back to structural inequalities" (38). The structural inequali-ties will be taken seriously by the American public when they see that Black feminists have turned their attention to more serious fundamental problems that affect the Black race and that is racism and inequality, especially in political representation in power and decision making.

Gouws (2018) analysis the #EndRapeCulture in South Africa. South African women have decried the rape culture that rocks the very foundation of the South African society for far too long a period. With the emergence of digitalization, and in this case South African university female students, the power of digital communication to raise awareness cannot be underestimated. Since rape is such a sensitive issue and if history is our inimitable teacher, victims are often ashamed to come forward to report instances of rape. The Internet seems to have simplified the process, whereby users can go under anonymous postings and expose culprits and of course Twitter has made it easy for hashtags to be created for victims to report incidences of rape. This process is far more effective than taking to the streets when the same victims are subject to harassment and other forms of psychological torture that will provide no relief.

Another political area that Black women are navigating, though cautiously, is the never-ending question of their "hair." Gill (2015) discusses the politics surrounding Black women's hair and the societal notion of what it means to have beautiful hair. The plethora of blogs and digital communicative windows that have spread their winds on the Internet has allowed women of African descent to visit sites that instruct, advice, expose, and discuss about their natural hair. As Tiffany Gills explores in her research article, this was not possible except toward the turn of the twenty-first century. Black women were using chemical products like straighteners to transform their kinky hair to resemble that of White or Asian women because that was what was deemed in society as "beautiful hair." Beauty Salons were profiting immensely from these chemical products that were mostly bought by Black women to straighten their hair. But as Gill reports in her article, most of these industries have experienced a downturn in their turnover. Most Black women are now proud to wear their natural hair and so sales from those chemical products are declining. The dawn of digital communication has witnessed free venues for these women to seek advice and get more relevant information about maintaining their natural hair than they have ever had before. The site that is mostly visited by these women is Nappturality.com. It is at this site that they meet other women of their race who are actively posting images of their hair and discussing how to maintain natural hair without using manufactured products that are meant to make them look anything other than themselves.

Women in Africa have another issue plaguing their lack of robust participation in cyberspace:

> Women and girls may also face increased risk of control and violence when they use digital ICTs. By taking advantage of new technology, women and girls may be seen as transgressing gender norms, threatening men's position and power in the family or society. Where ICTs give women access to means of private communication, they may lead to men's control and surveillance over women. (Cummings and O'Neil, 2015, 10)

According to Cummings and O'Neil (2015), this is prevalent in North African countries where cultural taboos and traditional gender roles prevent women from participating in some spaces like the Internet that is deemed to be a public space without finding themselves in collision courses with their male relatives and counterparts. This means that if they are going against gender-agreed norms as stated above, this could be an impediment for human freedom and progress from a patriarchal point of view. They are being denied a voice on the cybernetic sphere of political influence that could be the theater for representations and power sharing for all mankind. At the same time, it was the women, largely young women, who were politically active in North Africa during the Arab Spring revolution. Women played pivotal roles in their various digital groups in Facebook and other outlets (see chapter 5). Thus, in as much as African women face insurmountable hurdles to navigate the already polluted political minefield by men, a field they have manipulated and dominated in the open era, the women are equally playing political roles as seen with the Arab Spring uprising. The first female African president, Sirleaf Johnson, rose to power in Liberia and ruled for two consecutive terms before handing power to George Weah in 2018. Her rise to power in Liberia ushered a new political reality that gender equality in politics is the new route for Africa. The fact that her reign was not rocked by scandals but by numerous successes is testament to the fact that the future for women in politics in Africa is not only bright but glowing. Our eyes are now turned to the Tanzania first female president and Africa's second female president, Samia Suluhu Hassan who rose to power on March 2021. Before both women rose to power, there were other women in Africa who had occupied posts of responsibilities like prime minister in Rwanda, Minister of Finance in Nigeria, and Speakers of the National Assembly in various African countries. Even though the number of men in politics in Africa outweighs that of women, women are powerfully vocal and active behind the scenes in most African countries. The problem is that gender politics and the politics of representations have compounded the role of women in African politics. Another issue fueling women participation online on issues related to politics is that the heavy handedness that has often accompanied in-person politicization of activities, be they rallying opponents of the incumbents at city halls or town square as the case maybe, have been avoided. This time they can post materials on popular online sites incognito. The good thing about online participation is the opportunity to be anonymous. Anonymity online provides opportunities for a user under an alias to attack politicians without fear of retributions since online surveillance is still at an infant stage in most African countries and others in Latin America and the Caribbean. Women will no longer be under the physical veil; rather, they'll use the Internet platforms as a veil to offer criticisms of the status quo. The same fate that awaits some of these African women in Africa is similar to the ones that seem to engulf Black feminist because Watkins (2017) opens her chapter on Black feminism online in an edited volume "Africana, race and communication" by stating, inter alia that "(Black) feminism, for most of its existence, has not achieved widespread acceptance among the Black masses" (170). The Black masses here include African women and men, Black American women and men, Black Latin American women and men and Caribbean women and men, and all who fall under the description of the Black race.

Chapter 11

Blacks and Digital Activism

OFFLINE VS. ONLINE ACTIVISM

Activism is as old as humanity itself. Man has been fighting to survive the various man-made hurdles on planet earth since the beginning of time. The multiple ecosystemic impacts on our lives has triggered ways to yearn for survival. That survival can target man-made problems as well as invincible natural and supernatural impediments. As a result, we have actively been looking for safety valves to live a peaceful life every blessed day, but sometimes that peace eludes us because of one reason or the other. There have been countless human rights marches organized by people in almost all countries in all parts of the world just to achieve one objective, freedom. But all kinds of human chains have surfaced and resurfaced. The recent inhuman killing of George Floyd by a White police officer named Derek Chauvin in Minneapolis June 2020, brought an unprecedented global wave of protests against police brutality on unarmed Black civilians. That global action was triggered primarily because of the force of digital media dissemination through multiple platforms on the Internet. This time it was a march against racism on police actions against Blacks or people of color in the United States. The world has been made aware of the intolerant actions of police brutality, mostly against Blacks in the United States. This march has been in solidarity with all people of African descent living in the United States. Some African governments, including the African Union, have sent messages of condemnation through their embassies to the U.S. government hoping that it will help stop the killings. Most people who lived during the Rodney King riot in Los Angeles that began on April 29, 1992, are familiar with this. The streets of LA saw constant protests that pitted the policemen and the protesters against each other. It was a march against racism and some thought that this would cease forever because nothing seriously had been undertaken for close to twenty-eight years to dismantle systemic racism in the United States. That is why the murder of George Floyd has opened the wound once more. Offline activism is often the physical, in-person protests where the street has become another theater for repeated action though with various interrelated episodes. Speeches are delivered by prominent activists like Al Sharpton or the late John Lewis and of course looting and vandalism also become the order of the in-person protests. The online protest movement has another functionality and formality that is diametrically opposed to that of in-person. With online protest, there is no room for looting and violence that often result in property damage and loss of life. Online protest has its own dynamics, as will be discussed below.

COVID-19 AND ACTIVISM

Barbot (2020) has written an editorial page depicting the action of the White police officer Derek Chauvin kneeling on the neck of George Floyd for over nine minutes and killing him in the process as a "collective moral injury." Her characterization of that action as bordering on the precipice of our collective moral principles as humans in general being injured is very apt. This time it is not only the Black community that is licking its own wound that has been leaking and developing ulcers for more than 400 years when they were forcefully ejected from Africa and brought to the Americas without their consent; it is the entire human race that has mourned his death. The activism is manifested both virtually and on the streets of the world from Europe, Asia, Africa. and the Americas. All the online platforms, electronic transmission devices like radio and television, have all shown the brutal inhuman and callous killing of this Black armless individual on the streets of Minneapolis. That callous killing action has been likened to that of strangling a dog by a White police officer and has recalled years of similar animalistic killings of unarmed Black men and women in the United States. This time, it was our moral religious conscience calling for action, and the police officer was arrested and jailed with a bail set at a million dollars. While all these physical actions were going on, the entire population of the United States was experiencing a partial "shut down," like other countries because of an invisible virus called Corona that had attacked the country by invading lungs of humanity, causing in-person activities the world over to shut down. The only other activities allowed to go on unperturbed were those carried out through the Internet and that is where activism has registered the most impact. The combination of an invisible health pandemic and a human-imposed health crisis with the knee of Derek Chauvin on the neck of a Black person who is a father to a young girl and husband to woman created another pandemic of its own. Americans of all races, creed, political affiliations, sexual orientations, and ethnicity abandoned the six-feet distancing rule recommended by the Center for Disease Control (CDC) to stage various protest marches in the United States. Their rules to all those venturing out in public and to avoid crowds were never heeded to. Even though some wore masks as they mingled with the crowd, a sizeable number of people did not heed to any rule because their emotional outburst by the action of the police officer killing an innocent armless Black civilian outweighed any COVID-19 pandemic rules. The empathy exhibited this time was nothing compared to another similar police brutal killing of say Michael Brown, Trayvon Martin, or Freddie Gray. The online condemnation on all multiple platforms was not enough and so people decided on their own volition to invade the street and like most street protests, looting, and other violent behaviors ensued.

It should be borne in mind that there have been all sorts of people of color marches and other civil rights movements, especially in mostly developing countries that may not have gripped world attention as has been seen in cases in Europe and the United States. The radio, newspapers, and television have brought some attention to the rest of the world, but that could only be disseminated to those who could afford satellite dishes/TV sets to receive images from Western countries. Most of the images from the killing of George Floyd were on the digital gadgets on platforms like Facebook, Twitter, and Instagram that are now prevalent in Africa. When activists like students, lawyers, teachers, nurses are on strike in mostly developing countries, local media that are heavily controlled by the state governments do not broadcast to the people. But with online digital media, the story is now different. The concept of activism has shifted from the old paradigmatic public sphere structure propounded by Jurgen Habermas to the online public and counterpublic spheres mushrooming and catering to the needs of diverse populations and users.

ONLINE ACTIVISM

The birth of hashtagism (#BlackLivesMatter, #GirlsLikeUs, #OscarSoWhite, #TWiB, #RhodesMustFall, #FeesMustFall, etc.) that has mushroomed as a result of the Internet communication revolution, especially with respect to Black causes, has dubbed this era the one of digital civil rights activism. Social media success stories that emanated from Arab Spring revolution in MENA (Middle East and North Africa) regions of the world provided a magic wand for online communicative activism to burgeon. The #OccupyWallStreet and many others around the world were borne out of accumulated frustrations by the minorities the world over who, for centuries, have taken their anger to the streets but with minimal successes, since they were more often isolated and sometimes unmediated. The dawn of Internet communications whereby in-person, interpersonal, intercultural, group, and mass communication could now effectively be carried out effortlessly has changed activism forever. Activists are now employing the gift of the Internet to rally support for their various causes where necessary. Though the digital gap phenomenon continues to rock the boat of online participation, especially when we look at the continent of Africa, there are still pockets of resistance like #RhodesMustFall and others organized mostly by students who, by and large, are not affected by digital divides issues to sound the drumbeats of anger and frustrations with power wielders on the continent. This onslaught of active Internet communicative presence has re-energized the debate about free speech and freedom of the downtrodden. The BLM that started with the death of Travon Martin in Florida and exoneration of his White culprit, George Zimmerman, has catapulted the national debate of racism and marginalization of Black people in the United States. This is also when Black Twitter saw the light of day on the Twitter line of communication where people posted messages demanding justice and accountability, especially as Black people were being unfairly targeted by the policemen. As a consequence,

> Black women have created and popularized hashtags that observe the raced aspects of street harassment, center the experiences of incarcerated Black trans women, offer interventions to mainstream white feminist erasures of Black women's experiences, and critique the appropriation and commodification of Black women's styles. (Jackson, 2016, 377)

Many other counterpublics have been created on cyberspace to cater to the needs of groups from all walks of life mainly wanting their voices to be counted and be acted upon. It is not enough for the voices to be heard, but what happens after users read those messages posted on these weblogs and Twitter platforms is extremely important. Action for positive effects has to be the outcome. That is what activists want and yearn for. This new avenue for activism that is spreading widely on given digital platforms is transforming the entire format of human protest. Some school of thoughts do not see how such a format or direction can move the needle because the fundamental structures that more often than not prevents change from taking place in the offline world are still heavily entrenched in the system regardless of the "noise" on the online public sphere. So, change can only come about if the activists on the online platforms can use the same tactics to galvanize participation in the offline organizations. This argument became prevalent after the MENA Arab Spring revolutions when after the dictators were toppled

(Hosni Mubarak of Egypt, Ben Ali of Tunisia, and Colonel Mourmar Kaddafi of Libya) as a result of the ceaseless and resilient protests by their people, the systems are still heavily in place and the online public sphere was unable to plant those revolutionists in parliament, military, executive, or legislative branches of government. That is probably why those three countries are still not democratic in the strict sense of the word, and some have taken a turn for the worse like Libya with warlords omnipresent in the country and preventing reforms from taking place. Other schools say online activism do change the mindset and create a lasting impact. The online public space with virtual user-generated interaction has gained unprecedented momentum since the launch of the dot com era of communications. Humans now upload, download, send and receive texts, images, audio and video messages and that has completely shifted the communicative landscape. As a result, activists now have taken to that space on weblogs, social media platforms like Twitter, Facebook, Instagram, Snap Chat, WhatsApp, Tiktok and other locally driven sites to drum for followers to a given cause. Meetings are now being called online, and groups have become powerful in organizing and posting images and video clips of political and other action-related plans to people across the state boundaries. This era that has been dubbed the digital minefield, like that of globalization has witnessed growth in Black activism. People who subscribe to this school of a tsunami in communication have cited numerous examples of actions taken to improve human conditions that started as a Twitter chat or a Facebook wall posts or a WhatsApp or YouTube audio message transmission. To Ndlovu (2017), this just confirms the applaudable social media role in disseminating the Libyan people-driven revolution:

> Accessing information from within Libya during the uprisings offered a lot of challenges. Amid media censorship during the civil uprisings in Libya, people, expatriates, foreign media and the international community had to rely on citizen journalists and other social media sources, who were relaying messages with short messages, posting links, photos and video clips via Twitter and Facebook pages. Even though social media penetration was relatively lower in Libya, thousands of Tweets and Facebook posts were generated from the country. (Ndlovu, 2017, 40–41)

Social media have, therefore, become the middle person within the tug of war between state-controlled media and the people. The state in Africa has been known since independence in the 1960s of most states on the continent, to trumpet mainly the views of the government at the behest of the average person on the street. Social media communications have relieved them from this stranglehold censorship that government media have placed them under for decades. With social media, though limited in scope and access, the few messages that are sent by the media literate few can attract the attention of those in the Diaspora and the international community that can use satellite devices to authenticate the source and take action. This is what has resulted in the multinational intervention in the Libyan conflict with the United States under the leadership of President Barack Hussein Obama, leading the coalition forces that smoked out Colonel Mourmar Kaddafi from his hidden hole in his village in Libya.

SURVEILLANCE AND BLM

The age of surveillance using complex technological systems like Face Recognition (FR) software has disproportionately targeted the Black race and other minority groups, especially in the United States. Aziz and Beydoun (2020) state inter alia about another group that is being impacted by this. In their study, they found out that "undercover agents and their proxies create fake accounts by which to infiltrate online groups on #BlackLivesMatter, #MuslimLivesMatter, #NoBAN NO Wall" (1155). Netizens (those who are bonafide virtual savvy inhabitants) now collide with ordinary cyber-citizens bent on eavesdropping on their online activities in order to report those activities to law enforcement. The problem this poses is that some of these infiltrators may not accurately report these activities, making it almost impossible to ever lay hands on culprits who hack the system for unknown reasons. A good example is the facial recognition software that is more often than not contracted to a third party and then provided to law enforcement. Black people have been targeted falsely through this device. As far back as 2009 in a study by Gross (2009), facial recognition software tended to resolve that "having a black hairstyle, the face was generally perceived as being black" (129). This is the erroneous perception ingrained in one's mind, primarily being spoon-fed by years of accumulated stereotypical misdiagnoses of human anatomy that has crept into our cognition and then to the designers of face recognition software. No matter how technically advanced a system is to detect a human face, it must germinate from the human mind of the engineer of that product. This is the gross exaggeration created by this system that has resulted in extreme errors in arresting innocent Black people and throwing them behind bars simply because the system has been faulty. This is similar to what algorithmic gross errors captured by O'Neil (2016) cited in Nobles (2018) say about what she calls "weapons of math destruction":

The math-powered application powering the data economy were based on choices made by fallible human beings. Some of these choices were no doubt made with the best intentions. Nevertheless, many of these models encoded human prejudices, misunderstandings, and bias into the software systems that increasingly managed our lives. Like gods, these mathematic models were opaque, their workings invisible to all but the highest priest in their domain: mathematicians and computer scientists. Their verdicts, even when wrong or harmful, were beyond dispute or appeal. And they tended to punish the poor and the oppressed in our society, while making the rich richer. (Nobels, 2018, 27)

This "weapons of math destruction" as O'Neil (2016) aptly describes has been responsible to countless people of color behind bars, incarcerated wrongly and because of bureaucratic red tape, they are being made to serve their term because they lack funds to secure expert defense lawyers to tirelessly carryout unbiased investigation. The poor and oppressed, as opined in the last sentence of the above-mentioned quotation, according to multiple statistical data in the United States from the first President George Washington to Donald Trump, have been Blacks and Hispanics.

In most cases, these errors go unpunished as the minority groups like Blacks, Muslims, and Hispanics often bear the brunt of such malice. Aziz et al. (2020) again have extensively discussed a certain program called BIE (Black Identity Extremism) being used by the police force to track "some members" of the BLM. "BIE programs, meanwhile, do not hide behind the cover of community policing. They constitute a more direct targeting of BLM activists, or individuals perceived to be tied to BLM, as a presumptive public safety threat" (1160). This is the issue that creates online surveillance debate as to their effectiveness. Who is considered a BLM extremist when the purpose of the BLM is to chastise White police brutality on Black people? Does it, therefore, arrogate to itself the role targeting online activists with no criminal record who is angry and goes online and cry foul on police extremities? This perplexing situation has prompted Sturgis (2020) to affirm that this has been one of the reasons why Americans who have been protesting police brutality by marching in the cities have pleaded with photographers to delete their images on their systems because they may be targets. Since some people may think that Blacks look alike, wrongful facial recognition technology may result in another spiral of wrongful convictions.

These are some of the worrying issues that need to be ironed out otherwise Black race and other minority groups, as already mentioned, will continue to be the victim of software bias. For bias to be resolved, ownership of the tools that are often used to track down Black culprits should be owned, managed, and controlled by Black folks, but this is hardly the case because technology ownership directly correlates with power dynamics in any given societal structure. Schradie (2019) has shared some of these views when she states convincingly that:

The reality is that throughout history, communications tools that seemed to offer new voices are eventually owned or controlled by those with more resources. They eventually are used to consolidate power, rather than to smash it into pieces and redistribute it. (Schradie, 2019, 25)

The government and private companies in the United States are the owners and controllers of the surveillance technology on citizens digital gadgets. In a Pew research study published May 4, 2020 carried out by Auxier (2020), he outlines a statistical data on Blacks and Hispanics' views of surveillance during the COVID-19 pandemic. The study found out that 60 percent of Blacks and 56 percent of Hispanics in the United States believe that the government is tracking their phones and the same percentage say the same of companies. On the contrary, only 43 percent of White Americans believe that the government is spying on them, but a sizeable majority 77percent believe that companies are the ones tracking their every move. This study has provided clues as to the perception of the American public with regards to surveillance. If the majority of Whites think that it is the companies that provide the mobile services that spy on them while African Americans and Hispanics think that it is rather the government and not the companies, then something needs to be done by those two powerful entities to reduce the level of mistrust and restore public trust in their services. There is no gainsaying the fact that government and huge corporations are two conspiring organizations to safeguard the public good, but sometimes they may be perceived as playing independent roles, especially as evidenced in the way White Americans perceive surveillance as opposed to Blacks and Hispanics.

SURVEILLANCE IN AFRICA

The surveillance landscape as discussed in the United States with respect to the lives of minorities is quite different in Africa. Apart from a few isolated cases, majority of people in Africa are Blacks and are not been spied upon for the same reasons as the Blacks and Hispanics in the United States. Reasons for government and private companies' surveillance of mobile phone usage in Africa are largely due to the rampant criminal behaviors that are prevalent with mobile phone users. The emergence of mobile money transfer in Africa has revolutionized B2C online transactions. Business-to-Consumer transaction has been made possible in a way that it has rapidly narrowed the gap between the rural and the urban dwellers. At first, Africans had to travel with cash from the city to the rural parts of the country. Most of the rural inhabitants are unbanked and majority of cash flow was limited to the city centers. The cell phone and smartphone revolution whereby everyone has been able to procure one of these gadgets for electronic communication has also brought other additional benefits like in East Africa where M-Pesa, the name for the local money transfer, has been extremely popular. Each country in Africa has its own brand of money transfer. As money transfer has been made convenient and narrowed the digital divide gap between the rich and the poor, urban and the rural, government and the people, the private sector and the people there have been reports of criminal activities especially when money is being transacted between one person to the other. Martin (2019) has described some of the reasons why some companies had to install a software to monitor online activities. "M-Pesa's transaction monitoring software, called Minotaur, uses neural networks to analyze and investigate all types of user activity, including account openings, terminations, and changes, in order to identify suspicious behavior" (Martin, 2019, 216). So, it is quite clear that Minotaur only monitors suspicious activities online especially tracking down those who are stealing pin numbers or passcodes to cash money. This is quite different from the surveillance in the United States, as already discussed when both Whites and Blacks are crying foul against privacy. While White Americans are blaming the companies, the Blacks are blaming both the companies and the governments. In Africa, the companies are providing solutions for online consumers to have confidence in their services.

AFRICAN GOVERNMENTS AND ONLINE ACTIVISM

Governments in Africa have been known for cracking down on activists who take to the street for peaceful protest against the regime. Police are often deployed with tear gas, water cannon, and rubber bullets to quell down riots. They have done this with relative success as they have instilled fear in the minds of the populace to be aware of the consequences of street protest. This has not deterred most street movements on the continent as evidenced recently with the overthrow of the Malian president. But another dimension of this protest normally carried out online has equally been met with other means of deterrent by the forces of law and order, especially in Africa. Some African governments have shut down the Internet (Langmia, 2019) in response to what they've now decided to term "Internet terrorism." Even though other African governments have relaxed stringent rules as demonstrated in the article below by Mukhongo (2015), their attitudes toward online protests are similar to offline protests. At the same time, the same governments are encouraging voices of dissent among its citizenry:

Governments in Sub-Saharan Africa are becoming more tolerant towards the media. Un-fortunately, unlike print media, electronic media has remained under strict government control and owner-ship, and therefore the Sub-Saharan governments still have enormous control over the media and its coverage of political news . . . . This has been the case in countries such as Zambia, Zimbabwe, and Angola. In South Sudan, after 22 years of civil war, the government has committed itself to improve press freedom and guarantee the freedom of expressions of the citizens, however security forces still hold a lot of power in the nation, and so have a lot of leeway to manipulate and control the media. (Mukhongo, 2015, 6419).

As seen from the submission from Mukhongo (2015), there is apparently a disconnect between what the government say and what they've done. There is apparently a veneer of hidden psycho-cultural hypocrisy lurking within the corridors of power in Africa that believe that the people are in their pockets when they are frightened. This attitude has helped dictatorial regime for the last sixty years after the lesson they learned from the series of coup d'état that rocked the continent a few years after they gained independence from colonial powers in the 1960s. It has since been confirmed that it is still the same colonial powers who have exported lethal weapons for the police and military in Africa for their protection and to keep them in power. They have made the military and the police to be enemy of progress in Africa for the past sixty years. As stated above, the governments have had enormous powers that have encouraged them to use that power to monopolize electronic media (Radio and TV), including some of the newspapers that help disseminate propagandistic messages in support of the regime. The example from South Sudan in the article above is especially significant because this country has just recently gained its independence from Sudan after years of war with each other. Before South Sudan gained its independence on July 9, 2011, both countries were engaged in endless warfare, pitting the Dinkas and the Nueres. Millions lost their lives, but the same government today has pledged press freedom. The truth, especially with what the constitutions and governments of African countries say, is that when actions are taken by the public, the media, and in this case the electronic media are bias toward to the people because they are under the control of the state. This is why the author above mentions the heavy-handed way that the governments in Africa have been able to control the media. With the emergence of the digital media, they have resorted to look for other means to suppress the will of the people, especially when the people are asking for accountability. This is the reality now in Africa, as beautifully captured below:

According to one report, employees of Huawei, the Chinese telecom giant, have helped the oppressive regime of Yoweri Museveni, Uganda's President, to build a surveillance system that enables it to monitor and curb political opposition, including a "Smart City" encompassing thousands of CCTV cameras equipped with facial recognition software, phone tapping and hacking of personal devices. Authorities were therefore able to gain access to opposition leaders' password-protected phones through spyware, access encrypted conversations, and consequently amass and arrest protesters even before a scheduled protest had a chance to begin. In Zambia, Huawei staff reportedly helped authorities to pinpoint the location of opposition bloggers and guide police units deployed to arrest them. (Megiddo, 2019, 410)

This extract from Megiddo (2019) is the dramatization of political weakness by the same African government that is being bolstered by the external forces and in this case, China. This is the classic portrayal of suppressing the voice of dissent in supposedly democratic institutions like in Uganda and Zambia. The president of Uganda took power in a military takeover and has since then been in power for thirty-two years and has recently won a reelection to stay in power. To make matters even worse, he masterminded the parliament by making them remove the clause for term limits and they did and so he is able to run for the presidency for life. When such conditions prevail in a country where voting for new presidents has been a tradition, the psychological and traumatic effects on the electorate is everlastingly damning. Imagine going to the polls and feeling distraught that your votes will not count because the machinery like the surveillance mentioned above is going to be tempered with? These are not only challenging but a reflection of the political dead end that most Africans find themselves today as a result of seeking political help from China and the West to help them suppress the opposition. When surveillance cameras are set up in the city to monitor all those planning to protest any given government action and the people are aware of that, it gives room of autocracy to sow lasting seeds in the country like Uganda where freedom of speech and movements are preached on the media on the daily basis. These systems mentioned above are only effective if the population are also working with the government agents and police. The digital media devices are of course a blessing and a curse for the African continent. On the one hand, they help to regulate violent behaviors, criminal acts that seek to undermine the smooth functioning of the telecommunication systems for the greatest good. But on the other hand, they are being used to maintain dictatorial regime in power, like the case of Uganda and Zambia discussed above. These are relevant issues that go to the core of the role of surveillance, the role of government, the role of the military, and the role of the people for whom these new mediated services are supposed to help. Protest peaceful march is the only weapon for the people who are armless and are not allowed to confront governments with no other force but non-violent peaceful means. The fact that governments in Africa are using facial recognition and "hacking personal devices" (Megiddo, 2019, 410) implies that online activism is under attack. It is under attack because with the omnipresence of the COVID-19 virus pandemic, where most people in Africa are under lockdown with schools and businesses closed and the people can only manifest their discontent in the way the governments have handled the crisis online through WhatsApp, Facebook, NaijaPal, Chomi, Lenali App, Mxit, Twitter, Instagram, and so on. These are the platforms readily available through the Internet that the people are now using as the new public sphere. Now that with the Chinese technologies, the African governments are now hacking into these devices using facial recognition and encryption techniques, it only goes to buttress the view that freedom for the people has been asphyxiated from all directions and so hope has turned into despair and the future for African democracies, for lack of a better term, is uncertain. Unless and until something drastically changes for the democratic wind to shift direction toward the empowerment of the people, protests for meaningful change will only undergo the same fate in Africa as it did at the dawn of political independence with the onslaught of mutinies, riots, and coup d'état that characterized the African continent.

Bibliography

Akomolafe, F. (2014). Burkina Faso: You cannot kill ideas. *New African*, 66–67.

Alzouma, G. (2012). Far away from home . . . with a mobile phone! Reconnecting and regenerating the extended family in Africa. In P. H. Cheong, J. N. Martin and L. P. Macfadyen (Eds.), *New Media and Intercultural Communication*. New York, NY: Peter Lang, 193–208.

Ananthakrishnan, U. and V. Santhi Siri. (2018). Egyptian hieroglyphs to emojis: Pictographs as a universal language system and its role in creating the 'global brain.' *Languages in India*. Retrieved on July 24, 2019from http://www.language-inindia.com/june2018/mediacentresalemseminar/ananthakrishnanhieroglyphsemo-jis.pdf

AndreJevic, M. (2013). *Infloglut: How too Much Information is Changing the Way We Think and Know*. New York, NY: Routledge.

Asante, M. K. (2007). *An Afrocentric manifesto*: Toward an African renaissance. Malden, MA: Polity Press.

Asante, M. K. (2015). *African pyramids of knowledge: Kemet, Afrocentricity and Africology*. New York, NY: Universal Write Publications.

Asante, M.K. (2016). *Lynching Barack Obama: How Whites Tried to String up the President*. New York, NY: Universal Write Publications.

Asante, M. K. (2020). *Ama Mazama: The ogunic presence in Africology*. Lanham, MD: Lexington Books.

Asongu, S. A. (2018). Conditional determinants of mobile phones penetration and mobile banking in Sub-Saharan Africa. *Journal of the Knowledge Economy*, *9*(1), 81–135.

Auxier, B. (May 4, 2020). How Americans see digital privacy issues amid the COVID-19 outbreak. Pew Research Center. Retrieved from https://www.pewresearch.org/fact-tank/2020/05/04/how-americans-see-digital-privacy-issues-amid-the-covid-19-outbreak/

Aziz, S. F. and Beydoun, K. A. (2020). Fear of a Black and Brown Internet: Policing Online Activism. *Boston University Law Review, 100*, 1153–1193

Babou, D. (2004). "Interview with Molefi Kete Asante," Dakar (May 3).

Bangura, A. K. (2020). *Seshu nu per ankh:* The ancient Kemetian genesis of digital communication. In K. Langmia and A. L. Lando (Eds.), *Digital Communications at Crossroads in Africa: A Decolonial Approach.* Cham: Palgrave, 1–4.

Barbot, O. (2020). George Floyd and our collective moral injury. *AJPH* doi: 10.2105/ AJPH.2020.305850.

Becker, D. (2017). Instagram as the potential platform for alternative visual culture in South Africa. In M. Bunce, S. Franks and C. Paterson (Eds.), *Africa's Media Image in the 21ˢᵗ Century.* New York, NY: Routledge, 102–112.

Bell, D. (2001). *Introduction to Cybercultures.* New York, NY: Routledge.

Bornman, J., Bryen, D. N., Moolman, E., and Morris, J. (2016). Use of consumer wireless devices by South Africans with severe communication disability. *African Journal of Disability,* 5(1).

Bonilla-Silva, E. (2001). *White Supremacy and Racism in the Post-Civil Rights Era.* Boulder, CO: Lynne Rienner Publishers.

Bornman, J., Bryen, D. N., Moolman, E., and Morris, J. (2016). Use of consumer wireless devices by South Africans with severe communication disability. *African Journal of Disability,* 5(1), 202.

Borchert, M. (1998). The challenge of cyberspace: Internet access and persons with disabilities. In B. Ebo (Ed.), *Cyberghetto or Cybertopia.* Wesport, CT: Praeger, 45–64.

Bornman, J., Bryen, D. N., Moolman, E., and Morris, J. (2016). Use of consumer wireless devices by South Africans with severe communication disability. *African Journal of Disability,* 5(1), 202.

Boutros, A. (2015). Religion in the Afrosphere: The constitution of a blogging counterpublic. *Journal of Communication Inquiry, 39*(4), 319–337.

Bowers, C. A. (2014). *False Promises of the Digital Revolution.* New York, NY: Peter Lang.

Breen, M. (2011). *Uprising: The Internet Unintended Consequences.* Champaign, IL: Common Ground Publishing LLC.

Breen, M. (2011). The Internet, gender and identity: Proletarianization as selective essentialism. In P. Kalantzis-Cope and K. Gherab-Martin (Eds.), *Emerging digital spaces in contemporary society.* New York, NY: Palgrave Macmillan, 279–292.

Brenzinger, M., Heine, B., and Sommer, G. (1991). Language death in Africa. *Diogenes, 39*(153), 19–44.

Brock, A. (2018). Critical technocultural discourse analysis. *New Media & Society, 20*(3), 1012–1030.

Brown, A. (2002). Performing "truth": Black speech acts. *African American Review, 36*(2), 213–225.

Bruns, A., Highfield, T., and Burgess, J. (2014). The Arab Spring and its social media audiences: English and Arabic Twitter users and their networks. In M. McCaughey (ed). *Cyberactivism on the Participatory Web.* New York, NY: Routledge, 96–128.

Buku, M. W., and Mazer, R. (2017). *Fraud in Mobile Financial Services: Protecting Consumers, Providers, and the System* (No. 119208, pp. 1–4). The World Bank.

Bury, R. (2005). *Cyberspace of Their Own: Female Fandoms Online.* New York, NY: Peter Lang.

Byerly, C. and Valentin, A. (2017). Women's access to media: Legal dimensions of ownership and employment in the United States. In R. A. Lind (Ed.), *Race and Gender in Electronic Media.* New York, NY: Routledge, 267–292.

Carey, J. W. (1992). *Communication as Culture.* New York, NY: Routledge.

Casilli, A. A. (2017). Global Digital Culture| Digital Labor Studies Go Global: Toward a Digital Decolonial Turn. *International Journal of Communication, 11,* 21.

Casmore, E. (2012). *Beyond Black: Celebrity and Race in Obama's America.* New York, NY: Bloomsbury Academic.

Chen, G. M. (2017). Social media: From digital divide to empowerment. In C. P. Campbell (Ed.), *The Routledge Companion to Media and Race.* New York, NY: Routledge, 117–125.

Chetty, N. and Alethur, N. (2018). Hate speech review in the context of online social networks. *Aggression and Violent Behavior, 40,* 108–118

Cisse, M. (2018). Look to Africa to advance artificial intelligence. *Nature, 562*(7728), 461–462.

Clark, M. (2014). To tweet our own cause: A mixed method study of the online phenomenon "Black Twitter." Dissertation: The University of North Carolina at Chapel Hill, Proquest Dissertation Publishing.

Coetzee, J. (2016). A Johannesburg Company will build Africa's first homegrown smartphones. Retrieved from http://qz.com/856850/south-africas-onyx-connect -has-inked-a-deal-with-google-to-make-cheap-android-smartphones/

Contee, C. G. (1972). Du Bois, the NAACP, and the Pan-African Congress of 1919. *The Journal of Negro History, 57*(1), 13–28.

Craig, R. T. (2014). *African Americans and Mass Media: A Case for Diversity in Media Ownership.* Lanham, MD: Lexington Books.

Cummings, C. and O'Neil, T. (2015). *Do Digital Information and Communications Technologies Increase the Voice and Influence of Women and Girls? A Rapid Review of the Evidence.* London, UK: Overseas Development Institute.

Daniels, J. (2013). Race and racism in Internet studies: A review and critique. *New Media and Society, 15*(5), 695–719.

Daniels, J. (2008). Race, civil rights, and hate speech in the digital era. Learning race and ethnicity: Youth and digital media. In A. Everett (Ed.), *The John D. and Catherine T. MacArthur Foundation Series on Digital Media and Learning.* Cambridge, MA: The MIT Press,129–154. doi: 10.1162/dmal.9780262550673.129

Daniels, J. (2016). The trouble with white feminism: Whiteness, digital feminism and the intersectional internet. In S. U. Noble & B.M. Tynes (Eds.) *The intersectional Internet: Race, Sex, Class and Culture Online.* New York, NY: Peter Lang, 278–306.

Dates, J. L. and Ramirez, M. M. (2018). *From Blackface to Black Twitter: Reflections on Black humor, race, politics and gender.* New York, NY: Peter Lang.

Doueihi, M. (2011). *Digital Cultures.* Cambridge, MA: Harvard University Press

Du Bois, W. E. B. (2014). *Souls of Black Folks.* Tampa, FL: Millennium Publications.

Edwards, L., Kontstathis, A. E. and Fisher, C. (2016). Cyberbullying, race/ethnicity and mental health outcomes: A review of literature. *Media and Communication, 4*(3), 71–78

Ellison, T. L., and Solomon, M. (2019). Counter-storytelling vs. deficit thinking around African American children and families, digital literacies, race, and the digital divide. *Research in the Teaching of English, 53*(3), 223–244.

Eltantawy, N., and Wiest, J. B. (2011). The Arab spring| Social media in the Egyptian revolution: Reconsidering resource mobilization theory. *International Journal of Communication, 5,* 18.

Enck-Wanzer, D. (2011). Barack Obama, the Tea Party, and the threat of race: On racial neoliberalism and born again racism. *Communication, Culture & Critique, 4*(1), 23–30.

Everett, A. (2009). *Digital Diaspora: A Race for Cyberspace.* New York, NY: SUNY Press.

Eubanks, V. (2011). *Digital Dead End: Fighting for Social Justice in the Information age.* Cambridge, MA: The MIT Press.

Fadda-Conrey, C. (2011). Arab American citizenship in crisis: Destabilizing representations of Arabs and Muslims in the US after 9/11. *MFS Modern Fiction Studies, 57*(3), 532–555.

Fanon, F. (1967). *White Skin, Black Masks.* New York, NY: Grove Press.

Ferenbok, J. (2011). Configuring the face as a technology of citizenship: Biometrics, surveillance and the facialization of institutional identity. In In P. Kalantzis-Cope and K. Gherab-Martin (Eds.), *Emerging Digital Spaces in Contemporary Society.* New York, NY: Palgrave Macmillan, 126–128.

Fortunati, L. (2007). Immaterial labor and its machinization. *Ephemera, 7*(1), 139–157.

Franklin, M. I. (2013). *Digital Dilemmas: Power, Resistance, and the Internet.* New York, NY: Oxford University Press.

Fuchs, C., and Horak, E. (2008). Africa and the digital divide. *Telematics and Information, 25*(2), 99–116. doi: 10.1016/j.tele.2006.06.004

Gandy, O.H. (1998). *Communication and race: A structural perspective.* London, UK: Arnold.

Gajjala, R. (2000). Internet constructs of identity and ignorance: 'Third-world' contexts and cyberfeminism. *Works and Days, 33*(17&18), 117–137.

Gohil, N. S., and Sidhu, D. S. (2007). The Sikh turban: Post-911 challenges to this article of faith. *Rutgers JL & Religion, 9,* 1.

Ghosh, B. N. (2019). *Dependency Theory Revisited.* New York, NY: Routledge.

Gray, K. L. (2012a). Deviant bodies, stigmatized identities and racist acts: Examining the experiences of African-American gamers in Xbox live. *New Review of Hypermedia and Multimedia. 18(4),* 261–276.

Gray, K.L. (2012b). Intersecting oppressions and online communities. *Information, Communication and Society, 15*(3), 411–428.

Gray, K. L. (2017). The Internet: Oppression in digital spaces. In C. P. Campbell (Ed.), *The Routledge Companion to Media and Race.* New York, NY: Routledge, 107–116.

Gray, H. (2000). Black representation in the post network, post-civil rights world of global media. In S. Cottle (Ed.), *Ethnic Minorities and the Media*. Maidenhead, PA: Open University Press, 118–129.

Grosswiler, P. (2009). Continuing media controversies. In A. Debeer and J. C. Merrill (Eds.), *Global Journalism*. Boston, MA: Pearson, 115–130.

Grosswiller, P. (2013). *Old Media New Media: From Oral to Virtual Environments*. New York, NY: Peter Lang

Gill, T. M. (2015). # TeamNatural: Black Hair and the Politics of Community in Digital Media. *Journal of Contemporary African Art*, *2015*(37), 70–79.

Gorin, V. (2015). "A path into alternative models? The role of citizen journalism in global representation of humanitarianism," presentation, Global Humanitarianism and media culture, Sussex.

Gouws, A. (2018). # EndRapeCulture campaign in south Africa: Resisting sexual violence through protest and the politics of experience. *Politikon*, *45*(1), 3–15.

Guzman, A. (2016). The message of mute machines: Human-machine communication with industrial technologies. Communication +1, 5(1) 1–30.

Graham, M. and Dutton, W. H. (2014). *Society and the Internet: How Networks of Information and Communication Are Changing Our Lives*. Oxford, UK: Oxford University Press

Gross, T. F. (2009). Own-ethnicity bias in the recognition of Black, East Asian, Hispanic, and White faces. *Basic and Applied Social Psychology*, *31*(2), 128–135.

Guzman, A. L. (2018). Beyond extraordinary: Theorizing artificial intelligence and the self in daily life. In M. Graham & W.H. Dutton (Eds.) *A Networked Self and Human Augmentics, Artificial Intelligence, Sentience*. New York, NY: Routledge, 83–96.

Hafkin, N. J., and Huyer, S. (2007). Women and gender in ICT statistics and indicators for development. *Information Technologies and International Development*, 4(2), 1–25.

Hansen, M.B.N. (2006). *Bodies in Code: Interfaces with Digital Media*. New York, NY: Routledge

Hamdy, N., and Conlin, L. (2013). Women and social media in the Egyptian revolution. In R. D. Berenger (Ed.), *Social Media go to War: Rage, Rebellion and Revolution in the Age of Twitter*. Spokane, WA: Marquette Books, 487–500.

Hardy, J. (2014). *Critical Political Economy of the Media: An Introduction*. London, UK: Routledge.

Harris, A. (2015). Move, get out the way: "Black women-of-words" voyaging on the information superhighway. In K. E. Tassie and S. M. Givens (Eds.), *Women of Color and Social Media Multitasking: Blogs, Timelines, Feeds and Community*. Lanham, MD: Lexington Books, 69–90.

Harris, L. K. (2015). "Follow me on Instagram": "Best self" identity construction and gaze through hashtag activism and selfie self-love." In K. E. Tassie and S. M. Givens (Eds.), *Women of Color and social media multitasking: Blogs, timelines, feeds and community*. Lanham, MD: Lexington Books, 131–144.

Hilbert, M. (2011). Digital gender divide or technologically empowered women in developing countries? A case of lies, damned lies and statistics. *Women Studies International forum, 34*, 479–489.

Hochschield, A. (1998). *King Leopold's Ghost: A Story of Greed, Terror, and Heroism in Colonial Africa.* New York, NY: Houghton Mifflin Company.

Hope Michael, D., Raptis Constantine, A., Amar, S., Hammer Mark, M., and Henry Travis, S. (2020). A role for CT in COVID-19? What data really tell us so far. http://www. thelancet. com/article/S0140673620307285/pdf

Howard, P. N., and Hussain, M. M. (2013). *Democracy's Fourth Wave? Digital Media and the Arab Spring.* Oxford: Oxford University Press.

Halloway, J.E. (1991). *Africanisms in American Culture.* Bloomington, IN: Indiana University Press.

Harlow, S. and Benbrook, A. (2019). How #Blacklivesmatter: Exploring the role of hip-hop celebrities in constructing racial identity on Black Twitter. *Information, Communication & Society, 22*(3), 352–368.

Hollington, A. (2017). Emotions in Jamaican. *Consensus and Dissent: Negotiating Emotion in the Public Space, 19,* 81–104.

Jackson, J. S. and Banaszczyk, S. (2016). Digital standpoints: Debating gendered violence and racial exclusions in the feminist counterpublic. *Journal of Communication Inquiry, 40*(4), 391–407.

Jarrett, K. (2016). *Feminism, Labour and Digital Media: The Digital Housewife.* New York, NY: Routledge.

Jackson, S. J. (2016). Reimaging intersectional democracy from Black feminism to hashtag activism. *Women's Studies in Communication, 39*(4), 375–379.

James, G.G.M. (2017). *Stolen Legacy: The Egyptian Origins of Western Philosophy.* Allegro Editions.

Jin, S. W., Jones, T. V., and Lee, Y. (2019). Does resilience mediate the link between depression and internet addiction among African American University Students? *The Journal of Negro Education, 88*(2), 114–129.

Jones, E. G. (2013). *Social Media and Minority Languages.* Buffalo, NY: Multilingual Matters.

Jorden, E. N. (2018). The Alt-right's use of President Donald Trump's Twitter account as a propaganda device. Retrieved from https://mds.marshall.edu/etd/1152.

Joseph, R. P., Pekmezi, D., Dutton, G. R., Cherrington, A. L., Kim, Y. I., Allison, J. J., and Durant, N. H. (2016). Results of a culturally adapted Internet-enhanced physical activity pilot intervention for overweight and obese young adult African American women. *Journal of Transcultural Nursing, 27*(2), 136–146.

Keane, J. (2013). *Democracy and the Media Decadence.* Cambridge, UK: Cambridge University Press.

Khannous, T. (2011). Virtual gender: Moroccan and Saudi women's cyberspace. *Journal of Women of the Middle East and The Islamic World, 8,* 358–387.

Khondker, H. H. (2011). Role of the new media in the Arab Spring. *Globalizations, 8*(5), 675–679.

Kim, P. T. (2018). Big Data and Artificial Intelligence: New Challenges for Workplace Equality. *University of Louisville Law Review, 57,* 313–328.

Kirby, A. (2009). *Digimodernism: How New Technologies Dismantle the Postmodern and Reconfigure Our Culture.* New York, NY: The Continuum Publishing Group Inc.

Kolko, B., Nakaruma, L., and Rodman, G. (2000). *Race in Cyberspace*. London, UK: Routledge.

Karimi, F. (August 15, 2020). The father of a five-year-old boy killed in North Carolina says the suspect was a neighbor for eight years. Retrieved from https://www.cnn .com/2020/08/15/us/north-carolina-boy-killed-father-speaks-trnd/index.html

Katyal, S. K. (2019). Private Accountability in the Age of Artificial Intelligence. *University of Louisville Law Review, 66*, 54.

Koch, N. S. and Schockman, H.E. (1998). Democratizing Internet access in Lesbian, Gay, and Bisexual communities. In B. Ebo (Ed.), *Cyberghetto or Cybertopia*. Westport, CT: Praeger, 171–184.

Kshetri, N. (2006). *Big Data's Big Potential in Developing Countries*. Boston, MA: CABI.

Kress, T. M. (2009). In the shadow of Whiteness: (Re)exploring connections between history, enacted culture and identity in digital divide initiatives. *Cultural Studies of Science Education 4(1)*, 41–49.

Kubheka, B. Z., Carter, V., and Mwaura, J. (2020). Social media health promotion in South Africa: Opportunities and challenges. *African Journal of Primary Health Care and Family Medicine, 12*(1), 1–7.

Kwame, D. and Johnson III, O. A. (2019). *Contemporary racial politics in Latin America*. New York, NY: Routledge.

Lando, A. L. (2020). Africans and digital communication at crossroads: Rethinking existing Decolonial paradigms. In K. Langmia and A. L. Lando (Eds.), *Digital Communications at Crossroads in Africa: A Decolonial Approach*. Cham: Palgrave, 107–132.

Langmia, K., and Durham, E. (2007). Bridging the gap: African and African American communication in historically black colleges and universities. *Journal of Black Studies, 37*(6), 805–826.

Langmia, K, and Mpande, S. (2014). Social media and critical pedagogy. In K. Langmia, T.C.M Tyree, P. O'Brien, and I. Sturgis (Eds.), *Social Media: Pedagogy and Practice*. Lanham, MD: University Press of America, 56–72.

Langmia, K. Glass, A. (2014). Coping with smartphones in a college classroom: *Teaching Journalism and Mass Communication, 4* (1), 13–23.

Langmia, K. (2019). Confronting the lion with bare hands: Social media and the Anglophone Cameroonian Protest. In E. Ngwainbi (Ed.), *Media in the Global Context*. Cham: Palgrave Macmillan, 127–141.

Langmia, K. (2016). *Globalization and Cyberculture: An Afrocentric Perspective*. Switzerland: Palgrave.

Langmia, K. (2020). Pax-Africana versus W-estern digiculturalism: An ethnometh-odological study of selected mobile African Apps. In K. Langmia and A. L. Lando (Eds.), *Digital Communications at Crossroads in Africa: A Decolonial Approach*. Cham: Palgrave, 93–106.

Langmia, K., and Lando, A. (2020). *Digital Communications at Crossroads in Africa: A Decolonial Approach*. Cham: Palgrave.

Legewie, J., and Fagan, J. (2016). Group threat, police officer diversity and the deadly use of police force. *Columbia Public Law Research Paper*, (14-512).

Leung, L. (2017). *Virtual Ethnicity: Race, Resistance and the World Wide Web.* New York, NY: Routledge.

Lindridge, A., Henderson, G. R., and Ekpo, A. E. (2015). (Virtual) ethnicity, the Internet, and well-being. *Marketing Theory, 15*(2), 279–285.

Livingstone, S., and Helsper, E. (2010). Balancing opportunities and risks in teenagers' use of the internet: The role of online skills and internet self-efficacy. *New Media and Society* 12(2): 309–329.

Lohr, S. (February 2012). The age of big data, *The New York Times.* Retrieved from http://www.nytimes.com/2012/02/12/sunday-review/big-datas-impact-in-the-world.html?pagewanted=all

Luhan, M. (1994). *Understanding the Media: The Extension of Man.* Cambridge, MA: MIT Press.

Luke, T.W. (2011). Digital citizenship. In P. Kalantzis-Cope and K. Gherab-Martin (Eds.), *Emerging Digital Spaces in Contemporary Society.* New York, NY: Palgrave Macmillan, 83–96.

Maragh, R. S. (2018). Authenticity on "Black Twitter": Reading racial performance and social networking. *Television & New Media, 19*(7), 591–609.

Martin, A. (2019). Mobile money platform surveillance. *Surveillance and Society, 17*(1/2), 213–222.

Mashamba-Thompson, T. P., and Crayton, E. D. (2020). Blockchain and artificial intelligence technology for novel coronavirus disease-19 self-testing. *Diagnostics2020, 10,* 198. doi: 10.3390/diagnostics10040198.

Mazrui, A. (1986). *The African: A Triple Heritage.* Boston, MA: Little Brown and Company.

Mbiti, J. S. (1969, 2011). *African Religions & Philosophy.* Nairobi: East African Educational Publishers.

McChesney, R.W. (2008). *The Political Economy of Media: Enduring Issues, Emerging Dilemmas.* Monthly Review Press.

McLuhan, M., Mcluhan, M. A., and Lapham, L. H. (1994). *Understanding Media: The Extensions of Man.* MIT Press.

McPhail, T. (2006). *Global Communication: Theories, Stakeholders and Trends.* Oxford, UK: Blackwell.

Megiddo, T. (2019). Online activism, digital domination, and the rule of trolls: Mapping and theorizing technological oppression by government. *Columbia Journal of Transnational Law 58,* 394.

Milioni, D. L., Doudaki, V., and Demertzis, N. (2014). Youth, ethnicity, and a 'reverse digital divide' A study of Internet use in a divided country. *Convergence, 20*(3), 316–336.

Mhlanga, D. at Moloi, T. (2020). COVID 19 and the digital transformation of education: What we are learning in South Africa. Retrieved from doi 10.20944/preprints202004.0195.vt.

Mossberger, K., Tolbert, C. J., and Anderson, C. (2017). The mobile Internet and digital citizenship in African-American and Latino communities, *Information, Communication & Society, 20:10,* 1587–1606, DOI: 10.1080/1369118X.2016.1243142

Mukhongo, L. L. (2015). Online political activism among young people in sub-Saharan Africa. In *Encyclopedia of Information Science and Technology, Third Edition* (6419–6426). IGI Global.

Mckenzie, R. (2018). Bots, bias and big data: Artificial intelligence, algorithmic bias and disparate impact liability in hiring practices. *Arkansas Law Review, 71* (2), 529–570.

Miller, V. (2011). *Understanding Digital Culture.* Los Angeles, CA: Sage Publication.

Nakamura, L. (2002). *Cybertypes: Race, Ethnicity and Identity on the Internet.* New York, NY: Routledge.

Nkrumah, K. 1964. *Consciencism: Philosophy and Ideology for De-colonization.* New York, NY: Monthly Review Press.

Nichols, B. (2000). The age of culture in the age of cybernetic systems. In J. T. Cardwell (Ed.), *Electronic Media and Technoculture.* New Brunswick, NJ: Rutgers University Press, 90–114.

Nakamura, L., and Chow-White, P. (Eds.). (2013). *Race After the Internet.* New York, NY: Routledge.

Nakayama, T. K. (2017). What's next for whiteness and the Internet. *Critical Studies in Media Communication, 34*(1), 68–72.

Ndlovu, E. (2017). The Diaspora community's intervention in the Libyan uprising. In O. Ogunyemi (Ed.), *Media, Diaspora and Conflict.* Cham: Palgrave, 37–52.

Ndumu, A. (2020). Disrupting Digital Divide Narratives: Exploring the US Black Diasporic Immigrant Context. *Open Information Science, 4*(1), 75–84.

Nobles, S.U. (2018). *Algorithms of Oppression: How Search Engines Reinforce Racism.* New York, NY: New York University Press.

Nyamnjoh, F. (2012). Potted plants in green houses: A critical reflection on the resilience of colonial education in Africa. *Journal Asian and African Studies,47(2),* 129–154.

Omotoso, S. A. (2017). Communicating feminist ethics in the age of new media in Africa. *Gendering Knowledge in Africa and the African Diaspora,* 64–84.

O'Neil, C. (2016). *Weapons of Math Destruction: How Big Data Increases Inequality and Threatens Democracy.* London: Crown.

Osuagwu, O. E., Okide, S., Edebatu, D., and Udoka, E. (2013). Low and expensive bandwidth remains key bottleneck for Nigeria's internet diffusion: A proposal for a solution model. *West African Journal of Industrial and Academic Research, 7*(1), 14–30.

Onwumechili, C. and Amulega, S. (2020) Digital communications: Colonization or rationalization? In K. Langmia and A. Lando (Eds.), *Digital Communications at Crossroads in Africa: A Decolonial Approach.* Cham: Palgrave, 23–40.

Oyedemi, T. D. (2011). Digital inequalities and implications for social inequalities: A study of Internet penetration amongst university students in South Africa. *Telematics and Informatics, 29,* 302–313.

Oyewumi, O. (1997). *The Invention of Women: Making Sense of Western Gender Discourses.* Minneapolis, MN: University of Minnesota Press.

Pommerolle, M. and De Marie Heungoup, H. (2017). The Anglophone crisis: A tale of the Cameroonian post colony. *African Affairs, 116*(464), 526–538.

Prager, J. (2020). Do black lives matter? A psychoanalytic exploration of racism and American resistance to reparations. In *Post-Conflict Hauntings*. Cham: Palgrave Macmillan, 93–118.

Pritchard, G. W., and Vines, J. (2013, April). Digital apartheid: An ethnographic account of racialised HCI in Cape Town hip-hop. In *Proceedings of the SIGCHI Conference on Human Factors in Computing Systems*, 2537–2546.

Qi, Y. W., and Lemmer, E. M. (2013). Teaching Mandarin as a foreign language in Higher Education institutions in South Africa. *Per Linguam: A Journal of Language Learning= Per Linguam: Tydskrif vir Taalaanleer*, 29(1), 33–48.

Rabaka, R. (2009). *Africana critical theory: Reconstructing the Black radical tradition, from W. E.B. Du Bois and C.L.R. James to Frantz Fanon and Amilcar Cabral*. Lanham, MD: Lexington Books.

Radsch, C. (2012). Unveiling the revolutionaries: Cyberactivism and the role of women in the Arab uprisings. *Rice University James A. Baker III Institute for Public Policy Research Paper*.

Ragnedda, M. and Muschert, G.W. (2016). Theorizing digital divides and inequalities. In J. Servaes and B. A. Oyedemi (Eds.), *Social Inequalities, Media and Communication*. Lanham, MD: Lexington Books, 23–36.

Rai, G. (2017). Changing perceptions and meaning of cyberfeminism. *International Research Journal of Multidisciplinary Studies, 3* (4), 1–10.

Redd, L. N. (1988). Telecommunications, economics, and black families in America. *Journal of Black Studies, 19* (1), 111–123.

Rimini, F. (2011). The container project in rural Jamaica: Socializing technology and unleashing creativity along the digital divide. In K. St. Amant and B. A. Olaniran (Eds.), *Globalization and Digital Divide*. New York, NY: Cambria Press, 103–139.

Robinson, L., Cotten, S. R., Ono, H., Quan-Haase, A., Mesch, G., Chen, W., Schulz, J., Hale, T. M. and Stern, M. J. (2015). Digital inequalities and why they matter. *Information Communication & Society, 18*(5), 569–582. doi: 10.1080/1369118X.2015.1012532.

Ronson, J. (2015). How one stupid tweet blew up Justine Sacco's life The New York Times, February 12. Retrieved http://www.nytimes.com/2015/02/15/magazine/how--one-stupid-tweet-ruined-justine-saccos-life.html

Rabaka, R. (2009). *Africana critical theory: Reconstructing the Black radical tradition, from W.E.B. Du Bois and C. L. R. James to Frantz Fanon and Amilcar Cabral*. Lanham, MD: Lexington Books.

Ragnedda, M., and Mutsvairo, B. (2018). *Digital Inclusion: An International Comparative Analysis*. Lanham, MD: Lexington

Regan, P. (2012). Hans-Georg Gadamer's philosophical hermeneutics: Concepts of reading, understanding and interpretation. *Meta: Research in hermeneutics, phenomenology, and practical philosophy, 4*(2), 286–303.

Reiter, B. (2019). Recognition, reparations and political autonomy of Black and native communities in the Americas. In K. Dixon and O. A. Johnson (Eds.), *Comparative Racial Politics in Latin America*. New York, NY: Routledge, 44–63.

Rodney, G., and Wakeham, M. (2016). Social media marketing communications effect on attitudes among millennials in South Africa. *The African Journal of Information Systems*, *8*(3), 2.

Rodney, W. (1982). *How Europe underdeveloped Africa. Washington*, DC: Howard University Press.

Rosenbaum, J.E. (2018). *Constructing Digital Cultures: Tweets, Trends, Race and Gender.* Lanham, MD. Lexington Press

Sansone, L. (2017). Fragile heritage and digital memory in Africa. In P. B. Farnetti and C. D. Novelli (Eds.), *Images of Colonialism and Decolonisation in the Italian Media.* Newcastle upon Tyne: Cambridge Scholars Publishing, 8–21.

Sawyer, L. L. (2017). "Don't try and play me out": The performances and possibilities of digital Black womanhood (Doctoral dissertation). Retrieved from Proquest (10622458.)

Schapals, A. K., Bruns, A., and McNair, B. (2018). *Digitizing Democracy.* New York, NY: Routledge.

Scholz, T. (2013). Introduction: Why does digital labor matter now? In T. Scholz (Ed.), *Digital Labor: The Internet as Playground and Factory.* New York, NY: Routledge, 1–9

Schradie, J. (2019). *The Revolution that Wasn't: How Digital Activism Favors Conservatives.* Harvard University Press.

Shade, L.R. (2002). *Gender and Community in the Social Construction of the Internet.* New York, NY: Peter Lang.

Shah, S. and Widjaya, R. (2000). Post mentioning 'Black Lives Matter' spiked on law makers social media accounts after George Floyd. Retrieved from https://www.pewresearch.org/fact-tank/2020/07/16/posts-mentioning-black-lives-matter-spiked-on-lawmakers-social-media-accounts-after-george-floyd-killing/

Skalli, L. H. (2013). Young women and social media against sexual harassment. *The Journal of North African Studies, 2*, 244–258.

Smyth, T. N., and Best, M. L. (2013, December). Tweet to trust: Social media and elections in West Africa. In *Proceedings of the Sixth International Conference on Information and Communication Technologies and Development: Full Papers-Volume 1.* ACM, pp. 133–141.

Soyinka, W., Amin, A., Selassie, B. H., Mugo, M. G., and Mkandawire, T. (2015). *Reimagining Pan-Africanism.* Dar es Salam, Tanzania: Mkuki Na Nyota Publishers.

Stone, A. L. and Carlisle, S. K. (2015). Racial bullying and adolescent substance use: An examination of school-attending young adolescents in the United States. *Journal of Ethnicity in Substance Abuse, 15*(1), 1–20. doi: 10.1080/15332640.2015.1095666.

Strahler, D.C. and Flynn, T. R. (2013). Transparency, misrepresentation, and social media. In S. J. Drucker and G. Gumpert (Eds.), *Regulating Social Media: Legal and Ethical Considerations.* New York, NY: Peter Lang, 153–171.

Sturgis, I. (July 8, 2020). See something, say something. Really, with constant surveillance? *Digital Privacy News*

Suler, J. and Barak, A. (2008). Reflections on the psychology and social science of cyberspace. In A. Barak (Ed.), *Psychological Aspects of Cyberspace: Theory, Research, Applications.* Cambridge University Press.

Skinner, E. P. (1999). *The African Presence: In Defense of Africanity*. Chicago, IL: University of Illinois Press.

Skinner, E. P. (2001). The restoration of African identity for a new millennium. In I. O. Okpewho, C. B. Davies and A.A. Mazrui (Eds.), *The African Diaspora: African Origins and New World Identities*. Bloomington, IN: Indiana University Press, 28–45.

Soyinka, W. (1995). *Yoruba Astrophysics*. The Washington Post Newspaper.

Smith, A. (2014). African Americans and technology use. Pew Research Center. Retrieved from http://www.pewinternet.org/2014/01/06/african-americans-and -technology-use/

Smythe, D. W. (2014). Communications: Blindspot of Western Marxism. In L. McGuigan and V. Manzerolle (Eds.), *The Audience Commodity in a Digital Age: Revisiting a Critical Theory of Commercial Media*. New York, NY: Peter Lang, 29–53.

Tindongan, C. W. (2011). Negotiating Muslim youth identity in a post-9/11 world. *The High School Journal, 95*(1), 72–87.

Thiongo, N. (2009). *Something torn and new. An African Renaissance*. Civitas Books.

Thussu, D. (2007). *Media on the Move*. London, UK: Routledge.

Tufekci, Z. and Wilson, C. (2012). Social media and the decision to participate in public protest: Observations from Tahrir Square. *Journal of Communication, 62*, 363–379.

Turkle, S. (1997). Constructions and reconstructions of self in virtual reality: Playing in the MUDs. In S. Kiesler (Ed.), *Culture of the Internet*. New Jersey, NJ: Lawrence Erlbaum, 143–155.

Uribe-Jongbloed, E. (2013). Minority language media studies and communication for social change: Dialogue between Europe and Latin America. In E. G. Jones and E. Uribe-Jongbloed (Eds.), *Social Media and Minority Languages: Convergence and the Creative Industries*. Buffalo, NY: Multilingual Matters, 31–46.

Vaidhyanathan, S. (2011). *The Googlization of Everything (and why should worry)*. Los Angeles, CA: University of California Press.

van Reijswoud, V. and de Jager, A. (2011). The role of appropriate ICT in bridging the digital divide. In K. St. Amant and B.A. Olaniran (Eds.), *Globalization and Digital divide,* New York, NY: Cambria Press, 58–82.

Vernon, D. (2019). Robotics and Artificial Intelligence in Africa [Regional]. *IEEE Robotics & Automation Magazine, 26*(4), 131–135.

Vogels, E.A., Perrin, A., Rainie, L., and Anderson, M. (April, 30, 2020). 53% of Americans Say the Internet Has Been Essential During the COVID-19 Outbreak. Retrieved from Pew Research Center. https://www.pewresearch.org/internet/2020 /04/30/53-of-americans-say-the-internet-has-been-essential-during-the-covid-19 -outbreak/

Wafula-Kwake, A. K. and Ocholla, D. N. (2009). The feasibility of ICT diffu-sion amongst African rural women: A case study of South Africa and Kenya. *International Review of Ethics*, 7, 1–20.

wa Thiong'o, N. (2009). *Something Torn and New: An African Renaissance*. Basic Civitas Books.

Wa Thiongo, N. (2012). *Globaletics: Theory and the Politics of Knowing.* New York, NY: Columbia University Press.

Watkins, V. (2017). (Black) Feminism online: The political uses of social media and the implications for African Studies. In J.L. Conyers (Ed.), *Africana, Race and Communication: A Social Study of Film, Communication and Social Media.* Lanham, MD: Lexington, 169–195.

Weber, R. M. (2019). "Hey, Siri! Is Artificial Intelligence the Ultimate Oxymoron?" *Journal of Financial Service Professionals, 73*(4).

Welsing, F.C. (1991). *The Isis Papers: The Keys to the Colors.* Chicago, IL: Third World Press

Williams, S. (2016) #SayHerName: Using digital activism to document violence against black women, *Feminist Media Studies, 16*(5), 922–925. doi: 10.1080/14680777.2016.1213574.

Wilson II, C.C., Guttierrez, F. and Chao, L.M. (2003). *Racism, Sexism and the Media: The Rise of Class Communication in Multicultural America.* Thousand Oaks, CA: Sage Publications.

Whitehead, J. (2016). Book review: de Sousa Santos, B. (2014) Epistemologies of the South: Justice against Epistemicide. London; Paradigm Publishers. *Educational Journal of Living Theories, 9*(2), 87–98.

White, H. (1973). *Metahistory. The Historical Imagination in the Nineteenth- Century Europe.* Baltimore, MD: The Johns Hopkins University Press.

White, G. (Feb. 2019). What is Black Twitter and how is it changing the National conversation? *State News Service,* Waco, TX.

Wyche, S., and Olson, J. (2018). Gender, mobile, and mobile internet| Kenyan women's rural realities, mobile internet access, and "Africa rising." *Information Technologies & International Development, 14*, 15.

Yong J. D. (2015). *Digital Platforms, Imperialism and the Political Culture.* New York, NY: Routledge.

Index

About the Author

Dr. Kehbuma Langmia is a Fulbright scholar/professor and chair in the Department of Strategic, Legal and Management Communication, School of Communications, Howard University. He is the recipient of the prestigious 2020 National Communication Association Orlando Taylor Distinguished Scholar Award in Africana Communication. A graduate from the Communication and Media Studies Program at Howard University, Dr. Langmia has extensive knowledge and expertise in Information Communication Technology (ICT), Intercultural, Cross Cultural and International Communication, Black Diaspora Communication Theory, Decolonial Media Studies, Social Media, and Afrocentricity. Since earning his PhD in Communications and Media Studies from Howard University in 2006, he has authored, co-authored, and edited thirteen books, published seventeen book chapters, and ten peer-reviewed journal articles nationally and internationally. In November 2017, Dr. Langmia was awarded the prestigious Toyin Falola Africa Book Award in Marrakesh, Morocco, by the Association of Global South Studies for his book titled " Globalization and cyberculture: An Afrocentric Perspective." For the last four years he has been selected by Howard University to act as scholar coach for the Howard University Summer Writing Academy. This year, he was selected among the 35 U.S. professors chosen from a competitive pool of over 100 applicants to serve in the Visiting Professor Program at Fordham University in New York, organized by ANA. In addition, he regularly gives keynote speeches on Information Communication Technology, Black Diaspora–mediated communication, and Social Media in prominent national and international universities, including the Library of Congress, the National Intelligence University (Department of Defense, USA), and National Defense University (Department of Defense, USA); Morgan State University (Maryland, USA); Bowie State University (Maryland, USA); Melbourne

University (Australia); Buea University (Cameroon), Daystar University (Kenya), Madras Institute of Technology (India); ICT University (Cameroon) and Covenant University (Nigeria), Makerere, University Business School, MUBS (Uganda), and Temple University, Pennsylvania. He was the 2017 Maryland Communication Association Keynote Speaker holding at College of Southern Maryland, Waldorf, Maryland, and Communication Educators' Association Conference at Winneba, Ghana, in 2019. His most recent books are *Black/Africana Communication Theory*, published in 2018 by Palgrave/Macmillan Press; *Globalization and cyberculture: An Afrocentric perspective* and *Social Media: Culture and Identity*, published in 2017 by Palgrave, Macmillan Press and the latter co-edited with Tia Tyree published by Lexington Books. He is presently editing two books *Social Media: Safe Spaces or Dangerous Terrain* with Dr. Tia Tyree of Howard University, *Digital Communication at Crossroads in Africa: A Decolonial Approach* with Dr. Agnes Lucy Lando of Daystar University, Kenya, and self-authoring *Black Lives . . . and Digiculturalism* t published by the Lexington Press.

Website: drlangmia.net

www.ingramcontent.com/pod-product-compliance
Lightning Source LLC
Chambersburg PA
CBHW050650280326
41932CB00015B/2854